Orange County, Virginia
Order Book Abstracts
1747-1748

Ruth and Sam Sparacio

The Antient Press Collection
from
Colonial Roots
Millsboro, Delaware
2016

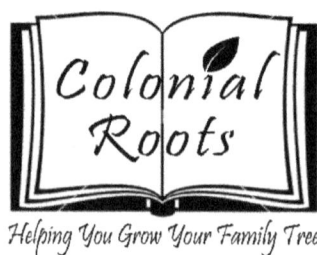

Colonial Roots

Helping You Grow Your Family Tree

ISBN 978-1-68034-326-7

p.
1

- <u>At a Court held for Orange County on Thursday the 23d day of July in the</u> twenty fourth year of the Reign of our Sovereign Lord George the Second of Great Britain, &c., Annoq: Domini 1747, before his Majesty's Justices of the Peace for the said County, (to wit);

ROBERT SLAUGHTER	SAMUEL BALL
ABRAHAM FIELD	FRANCIS SLAUGHTER
JOHN FINLESON &	GEORGE TAYLOR Gentlemen

- Upon the Petition of HENRY DOWNES, Gent. and WILLIAM McDONAUGH against JOANNA SIMS, Administratrix, &c. of RICHARD SIMS, deced., to be relieved on a Bond entered into by the said JOANNA, HENRY and WILLIAM for said JOANNA's due and faithfull administration of the Estate of the said RICHARD. On consideration whereof, it is ordered and decreed that the said JOANNA give said HENRY and WILLIAM Security to Indemnify them from said Bond or deliver up to them the said Estate

- Upon Petition of CHRISTOPHER ZIMMERMAN, who made Oath according to Law, Certificate is granted him for obtaining Letters of Administration of the Estate of JOHN NEWPORT, deced., on giving Security, on which he with JOHN FINLESON, Gent., entered into and acknowledged his Bond for his, the said CHRIS-TOPHER's, due and faithfull administration of the said Decedent's Estate

- Ordered that CHARLES MORGAN, DANIEL UNDERWOOD, RICHARD WRIGHT and BRYANT THORNHILL or any three of them being first sworn before a Justice of this County, do appraise in current money the slaves, if any, and personal Estate of JOHN NEWPORT, deced., and return the appraisment to the next Court

- Present. ROBERT GREEN and HENRY FIELD, Gent.

- A Lease between WILLIAM LUCAS of one part and WILLIAM SCELTON of the other part was acknowledged by the said LUCAS and ordered to be recorded

- DANIEL CARTER is hereby appointed CONSTABLE in this County in the room of JAMES ABBIT, who is discharged from that Office, and it is ordered that he be sworn into his said Office at the next Court

- An Indenture of Feoffment between THOMAS WATTS of one part and BENJAMIN CAVE of other part and a Memorandum of Livery of Seisen thereon endorsed were acknowledged by said THOMAS and ordered to be recorded, And EASTHER, the Wife of said THOMAS, personally appeared in court and being privilly examined as the Law directs, voluntarily relinquished her right of Dower to the Estate conveyed by the said Indenture

- A Deed of Gift from DARBY QUINN to RICHARD QUIN proved by the Oaths of ROBERT SHERMAN and LUCY SHERMAN, the witnesses thereto, and ordered to be recorded

- A Deed of Gift from DARBY QUIN to ELIZABETH BRUCE proved by the Oaths of ROBERT SHERMAN and LUCY SHERMAN, the witnesses thereto, and ordered to be recorded

p.   Orange County Court 23d of July 1747
2   - Upon the Petition of BENJAMIN CAVE, Gent., he is allowed to keep an
ORDINARY at his House in this County for the space of one year from this
time on giving Security. Thereupon he with HENRY FIELD, Gent., his Security,
entered into and acknowledged his Bond for his keeping the said ORDINARY according to Law and it is ordered that the Clerk of the Court do prepare a Licence for him
accordingly
           - An Inventory and Appraisment of the Estate of JOHN BOTTS, deced.,
returned into Court and ordered to be recorded
           - ZACHARY BLANKENBECKLER as a Constable in this County in the room
of RICHARD BURDYNE and WILLIAM WHITE in the room of SAMUEL SCOTT
took the Oaths to his Majesty's Person and Government and took and subscribed the
Oath of Abjuration and the Test were Constables and took the Oath appointed by the
Tobacco Law
           - THOMAS PETTY, JUNR., upon his Petition is exempted from paying Levies
           - JOHN YANCEY is by the Court appointed Overseer of the Highway from
STONEHOUSE's Plantation to BATTLE SPRING RUN in the room of JOHN REY-
NOLDS, who is discharged from that Office and it is ordered that the male labouring
Tithables which worked under the said REYNOLDS do attend and obey the said
YANCEY's directions in clearing and keeping the said way in repair
             - Present JAMES PENDLETON, Gent.
           - Upon the Attachment brought by GEORGE BUCHANNON & COMPANY
against WILLIAM PETTY, ordered that an Attachment issue against THOMAS
SIMS, the Garnishee, returnable to the next Court
             - Absent. ABRAHAM FIELD, Gent.
           - Upon Petitin of ABRAHAM FIELD, Gent., against CHRISTOPHER ZIM-
MERMAN, JUNR., this day came the parties by their Attorneys who being fully
heard, it is considered that the Plt. recover against Deft. eight hundred thirty pounds
of tobacco and his costs by him about his suit in this behalf expended
           - The Attachment brought by WILLIAM McDONAUGH against ROBERT
SIMS, JUNR. is dismissed
           - Upon the Presentment of the Grandjury against MICAJAH PICKET for
gaming on the Sabbath day, the said PICKET being heard, it is considered that he
forfeit and pay five shillings to the Churchwardens of Saint Thomas Parish where the
offence was supposed to have been committed for the use of the poor of the said
Parish, and that he also pay the costs of this Presentment

p.   Orange County Court 23d of July 1747
3   - ROBERT RAE and DANIEL CAMPBELL, Merchants, Plts. agst.
ABRAHAM COOPER, Deft.   In Case
This day came the Plts. by their Attorney and thereupon came also a Jury, to wit
    WILLIAM CHRISTOPHER   ZACHARIAH GIBBS   DAVID GRIFFIN
    WILLIAM JONES   THOMAS SLAUGHTER   JOHN WHARTON
    LEONARD TERRENCE   JOHN REYNOLDS   JOSEPH KIRK
    JAMES SUGGITT   THOMAS GIBSON   &   HENRY PENDLETON
who being sworn well and truly to Enquire of damages in this Cause, upon their Oath
do say that the Plts. have sustained damages by occasion of Deft.'s breach of promise in the Declaration mentioned to seven pounds, twelve shillings and five pence

besides their costs; Therefore it is considered by the Court that Plt. recover against Deft. and JAMES WILLIAMS and JOHN COOPER, his Securities, and THOMAS CHEW, Gent., Sherif of Orange County, their damages aforesaid in form aforesaid assessed and their costs by them about their suit in this behalf expended, and the Deft. in mercy, &c.

- Upon the Presentment of the Grandjury against WILLIAM COFEY, JUNR. for gaming on the Sabbath day, the said COFEY not appearing, it is considered by the Court that he forfeit and pay five shillings to the Churchwardens of Saint Thomas Parish where the offence was supposed to have been committed for the use of the poor of the said Parish and that he laso pay the costs of this Presentment

- Upon the Presentment of the Grandjury against NICHOLAS JONES for prophane swearing the said JONES being heard, it is considered that he forfeit and pay to the Churchwardens of Saint Thomas Parish five shillings for his offence for the use of the poor of the said Parish and that he also pay the costs of this Presentment

- The Presentment of the Grandjury against MUNGO PRICE is dismissed

- The King agst. JOHN WILSON   On an Information
The said WILSON not appearing another summons is awarded against him returnable to the next Court

- The King agst. JOSEPH CAVE   On an Information
The said CAVE not appearing another Attachment is awarded against him returnable to the next Court

- RICHARD SHIP, Admr. &c. of THOMAS SHIP, deced., Plt. agst.
CHRISTOPHER STROTHER, Deft.   On a Scire Facias
FRANCIS STROTHER came into Court and undertook for the Deft. that in case he is cast in this suit he shall pay the condemnation of the Court or render his body to Prison in discharge thereof, or that he, the said FRANCIS will do it for him, and thereupon the Defendant comes and defends the force and injury when &c., and pleads the general issue, the Triall whereof is continued til the next Court

p.   Orange County Court 23d of July 1747
4   - ANDREW GLASPY who has remained in Prison upwards of twenty days
         charged in execution at the suit of PHILIP LUDWELL, Esqr., being brought into Court by virtue of a Warrant from EDWARD SPENCER, Gent., one of the Justices of this County, submitted and delivered in a Schedule of his Estate made according to Law in such case made and provided, Wherepon it is ordered that the Schedule remain in the Clerk's Office of this County and that the Sherif forthwith set the said ANDREW at liberty

- OLIVER SMALL who have remained in Prison upwards to twenty days charged in execution at the suit of WILLIAM WROE, Exr. &c. of WILLIAM BRIDGES, deced., being brought into Court by Warrant from EDWARD SPENCER, Gent., one of the Justices of this County, subscribed and delivered in a Schedule of his Estate, made Oath according to Law in that case made and provided, whereupon it is ordered that the Schedule remain with the Clerk of this County and that the Sherif forthwith set the said OLIVER at liberty

- THOMAS CHEW, Gent., Plt. agst. JACOB SHOVER, Admr. &c. of JACOB SHOVER, deced., HENRY DOWNES and JACOB CASSELL, Defts.
In Chancery

This Cause by consent is set for hearing on the Bill and Demurrer and to be argued at the next Court
   - The King, agst. EDWARD ERWIN   On an Information
Dismissed
   - CHARLES DEWITT, Plt. agst. THOMAS BURK, Deft.   In Case
This day came the parties by their Attornies and Deft. saith he is Not Guilty of the Slander in the Declaration specified and of this he puts himself upon the Country, and Plt. likewise, theTrial of the issue is referred til the next Court and Plt. agrees that Deft.may give the special matter in evidence at the Trial
   - The Indictment of JAMES HEMPHILL is continued till the next Court
   - JOHN CHAMPE, Gent., Plt. agst. WILLIAM RUMSEY, Deft.   In Debt
Dismissed
   - JOHN CHAMPE, Gent., Plt. agst. DAVID KINKEAD, Deft.   In Case
Dismissed

p. 5   Orange County Court 23d of July 1747
   - JOHN NEALAND, Plt. agst. JOHN FORRESTER, Deft.   In Case
This suit is dismissed and it is ordered that Plt. pay unto Deft. his costs
   - WILLIAM BEVERLEY, Gent., Plt. agst GEORGE HOME, Deft. In Case
The Deft. being not arrested, on motion of Plt. a Plurius Capius is awarded him against Deft. returnable to the next Court
   - MARY YOUNGER, Executrix, &c. of JOSEPH YOUNGER, deced., Plt. agst. WILLIAM MINOR, Deft.   In Debt
Dismissed
   - JOHN BRAMHAM, Plt. agst WILLIAM RUSSELL, Gent., Deft.
In Case & in Covenant
Continued till the next Court for the Auditors to make Report
   - THOMAS COVINGTON, Plt. agst. DOUGALD CAMPBELL, Deft. In Debt
Dismissed
   - JAMES PICKETT, Plt. agst. FRANCIS WILLIAMS, Deft.   In Case
This suit abates for Bond and Security
   - RICHARD WINSLOW, Gent., Plt. agst WILLIAM RUSSELL, Gent., Deft. In Case
Continued till the next Court for the Auditors to make their Report
   - WILLIAM RUSSELL, Plt. agst. THOMAS WRIGHT, Deft.   In Case
Continued till the next Court

p. 6   Orange County Court 23d of July 1747
   - The Attachment of JAMES HUNTER against VALLENTINE BOSTICK is continued till next Court
   - The Attachment of ROBERT SEAYRES against WILLIAM JONES is continued till next Court
   - The Indenture of Lease and Release between FRANCIS THORNTON, Gent. and FRANCES his Wife and HANCOCK LEE, Gent. and MARY his Wife of one part and JOHN FROGG & MICHAEL WALLACE, Gent. of the other part and a Receipt endorsed on the Release were further proved by the Oath of ANTHONY STROTHER another of the witnesses thereto

- JAMES BARBOUR, Gent., Plt. agst JOHN SMITH JUNR., & TULLY
CHOICE, otherwise called JOHN SMITH, JUNR. of Orange County and
TULLY CHOICE of the said County, Defts. In Debt
This day came Plt. by his Attorney and thereupon it is considered by the Court that
Plt. recover against Defts. one hundred pounds current money of Virginia, the Debt in
the Declaration mentioned, and his costs by him about his suit in this behalf expended
and the Defts. in mercy, &c., But this Judgment, the costs excepted, is to be discharged by paiment of twenty five pounds, ten shillilngs and six pence half penny with
Interest on fifty pounds after the rate of five percent per annum from the thirtieth
day of June 1744 to the thirtieth day of June 1745, and on forty pounds from the thirtieth day of June 1745 to the thirtieth day of June 1746; and on thirty pounds from
the thirtieth day of June 1746 to the thirtieth day of June 1747; And on the said
twenty five pounds, ten shillings and six pence half penny from thence to the time of
paiment and costs; And this Judgment is to remain as a Security in case another
Breach of the Obligation in the Declaration mentioned shall happen
    - JOHN HOGG & ELEANOR his Wife, Admrx. of JOHN SAVAGE, deced.,
    Plts. agst GEORGE SMITH, SENR., Deft.   In Case
This day came the parties by their Attornies and thereupon came also a Jury to
wit   WILLIAM CHRISTOPHER   ZACHARIA GIBBS   DAVID GRIFFIN
        WILLIAM JONES   THOMAS SLAUGHTER   SAMUEL SHORT
        LEONARD TERRENCE   JOHN REYNOLDS   THOMAS GIBSON
        THOMAS SIMS   STOCKELY TOWLES   GEORGE DOGGETT
who being elected tried and sworn the truth to speak upon the issue joined, upon their
Oath do say that the Deft. did assume upon himself in manner and form as Plts.
against him hath declared and they do assess the Plts.'s damages by occasion of the
non performance of that assumption to three pounds current money besides his costs
Therefore it is considered by the Court that Plts. recover against Deft. their damages
aforesaid in form aforesaid assessed and their costs by them about their suit in this
behalf expended, and Deft. in mercy, &c.

p.   Orange County Court 23d of July 1747
7   - Sucky, a Negro girl, is by the Court adjudged to be three years old, Gregory
       and Jack five years old each, (   ) and Esther eight years each belonging to
WILLIAM PANNILL
       - On motion of JANE HUBBARD, a witness for JOHN HOG & ELEANOR his
Wife, Admrx. of JOHN SAVAGE, deced., Plts. against GEORGE SMITH, SENR., it is
ordered that said JOHN & ELEANOR pay her one hundred nine pounds of toacco for
one days attendance at this Court and for coming twenty eight miles from KING
GEORGE County and returning according to Law
       - ANTHONY STROTHER, Gent., Plt. agst WILLIAM NASH, Deft. In Debt
This day came the parties by their Attornies and thereupon came also a Jury, to
wit   WILLIAM CHRISTOPHER   ZACHARIA GIBBS   DAVID GRIFFIN
        WILLIAM JONES   AMBROSE POWELL   SAMUEL SHORT
        LEONARD TERRENCE   JOHN REYNOLDS   THOMAS GIBSON
        THOMAS SIMS   STOCKLEY TOWLES   GEORGE DOGGETT
who being elected tried and sworn the truth to speak upon the issue joined, upon their
Oath do say that the Deft. hath not paid the Debt in the Declaration mentioned and
that the ballance thereof is thirty pounds and six pence half penny. Therefore it is

considered by the Court that Plt. recover against Deft. the thirty pounds and six pence half penny and his costs by him about his suit in this behalf expended, and Deft. in mercy, &c.

- ANTHONY STROTHER, Merchant, Plt. agst
NICHOLAS CHRISTOPHER, Deft.   In Case

The Sherif making return that he had attached one old Plate and Deft. not appearing to replevy the same, whereupon Plt. made Oath to his Account against the Deft., the ballance thereof appearing to be five pounds, eighteen shillings and eleven pence. Therefore it is considered by the Court that Plt. recover against Deft. the five pounds, eighteen shillings and eleven pence and his costs by him about his suit in this behalf expended, and the Deft. in mercy, &c., and it is ordered that the Sherif make sale of the Plate according to Law and the money arising from such sale to pay to the Plt. in discharge of so much of this Judgment

- MICHAEL COOK, JOHN ZIMMERMAN and ZACHARIAS BLANKEN-BEKER in pursuance of an order of this Court for Viewing a Way, this day made return, "that according to an Order of this Worshipfull Court of the County of Orange, we the Subscribers have viewed the new Road beginning at a Poplar by the corner of ROBERT KING's Plantation, and runing along their Old Rolling Road to JAMES YOWELL's Plantation and turn out of the said Road on the tp of a Hill and runing a straight course to JOHN THOMAS's Rolling Road and along the said Road upon PETER FLESHMAN's land and tenement of the said Road by the side of a Branch and up a bottom on top of a hill into JOHN THOMAS's Old Rolling Road and alaong the said Road unto JOHN ZIMMERMAN's Plantation and turns out of the said Road into JOHN ZIMMERMAN's Path along the said Plath and turns out of the Path in a bottom

p.   Orange County Court 23d of July 1747
8   and runs across the CATTAIL BRANCH to BLOODWORTH's ROAD in a
         bottom by a Ring Oak. Whereupon it is ordred that ROBERT KING, JOSEPH KING, JOHN THOMAS, JOHN SHEPPARD, CHRISTOPHER YOWELL, JAMES YOUELL, DAVID YOUELL, THOMAS GARRETT, RICHARD MULLIN, ANTHONY HEAD, WILLIAM CARROL. JOHN SAMPSON do clear the said Way and keep in repair

- ROBERT GREEN & WILLIAM RUSSELL, Gent., Churchwardens of
Saint Mark's Parish, Plts. agst ANNE LOVELL, Single Woman, Deft. In Debt

This day came Plts. by their Attorney and Deft. being again solemnly called came not. Therefore it is considered by the Court that Plts. recover against the Deft. and GABRIEL LOVELL, her Security, five hundred pounds of tobacco and cask or fifty shillings for the use of the said Parish and their costs by them about their suit in this behalf expended, and Deft. in mercy, &c.

- ROBERT GREEN & WILLIAM RUSSELL, Gent., Churchwardens of Saint
Mark's Parish, Plts agst JEMIMA WILLIAMS, Single Woman, Deft. In Debt

This day came Plts. by their Attorney and Deft. being again solemnly called came not; Therefore it is considered by the Court that Plts. recover against Deft. and JAMES WILLIAMS, her Security, five hundred pounds of tobacco and cask or fifty shillings or the use of the said Parish and their costs by them about their suit in this behalf expended, and Deft. in mercy, &c.

- ROBERT RAE & DANIEL CAMPBELL, Merchants, Plts. agst.
GEORGE HOME, Deft.   In Case
The Deft. not being arrested, on Plts.'s motion, a Plurius Capias is awarded them
against the Deft. returnable to the next Court
      - JOHN SMITH, JUNR., Plt. agst. THOMAS YATES, Deft.   In Debt
CHRISTOPHER ZIMMERMAN, Security for Deft.'s appearance, came into Court
and delivered the Deft. up in discharge of himself and thereupon Deft. comes and
defends the force and injury when, &c., and saith that he hath paid the Debt in the
Writing Obligatory in the Declaration mentioned and further that he did not assume
upon himself in manner and form as Plt. against him hath complained and of this he
puts himself upon the Country and Plt. likewise. Therefore the Trial of the issue is
referred til the next Court
      - Present. ROBERT EASTHAM, Gent.

p.   Orange County Court 23d of July 1747
9   - JUDITH CHEEK, the Wife of JOHN CHEEK, being brought before the
      Court on Suspicion of being Guilty of felonious stealing several goods belonging
to SAMUEL HILDRUP of the Town of FREDERICKSBURG and upon examination
denied the fact. Whereupon it is the oppinion of the Court that she is Guilty of a mis-
demeanor and thereupon it is ordered that she be committed to the Goal of this County there to remain until she finds two Securities to be bound in Recognizance with her,
herself in the sum of twenty pounds, and her Securities in ten pounds each, to be on
condition that she shall appear at the next Grand Jury Court to answer what shall be
objected to her
      - Ordered that the Court be adjourned till tomorrow morning 8 o'clock
      - The Minutes of these Proceedings were signed
                              R. EASTHAM

- At a Court continued and held for Orange County on Fryday the 24th day
of July 1747   Present

ROBERT GREEN	WILLIAM RUSSELL	
SAMUEL BALL	HENRY FIELD	Gentlemen
FRANCIS SLAUGHTER	PHILLIP CLAYTON &	
	JAMES PENDLETON	

      - Upon the Attachment brought by GEORGE BUCKHANNON & COMPANY
against the Estate of WILLIAM PETTY, THOMAS SIMS, the Garnishee, appeared
in Court and being sworn declared that he owes Deft. one pound, four shillings and
eight pence which he is ordered to keep in his hands till further orders
      - JOHN PENDERGRASS, Plt. agst. WILLIAM RUSSELL, Gent., Deft.
In Case
This suit is dismissed and it is ordered that Plt. pay unto Deft. his costs
      - The Petition of JOHN GRYMES, Esqr. & FRANCIS WILLIS, Gent. Execu-
tors, &c. of HENRY WILLIS, Gent., deced., against TULLY CHOICE is dismissed
being agreed by the parties
      - The King agst MICHAEL COOK   On an Information
Continued till next Court

p.   Orange County Court 24th of July 1747
10   - JOHN RAINS, Plt. agst. JOHN FINNEL, Deft. In Assault & Battery
        This day came the parties by their Attornies and thereupon came also a Jury
to wit THOMAS SIMS   THOMAS THORNTON   DAVID GRIFFIN
       JOHN BOURNE   JOSEPH REYNOLDS   BRYAN SYSON
       JAMES SUGGITT   AMBROSE POWEL   MICHAEL WHATLEY
       JOHN CHRISTOPHER   JOHN MORPHIS   HARBIN MOOR

who being elected tried and sworn the truth to speak upon the issue joined, upon their
Oath do say that Deft. is Guilty of the Assault and Battery in the Declaration mentioned and they do assess the Plt.'s damages by occasion thereof to twenty shillings
Sterling. Therefore it is considered by the Court that Plt. recover against Deft. his
damages aforesaid in form aforesaid assessed and the Deft. in mercy, &c.
        - The Churchwardens of Saint Mark's Parish, Plts. agst.
        ANNE STUART, Single Woman, Deft.   In Debt
    This day came the Plts. by their Attorney and Deft. being again solemnly called
came not. Therefore it is considered by the Court that Plts. recover against Deft. and
CHRISTOPHER ZIMMERMAN, her Security, five hundred pounds of tobacco and
cask or fifty shillings, the Debt in the Declaration mentioned, for the use of the said
Parish and their costs by them about their suit in this behalf expended, and Deft. in
mercy, &c.
        - JOHN NEWPORT, Plt. agst. WILLIAM HUGHES, Deft.   In Detinue
    This day came the parties by their Attornies and thereupon the matters of Law
arising upon the Special Verdict in this Cause being argued, it seems to the Court
that the Law is for the Plt. Therefore it is considered by the Court that Plt. recover
against Deft. four pounds current money, the damages in the Verdict aforesaid for the
detaining the Gelding in the Declaration mentioned assessed and his costs by him
about his suit in this behalf expended, and Deft. in mercy, &c.
        - On motion of JOSEPH KIRK, a witness for JOHN RAINS, Plt. against
JOHN FINNEL, Deft., who made Oath that he had attended sixteen dayes as an
evidence in that suit. It is ordered that the said RAINS pay him four hundred pounds
of tobacco for his said attendance according to Law

p.   Orange County Court 24th of July 1747
11   - Upon Petition of HUMPHREY BELL against HUGH MARTIN for three
        pounds, ten shillings and two pence said to be due by Account, this day came
Plt. by his Attorney and Deft. not appearing and Plt.'s Account being proved by the
Oath of WILLIAM COWNE, Gent., therefore it is considered by the Court that Plt.
recover against Deft. the three pounds, ten shillings and two pence and his costs by
him about his suit in this behalf expended, together with a Lawyer's fee
        - The Presentment of the Grandjury against MARY THORNTON, the said
MARY not appearing, another Attachment is awarded against her returnable to next
Court
        - The Presentment of the Grandjury against THOMAS FOX is continued till
next Court
        - The Presentment of the Grandjury against JOHN INGRAM is continued till
next Court
        - The Presentment of the Grandjury against JOHN WILLIS is continued till
next Court

- Present. ROBERT SLAUGHTER, Gent.
- JOHN GRYMES Esqr., & FRANCIS WILLIS, Gent., Executors &c. of
HENRY WILLIS, Gent., Plts. agst GEORGE HOME, Deft.   In Case
Continued till next Court
- HUMPHREY BELL of London, Mercht., Plt. agst. DAVID MOOR, Deft.
In Case
This day came the parties by their Attorneys and thereupon came a Jury, to wit

THOMAS SIMS	THOMAS THORNTON	DAVID GRIFFIN
JOHN BOURNE	JOSEPH REYNOLDS	BRYAN SYSON
JAMES SUGGITT	AMBROSE POWEL	MICHAEL WHATLEY
JOHN CHRISTOPHER	JOHN MORPHIS	HARBIN MOOR

who being elected tried and sworn the truth to speak upon the issue joined, upon their
Oath do say that Deft. did assume upon himself in manner and form as Plt. against
him hath declared and they do assess the Plt.'s damages by occasion of the non performance of that assumption to five pounds, seventeen shillings three pence three
farthings, besides his costs. Therefore it is considered by the Court that Plt. recover
against Deft. his damages aforesaid in form aforesaid assessed and his costs by him
about his suit in this behalf expended, and Deft. in mercy, &c.
- ISAAC SMITH, Plt. agst. ROBERT BOHANNON, Deft.   In Chancery
On motion of Plt. by his Council a Commission is awarded him to take the Deposition of his witnesses in this Cause giving Deft. legal notice of the time and place of
executing the same, and the Cause is continued till next Court at the costs of Plt.

p.   Orange County Court 24th of July 1747
12   - EDWARD TEAL, Plt. agst. JOHN MISCAL, PHILLIP CLAYTON and
       WILLIAM BEVERLEY, Gent., Defts. In Chancery
Continued till next Court
- RICHARD WINSLOW, Plt. agst DENNIS BYRNE, EDWARD SPENCER
and ISAAC SMITH, Defts.   In Debt
Continued till next Court at the motion and costs of Plt. By consent of the parties
by their Attornies, Commissions are awarded them to examine and take the Depo-
sitions of JOSEPH MORTON, Gent., a witness for the Plt. to be directed to some of
the Justices of KING GEORGE County Court, each party giving the other legal
notice of the time and place of executing the same
- CHARLES DICK, Mercht., Plt. agst WILLIAM RUSH, Deft.   In Case
Dismissed being agreed by the parties
- BENJAMIN BORDEN, Plt. agst JAMES ARMSTRONG, Deft.   In Debt
Continued till the next Court
- JAMES BELL, Plt. agst. GEORGE HOME, Deft. In Case
The Deft. not appearing, on motion of Plt. by his Attorney, another Attachment is
awarded him against Deft.'s Estate returnable to the next Court
- Absent. PHILLIP CLAYTON & JAMES PENDLETON, Gent.
- Present. GOODRICH LIGHTFOOT, Gent.
- JAMES PENDLETON and PHILLIP CLAYTON, Gent., Plts. agst
JOHN RAY, Deft.   In Debt
The Deft. not appearing, on motion of Plts. by their Attorney, another Attachment
is awarded them against Deft.'s Estate returnable to next Court

p.   Orange County Court 24th of July 1747
13   - The Attachment brought by PHILLIP CLAYTON and JAMES PENDLE-
      TON, Gent., against the Estate of THOMAS HANNAN is continued till next
Court
      - On motion of ISAAC SMITH, a witness for JOHN FINNEL at the suit of
JOHN RAINS, who made Oath that he had attended this Court nineteen days as an
evidence in that suit, it is ordered that said FINNEL pay him four hundred seventy
five pounds of tobacco for his said attendance according to Law
      - ROBERT HILL, Plt. agst ALEXANDER WAUGH, Deft.   In Case
This day came the parties by their Attornies and thereupon came a Jury, to wit,

THOMAS SIMS	THOMAS THORNTON	DAVID GRIFFIN
JOHN FINELL	JOSEPH REYNOLDS	BRYAN SYSON
JAMES SUGGITT	AMBROSE POWELL	MICHAEL WHATLEY
THOMAS HOUISON	JOHN MORPHIS	HARBIN MOOR

who being elected tried and sworn the truth to speak upon the issue joined, (the Plt.
offered a list of a hogshead of tobacco signed by JOSEPH STEWART, an Inspector at
ROYSTON's WAREHOUSE as evidence in this Cause, which was approved by the
Deft. but the same was allowed to be given as evidence) upon their Oath do say that
Deft. did assume upon himself in manner and form as Plt. against him hath declared
and they do assess the Plt.'s damages by occasion of the non performance of that
assumption to two thousand three hundred seventy five pounds of tobacco besides his
costs. Whereupon the Deft. to stay the Judgment thereon filed his Plea in arrest
thereof and the Cause is continued to the next Court for the matters of Law arising
thereupon to be argued
      - RICHARD BREEDIN CROSS having been summoned to attend as a
witness for ROBERT HILL, Plt. against ALEXANDER WAUGH, Deft. and not
appearing, it is ordered that he forfeit and pay to said ROBERT three hundred fifty
pounds of tobacco unless at the next Court he shew cause to the contrary
      - Present. PHILLIP CLAYTON & JAMES PENDLETON, Gent.
      - HUMPHREY BELL, Plt. agst. WILLIAM COX, Deft.   In Debt
The Deft. being not arrested, on motion of Plt. by his Attorney another Plurius
Capias is awared against him returnable to the next Court
      - JOHN BELFIELD and WILLIAM JORDAN, Executors, &c., of THOMAS
      WRIGHT BELFIELD, Gent., deced., Plts. agst WILLIAM MORTON, Deft.
      In Chancery
Continued for the Auditors to make return of their Proceedings to the next Court
      - DANIEL HORNBY, Gent.,Plt. agst WILLIAM MORTON, Deft.   In Debt
Continued for the Auditors to make return of their Proceedings to the next Court

p.   Culpeper County Court 24th of July 1747
14   - JANE WHARTON, Widow and Admrx., &c. of THOMAS WHARTON,
      deced., Plt. agst   THOMAS CHEW, Gent., Sherif of Orange County, Deft.
      In Case
The Deft. not appearing, on motion of Plt. by her Attorney, an Attachament is
awarded her against Deft.'s Estate returnable to next Court
      - The Petition of THOMAS CHEW, Gent., against ROBERT GREEN, Gent. is
continued till the next Court at motion and costs of Plt.

- DIANA WHEELER, Exrx., &c. of JOHN WHEELER, deced., Plt. agst
DAVID KINKEAD, Admr. &c. of JOHN HOBSON, deced., Deft.
On a Scire Facias

This day came Plt. by ZACHARY LEWIS, Gent., her Attorney, and the Sherif
returning that the Deft. hath nothing in his Bailiwick whereby he could cause him to
know nor is he found within the same; on motion of Plt. an Alias Scire Facias is
awarded her against the Deft. returnable to the next Court

- WILLIAM WROE, Exr. &c. of WILLIAM BRIDGES, deced., Plt. agst.
WILLIAM WHITE, Deft.   On a Scire Facias

This day came Plt. by ZACHARY LEWIS, Gent., his Attorney, and the Sherif
returning that the Deft. hath nothing in his Bailiwick whereby he could cause him to
know nor is he found within the same, on motion of Plt. an Alias Scire Facias is
awarded im against the Deft. returnable to the next Court

- JOHN WHARTON, Plt. agst. JANE WHARTON, Admrx. &c. of THOMAS
WHARTON, deced., Deft. In Case

This day came Plt. by ZACHARY LEWIS, Gent., his Attorney, and Deft. being
returned arrested was solemnly called but came not. Therefore on the motion of Plt.,
it is ordered that unless she appear her at the next Court to answer Plt.'s action
Judgment shall then be entered for Plt. against her, the Deft., for the Debt in the
Declaration mentioned and costs

p.   Orange County Court 24th of July 1747
15   - RICHARD DOGGETT by GEORGE DOGGETT his next Friend, Plt. agst
        WILLIAM BUNTINE, Deft.   In Assault and Battery

This day came Plt. by ZACHARY LEWIS, Gent., his Attorny, and Deft. not being
arrested, on motion of Plt. an Alias Capias is awarded him against the Deft., returnable to the next Court

- MARTIN DEWITT, Plt. agst. MICAJAH PICKET, Deft.
In Assault and Battery

This day came Plt. by ZACHARY LEWIS, Gent. his Attorney, and Deft. not being
arrested, on motion of Plt. an Alias Capias is awarded him against the Deft. returnable to the next Court

- KEENE FIELD Quitam &c. Plt. agst. WILLIAM RUSSELL, Gent., Deft.
In Debt

This day came Plt. who as well, &c., by ZACHARY LEWIS, Gent., his Attorney,
and Deft. by GEORGE WYTHE, Gent., his Attorney, and Deft. defends the force and
injury when, &c., and prays and has leave to imparl til the next Court and then to
plead

- HUMPHREY BELL of London, Mercht., Plt. agst.
WILLIAM NASH, Deft. In Case

This day came Plt. by ZACHARY LEWIS, Gent., his Attorney, and Deft. being
returned arrested was solemnly called but came not. Therefore on motion of Plt., it is
ordered that unless he appears here at the next Court and answers Plts. action,
Judgment shall then be entered for Plt. against him, the Deft., and JAMES
POLLARD, his Security, for the Debt in the Declaration

- JOHN ALLAN, Merchant, Plt. agst. WILLIAM McDONAUGH, Deft. In Debt

This day came Plt. by ZACHARY LEWIS, Gent., his Attorney and Deft. being arrested was solemnly called but came not. Therefore it is ordered that unless he appears at the next Court and answers Plt.'s action, Judgment shall then be entered for Plt. against him, the Deft. and WILLIAM CRAWFORD, his Security, and THOMAS CHEW, Gent., Sherif of Orange County, for the Debt in the Declaration mentioned and costs

p.   Culpeper County Court 24th of July 1747
16   - On the motion of GEORGE DOGGETT, a witness for ROBERT HILL, Plt. against ALEXANDER WAUGH, Deft., it is ordered that said ROBERT pay him fifty pounds of tobacco for two days attendance according to Law

- On motion of JOHN LYNCH, a witness for ALEXANDER WAUGH at the suit of ROBERT HILL, who made Oath that he had attended five days as an evidence in that suit, it is ordered that the said ALEXANDER pay him one hundred twenty five pounds of tobacco for his said attendance according to Law

- On motion of WILLIAM MILLER, a winess for ROBERT HILL, Plt. against ALEXANDER WAUGH, Deft., it is ordered that said ROBERT pay him one hundred sixty four pounds of tobacco for two days attendance and for coming thirty eight miles from SPOTSYLVANIA County, and returning according to Law

- Upon Petition of JAMES SUGGITT against WILLIAM KIRTLEY for four hundred forty four pounds of tobacco and three shillings said to be due by Account, this day came Plt. and Deft. being served with a copy of the Petition and summoned to appear was called but came not. Therefore it is considered by the Court that Plt. recover against Deft. the four hundred forty four pounds of tobacco and three shillings and his costs by him about his suit in this behalf expended

- Upon Petition of HUMPHREY BELL against JOSEPH REYNOLDS for a Debt therein said to be due by Account, this day came the parties by their Attornies who being fully heard, it is ordered that the Petition be dismissed

- JOHN COBURN, Plt. agst. WILLIAM LONG, Deft.   In Case
This day came Plt. by ZACHARY LEWIS, Gent., his Attorney, and Plt. moved that Deft. might give Special Bail which was opposed but the same was granted and Deft. being solemnly called came not. Whereupon GEORGE LIVINGSTON, Security for Deft.'s appearance, by GEORGE WYTHE, Gent., his Attorney, comes and defends the force and injury when, &c., and prays and has leave to imparl thereof til the next Court and then to plead

- Upon Petition of ANDREW RAY against SAMUEL POUND for three pounds, one shilling and one penny said to be due by Account, this day came Plt. by ZACHARY LEWIS, Gent., his Attorney, and Deft. being served with a copy of the Petition and summoned to appear was called but came not. Therefore it is considered by the Court that Plt. recover against Deft. the three pounds, one shilling and one penny and his costs by him about his suit in this behalf expended

p.   Orange County Court 24th of July 1747
17   - Upon Petition of CHARLES DICK against JOHN SMITH, JUNR. for four pounds four and two pence half penny therein said to be due by Bill, this day came Plt. by ZACHARY LEWIS, Gent, his Attorney, and Deft. having been served with a copy of the Petition and summoned to appear was called but came not. Therefore it is considered by the Court that Plt. recover against Deft. the four pounds, four

shillings and two pence half penny and his costs by him about his suit in this behalf
expended, together with a Lawyer's fee

- Upon Petition of THOMAS HOUISON against SUSANNAH ANDERSON,
Admrx. &c. of GEORGE ANDERSON, deced., for two pounds, thirteen shillings and
six pence therein said to be due by Account, this day came the parties by their Attornies who being fully heard, it seems to the Court that the Intestate was in his life
time indebted to Plt. Therefore it is considered by the Court that Plt. recover against
Deft. twenty six shillings and his costs by him about his suit in this behalf expended,
to be levied of the goods and chattels of the said GEORGE in the hands of the said
SUSANNAH to be administered if so much she hath, if not that then the costs to be
levied of the proper goods and chattels of the said SUSANNAH

- THOMAS THORNTON, Plt. agst. JOHN CHRISTOPHER, Deft.   In Debt
This day came Plt. by ZACHARY LEWIS, Gent., his Attorney and Deft. being returned arrested was solemnly called but came not. Therefore on moton of Plt., it is
ordered that unless he appears at next Court and answers Plt.'s action Judgment
shall then be entered for Plt. against him, the Deft., and THOMA CHEW, Gent.,
Sherif of Orange County, for the Debt in the Declaration mentioned and costs

- HUMPHREY BELL Merchant Plt. agst. RICHARD WINSLOW, Deft.
In Case
This day came Plt. by ZACHARY LEWIS, Gent., his Attorney, and Deft. by
GEORGE WYTHE, Gent. his Attorney and Deft. prays and has leave to imparl there-
of til the next Court and then to plead

- The Petition of HUMPHREY BELL against JOHN SMITH, JUNR, is continued till next Court

- WILLIAM KELLY, Plt. agst JOHN LATHAM, Deft.
Dismissed

p.   Orange County Court 24th of July 1747
18   - WILLIAM RUSSELL, Gent., Plt. agst JANE WHARTON, Admrx. &c. of
        THOMAS WHARTON, deced., Deft.   In Case
This day came as well Plt. by GEORGE WYTHE, Gent., his Attorney as Deft. by
ZACHARY LEWIS, Gent. her Attorney and Deft. prays and has leave to imparl
thereof til next Court and then to plead

- Ordered that the Court be adjourned til tomorrow morning 8 o'clock
- The Minutes of these Proceedings were signed
                        ROBERT SLAUGHTER

- At a Court continued and held for Orange County on Saturday the 25th day
of July 1747   Present
WILLIAM RUSSELL   EDWARD SPENCER
HENRY FIELD   GOODRICH LIGHTFOOT   Gentlemen

- EDWARD WARE, Plt. agst WILLIAM CUDDEN, Deft.   On a Writ of Scire
Facias on a Judgment of this Court obtained the 23d day of March 1743 by Plt.
against Deft. for two pounds, eleven shillings and two pence half penny and
fifty nine pounds of nett tobacco and seven shillings and six pence
The Sherif again returning that Deft. hath nothing in his Bailiwick whereby he could

cause him to know neither is he found in the same. Therefore on motion of Plt. it is ordered that Judgment be entered for Plt. that he have Execution against Deft. according to the force form and effect of the recovery aforesaid for his costs expended in suing for and prosecuting this Writ

    - The Petition of PHILLIP CLAYTON and JAMES PENDLETON, Gent., against JAMES POLLARD is dismissed

p.
19
    Orange County Court 25th of July 1747

    - The Petition of WILLIAM FRAZIER against ISAAC SMITH is continued till the next Court

    - JOHN LEWIS, BEVERLEY WHITING and WARNER WASHINGTON, Gent., Exrs. &c. of JOHN WASHINGTON, Gent., late Sherif of GLOUCES-TER County, deced., Plts. agst. ROBERT FREEMAN, Deft.   In Case

This day came Plts. by GEORGE WYTHE, Gent., their Attorney and Deft. being returned arrested was solemnly called but came not. Thererfore on motion of Plts. it is ordered that unless he appears here at the next Court and answers Plts.'s action, Judgment shall then be entered for Plts. against him, the Deft. and THOMAS CHEW, Gent., Sherif of Orange County, for the Debt in the Declaration mentioned and costs

    - JOHN BEAZLEY, Plt. agst. SPENCER BRAMHAM, Deft.

    In Assault and Battery

This day came as well Plt. by GEORGE WYTHE, Gent., his Attorney as Deft. by ZACHARY LEWIS, Gent., his Attorney and Deft. saving and reserving to himself all advantages as well to the Writ as Declaration prays and has leave to imparl thereof til the next Court and then to plead

    - BATTAIL HARRISON, Plt. agst. THOMAS EDMONDSON, Deft. In Case

Dismissed being agreed by the parties

    - RICHARD VERNON, Plt. agst. JAMES McDANIEL, Deft.   In Debt

Dismissed be agreed by the parties

    - JOHN BLANTON, Plt. agst GEORGE DOGGETT, Deft. In Debt

This day came Plt. by his Attorney and Deft. not being arrested, on motion of Plt. an Alias Capias is awarded him against Deft. returnable to next Court

    - JOHN BRAMHAM, Plt. agst EDWARD WHITE, Deft.   In Trespass

Dismissed being agreed by the parties

p.
20
    Orange County Court 25th of July 1747

    - The Attachment brought by ROBERT RAE and DANIEL CAMPBELL against the Estate of NATHANIEL HEDGMAN is continued til next Court

    - The Attachment brought by ANDREW ROSS against the Estate of NATHANIEL HEDGMAN is continued til next Court

    - The Attachment brought by CHRISTOPHER HOMES and others against the Estate of RICHARD YARBROUGH is continued til next Court

    - JAMES HUNTON, Merchant, Plt. agst THOMAS COVINGTON, Deft.

    In Case

Dismissed

    - RICHARD BRIDGES, Plt. agst. THOMAS CHEW, Deft. In Debt

Continued til next Court at motion and costs of Plt.

- ISAAC SMITH, Plt. agst TIMOTHY CROSTHWAIT, Deft.   In Case
Continued till next Court
- The Petition of GEORGE BUCKHANNON and WILLIAM HAMILTON,
Executors, &c. of NEIL BUCKHANNON, deced., against THOMAS PETTY is continued til next Court at costs of Plts.
- The Petition of RICHARD WINSLOW against ISAAC SMITH is continued til next Court
- The Petition of GEORGE BUCKHANNON and WILLIAM HAMILTON,
Executors, &c. of NEIL BUCKHANNON, deced. against ROBERT HILL is continued til next Court at costs of Plts.
- ROBERT HARRIS, Plt. agst JOSEPH WALSH, Deft.   In Case
Continued til next Court at costs of Plt.
- ANTHONY STROTHER, Merchant, Plt. agst NICHOLAS CHRISTOPHER
Deft. In Case
Dismissed

p.   Orange County Court 25th of July 1747
21   - ANDREW ROSS, Merchant, Plt. agst GEORGE SMITH, JUNR., Deft.
        In Case
The Sherif having returned executed on the Capias, and Deft. in Goal and it appearing to the Court that he was sent to the Public Goal on suspicion of Felony after the taking by virtue of the Capias aforesaid, from whence has not returned from the Goal of thsi County, and he being solemnly called and not appearing, this suit is discontinued
- ANTHONY STROTHER, Merchant, Plt. agst SAMUEL FARGUSON,
Deft. In Case
This day came the parties by their Attorneys and Deft. relinquishing his former Plea saith he cannot gainsay Plt.'s action nor but that he is indebted to him one hundred six pounds, thirteen shillings and eleven pence farthing. Therefore it is considered by the Court that Plt. recover against Deft. the one hundred six pounds, thirteen shillings and eleven pence farthing and his costs by him about his suit in this behalf expended, and Deft. in mercy, &c., And the Plt. agrees that the Execution of this Judgment shall be stayed til the Court to be held for this County in June next
- THOMAS CHEW, Gent., Plt. agst SUSANNAH RUCKER, Exrx. &c. of
PETER RUCKER, Exr. &c. of JOHN RUCKER, deced., Deft.   In Case
Continued til next Court
- RICHARD WINSLOW, Gent., Plt. agst THOMAS WHARTON, Deft. In Case
Continued til next Court at motion and costs of Plt.
- ROBERT GREEN, Gent., Plt. agst GABRIEL LOVING, Deft.   In Case
Continued til next Court
- Upon the Presentment of the Grandjury against ANNE BRIDGES, the said ANNE not appearing, another summons is awarded against her returnable to the next Court

p.   Orange County Court 25th of July 1747
22   - MATHEW TOOL, Plt. agst MARTIN WALLOCK, Deft.   In Trespass
        Continued til next Court at motion and costs of Deft.

- THOMAS CHEW, Gent., Plt. agst JAMES BARBOUR, Gent., Deft.
In Trespass

This suit is dismissed and it is ordered that Plt. pay unto Deft. his costs

- The Petition of EDWARD WARE against WILLIAM STEVENS is continued til the next Court at the costs of the Plaintif

- ANDREW HARRISON who hath been summoned as a witness for EDWARD WARE against WILLIAM STEVENS was called and not appearing, it is ordered that he forfeit and pay to the said EDWARD three hundred fifty pounds of tobacco unless at next Court he shew cause to the contrary

- RICHARD WINSLOW, Gent., Plt. agst ROBERT SEAYRES and JOHN SEAYRES, Defts. In Case

This day came Plt. by his Attorney and Defts. being again solemnly called came not. Therefore it is ordered that Judgment be entered for Plt. against them, the Defts. and THOMAS CHEW, Gent., Sherif of Orange County, for the Debt in the Declaration mentioned and his costs to be ascertained on Inquiry by a Jury at next Court

- JOHN MORGAN and MARY his Wife, Plts. agst WILLIAM LIGHTFOOT, Deft. In Case

This day came as well Plts. by ZACHARY LEWIS, Gent., their Attorney, as Deft. by GEORGE WYTHE, Gent., his Attorney, and Deft. prays and has leave to imparl til next Court and then to plead

- WILLIAM HUGHES, Plt. agst THOMAS SANDERS, Deft. In Debt

The Deft. not being yet arrested, on motion of Plt. a Plurius Capias is awarded against him returnable to next Court

p.
23
    Orange County Court 25th of July 1747
- DANIEL HORNBY, Gent., Plt. agst CHRISTOPHER HOOMES, JOHN NEWPORT, GEORGE HOME, JEREMIAH ROSSON and RUSSELL HILL, Defts.   On a Scire Facias in a Recognizance entered into by Defts. in Orange County Court the 26th day of July 1745 whereby they undertook that if RICHARD YARBROUGH shold be convicted in an action then depending between the Plt. and said YARBROUGH that he should pay such Debt, damages and costs as should be adjudged to the Plt. or render his body to Prison for the same or that they the Defts. should do it for him; And Plt. having at a Court held for Orange County recovered against the said YARBROUGH thirty three pounds, seventeen shillings and five pence for Debt, one hundred eighty two pounds of nett tobacco and fifteen shillings or one hundred fifty pounds of tobacco for his costs; But to be discharged by payment of nineteen pounds, eighteen shillings and eight pence with Interest thereon at the rate of five percent per annum from the twenty ninth day of September 1743 to the time of paiment and costs which said YARBROUGH hath not paid nor surrendered his body to Prison as aforesaid.

This day came the Plt. by his Attorney and Defts. HOMES, ROSSON and HILL being warned and not appearing and the Sherif as to the Deft. HOME having twice returned that he hath nothing in his Bailiwick, whereby he could cause him to know neither is he found within the same and as to the other Deft., NEWPORT, this suit abates by his death; Therefore it is considered by the Court that Plt. recover against CHRISTOPHER HOMES, GEORGE HOME, JEREMIAH ROSSON and

RUSSELL HILL the sums aforesaid according to the force form and effect of the recovery against the said YARBROUGH and his costs by him expened in suing forth and prosecuting this Writ

- ROBERT BOURN Plt. agst. ARJALON PRICE, Deft. In Case

This day came the parties by their Attornies and thereupon came also a Jury, to

wit	MATHEW TOOL	THOMAS HUGHES	WILLIAM POUND
	WILLIAM PINNION	JOHN BRAMHAM	THOMAS FOX
	JOHN SMITH	SAMUEL SHORT	ELI GRIFFIN
	RICHARD SHIP	MICHAEL WHATLEY &	SAMUEL POUND

who being elected tried and sworn the truth to speak upon the issue joined, upon their Oath do say that Deft. did assume upon himself in manner and form as Plt. against him hath supposed and they do assess Plt.'s damages by occasion of the non performance of that assumption to four pounds, nineteen shillings and one penny besides his costs. Therefore it is considered by the Court that Plt. recover against Deft. his damages aforesaid in form aforesaid assessed and his costs by him about his suit in this behalf expended, and Deft. in mercy, &c.

p.   Orange County Court 25th of July 1747
24   - THOMAS GRAVES, Plt. agst ANDREW BOURN, Deft.   In Case
Continued til next Court
   - MARGARET RICE, Admrx. &c. of HENRY RICE, deced., Plt. agst.
NICHOLAS JONES, Deft.   In Debt

This day came Plt. by her Attorney and Deft. being again solemnly called came not; Therefore it is considered by the Court that Plt. recover against Deft. and THOMAS CHEW, Gent., Sherif of Orange County, ten pounds, twelve shilings and six pence current money of Virginia, the Debt in the Declaration mentioned, and her costs by her about her suit in this behalf expended, and Deft. in mercy, &c.

   - THOMAS PARK, Plt. agst. JOHN ASHER, ROBERT LYONS and
JOSEPH PHILLIPS, Defts.   In Trespass

This day came as well Plt. by ZACHARY LEWIS, Gent., his Attorney, as Defts. by GEORGE WYTHE, Gent., their Attorney, and Defts. pray and have leave to imparl hereof til the next Court and then to plead

   - HENRY PICKETT, Plt. agst THOMAS COLEMAN, Deft.   In Case

This day came as well Plt. by ZACHARY LEWIS, his Attorney as Deft. by GEORGE WYTHE, Gent., his Attorney and Deft. prays and has leave to imparl hereof til the next Court and then to plead

   - WILLIAM STROTHER, Plt. agst. WILLIAM KELLY, Deft.   In Debt
Dismissed
   - JAMES DUN, Plt. agst JOHN SMITH, JUNR., Deft.   In Debt

This day came Plt. by ZACHARY LEWIS, his Attorney, and Deft. being returned arrested was solemnly called but came not. Therefore on motion of Plt. it is ordered that unless he appears at next Court and answers Plt.'s action, Judgment shall then be entered for Plt. against him, the Deft. and JOHN SMITH, his Security, for the Debt in the Declaration mentioned and costs

p.   Orange County Court 25th of July 1747
25   - JOHN SPOTSWOOD, Gent. Plt. agst JOHN CHRISTOPHER, Deft. In Debt
This day came Plt. by ZACHARY LEWIS, Gent., his Attorney and Deft. being

returned arrested was solemnly called but came not. Therefore on motion of Plt., it is ordered that unless he appears here at next Court and answers Plt.'s action, Judgment shall then be entered for Plt. against him, the Deft., and THOMAS CHEW, Gent., Sherif of Orange County, for the Debt in the Declaration mentioned and costs

  - JOHN SPOTSWOOD, Gent., Plt. agst FRANCIS KIRTLEY, JUNR. and JAMES EARLY, Defts.   In Trespass

This day came Plt. by ZACHARY LEWIS, Gent., his Attorney and Deft., KIRTLEY being returned arrested was solemnly called but came not. Therefore on motion of Plt. it is ordered that unless he appears at next Court and answers Plt.'s action, Judgment shall then be entered for Plt. against him, the Deft., and FRANCIS KIRTLEY, his Security, for the Debt in the Declaration mentioned and costs; And Deft., EARLY, not being arrested, on Plt.'s motion an Alias Capias is awarded him against Deft. returnable to next Court

  - ROBERT HILL, Plt. agst. DANIEL CARTER and WILLIAM NASH, Defts. In Assault and Battery

This day came Plt. by ZACHARY LEWIS, Gent., his Attorney and Deft., NASH, being returned arrested was solemnly called but came not. Therefore on motion of Plt. it is ordered that unless he appears at next Court and answers Plt.'s action, Judgment shall then be entered for Plt. against him, the Deft., and THOMAS CHEW, Gent., Sherif of Orange County, for the Debt in the Declaration mentioned and costs; And the Deft., CARTER, not being arrested, on motion of Plt. an Alias Capias is awarded him against the Deft. returnable to the next Court

  - Upon Petition of WILLIAM LYNN against GEORGE DOGGET for three pounds, four shillings and ten pence therein said to be due by Bill, this day came Plt. by his Attorney and Deft. having been served with a copy of the Petition and summoned to appear was called but came not. Therefore it is considered by the Court that Plt. recover against Deft. the three pounds, four shillings and ten pence and his costs by him about his suit in this behalf expended, and the Deft. in mercy, &c.

  - Upon Petition of SAMUEL SHORT against JAMES McDANIEL for three pounds, five shillings therein said to be due by Note of Hand, this day came Plt. by his Attorney and Deft. having been served with a copy of the Petition and summoned to appear was called but came not. Therefore it is considered by the Court that Plt. recover against Deft. the three pounds, five shillings, and his costs by him about his suit in this behalf expended

p.   Orange County Court 25th of July 1747
26   - The Petition of JAMES DUN against JOHN WILLIS is dismissed
        - The Petition of WILLIAM STROTHER against JACOB MILLER is dismissed
        - The Petition brought by the Executors of NEIL BUCKHANNON, deced. against WILLIAM PETTY is dismissed
        - ANTHONY STROTHER, Gent., Plt. agst ELLIS MARCUS, Deft. In Case Continued til next Court
        - ANTHONY STROTHER, Gent., Plt. agst MICHAEL WHATLEY, Deft. In Case
Continued til next Court

- JOHN SMITH, JUNR., Plt. agst WILLIAM STROTHER, Deft.
In Assault and Battery
This day came Deft. by his Attorney and Plt. tho solemnly called came not but
made default; nor is his suit further prosecuted, Therefore on the prayer of Deft., it is
considered that the Plt. be non suit and pay the Deft. five shillings damages according
to Law and his costs by him about his defence in this behalf expended
- CHRISTOPHER ZIMMERMAN, Plt. agst. ROBERT APPLEBY, Deft.
In Case
Dismissed
- A List of Surveys made in this County between June 1746 and June 1747
returned by the Surveyor and ordered to be recorded
- On motion of FRANCIS MOOR, a witness for ARJALON PRICE at the suit
of ROBERT BOURN, it is ordered that said ARJALON pay him seventy five pounds
of tobacco for three days attendance as an Evidence at this Court according to Law
- On motion of EDWARD PRICE, a witness for ARJALON PRICE at the suit
of ROBERT BOURN, it is ordered that said ARJALON pay him seventy five pounds
of tobacco for three days attendance as an Evidence at this Court according to Law
- On motion of HARBIN MOOR, a witness for ARJALON PRICE at the suit of
ROBERT BOURN, it is ordered that said ARJALON pay him seventy five pounds of
tobacco for three days attendance as an Evidence at this Court according to Law

p.   Orange County Court 25th of July 1747
27   - On motion of LUKE THORNTON, a witness for ARJALON PRICE at the
      suit of ROBERT BOURN, it is ordered that said ARJALON pay him seventy
five pounds of tobacco for three days attendance as an Evidence at this Court according to Law
- On motion of JOHN MARSH, a witness for ROBERT BOURN against AR-
JALON PRICE, ordered that said ROBERT pay him fifty pounds of tobacco for two
days attendance ast this Court according to Law
- The Petition of MARGARET GIBSON against JOHN SMITH is continued til
next Court
- ELIZABETH BUCKHAM, Admrx., &c. of SIMON BUCKHAM, deced., Plt.
agst MICHAEL WHATLEY, Deft.   In Case
This day came the parties by their Attornies and thereupon came a Jury, to wit,

FRANCIS MOOR	HARBIN MOOR	THOMAS HUGHES
JOHN BRAMHAM	THOMAS FOX	JOHN MARSH
LUKE THORNTON	BRYANT SYSON	JOHN SMITH
SAMUEL SHORT	EDWARD PRICE &	ROBERT BOURN

who being elected tried and sworn the truth to speak upon the issue joined, upon their
Oath do day that Deft. is Guilty of the Trover and Conversion in the Declaration
specified and they do assess Plt.'s damages by occasion thereof to eight pounds, five
shillings current money, besides her costs. Therefore it is considered by the Court
that Plt. recover against Deft. her damages aforesaid in form aforesaid assessed and
her costs by her about her suit in this behalf expended, and Deft. in mercy, &c.
- ELIZABETH HARDIN, Plt. agst MICHAEL WHATLEY, Deft.   In Debt
This day came Plt. by GEORGE WYTHE, Gent., her Attorney, and Plt. moved that
Deft. should give Special Bail which was granted, and thereupon JOHN CHRISTO-
PHER, Security for Deft.'s appearance, by ZACHARY LEWIS, Gent., prays and has

leave to imparl hereof til next Court and then to plead

    - FRANCIS THORNTON, Gent., Plt. agst SAMUEL POUND, Deft. In Debt BRYANT SYSON comes and undertakes for Deft. that in case he should be cast in this suit, he shall pay the condemnation of the Court or render his body to Prison or that said BRYANT will do it for him, Therefore Deft. comes and says he cannot gainsay Plt.'s action. Therefore it is considered by the Court that Plt. recover against Deft. eight pounds, twelve shillings, the Debt in the Declaration mentioned, and his costs by him about his suit in this behalf expended, and Deft. in mercy, &c., But this Judgment, the costs excepted, is to be discharged by paiment of four pounds six shillings with Interest thereon at the rate of five percent per annum to be computed from the twenty sixth day of last June to the time of paiment and costs

p.
28
    <u>Orange County Court 25th of July 1747</u>

    - On motion of THOMAS CHEW, Gent. Sherif of Orange County complaining of the insufficiency of the Goal of this County, which being seen by the Court, it is ordered that it be repaired. Whereupon EDWARD SPENCER, Gent., in open Court undertakes the repairs and he is to bring his charges for the same at laying the next County Levy

    - On motion of THOMAS WEATHERBY, a witness for ELIZABETH BUCKHAM, Admrx. &c. of SIMON BUCKHAM, deced.,Plt. against MICHAEL WHATLEY Deft., it is ordered that said ELIZABETH pay him seventy five pounds of tobacco for three days attendance at this Court according to Law

    - On motion of JOHN SLEET, a witness for ELIZABETH BUCKHAM, Admrx. &c. of SIMON BUCKHAM, deced., Plt. against MICHAEL WHATLEY, Deft. it is ordered that said ELIZABETH pay him seventy five pounds of tobacco for three days attendance at this Court according to Law

    - On motion of STEPHEN BUCKHAM, a witness for ELIZABETH BUCKHAM, Admrx. &c. of SIMON BUCKHAM, deced., Plt. against MICHAEL WHATLEY, Deft. it is ordered that said ELIZABETH pay him fifty pounds of tobacco for two days attendance at this Court according to Law

    - ARCHIBALD GORDON and ALEXANDER SCOTT, Plts. agst. WILLIAM PETTY, Deft. In Debt

The Deft. not being arrested, on motion of Plt. by his Attorney, an Alias Capias is awarded him against the Deft. returnable to the next Court

    - Ordered that the Court be adjourned til the fourth Thursday in next month

    - The Minutes of these Proceedings were signed

                        W. RUSSELL

p.
29
    <u>- At a Court held at Orange County Courthouse on the Eighteenth day of</u> August in the Twenty First year of the Reign of our Sovereign Lord George the Second, King of Great Britain, &c., Annoque Domini MDCCXLVII for the Examination of CATHARINE GRANT on Suspicion of her being Guilty of feloniously taking and carrying away goods of the property of FRANCIS TYLER

                     Present

ROBERT SLAUGHTER   GOODRICH LIGHTFOOT

JOHN FINLESON   &   PHILIP CLAYTON   Gentlemen

The said CATHARINE was led to the Bar under the custody of the Keeper of the Goal of this County. Upon Examination denied the fact with which she stood charged. Whereupon divers witnesses were sworn and examined touching the premises and the Prisoner heard in her own defence. On consideration whereof, it is the oppinion of the Court here that she ought to be further prosecuted and on the prayer of the said CATHARINE for immediate punishment, it is ordered that the Sherif take her from the Bar and give her ten Lashes on her bare back at the Common Whipping Post well laid on and it is said to him that he cause execution hereof to be done immediately

The Minutes of these Proceedings were signed

ROBT. SLAUGHTER

- At a Court held for Orange County on Thursday the 27th day of August in the Twenty First year of the Reign of our Sovereign Lord, George the Second, &c., Annoque Domini 1747, before his Majesties Justices of the Peace for the said County, to wit;

ROBERT SLAUGHTER	SAMUEL BALL	FRANCIS SLAUGHTER
GEORGE TAYLOR	JOHN FINLESON	ROBERT GREEN
HENRY FIELD	GOODRICH LIGHTFOOT	Gentlemen

- A Deed Poll from DANIEL COOK to ELIZABETH HARRIS, Wife of ROBERT HARRIS, was acknowledged by said DANIEL and ordered to be recorded

- HENRY FIELD, Gent. Guardian of WILLIAM STANTON, Infant, Orphan of THOMAS STANTON, deced., rendered an Account of his Estate which he made oath and the same was examined and approved of by the Court and ordered to be recorded

- An Inventory and Appraisment of the Estate of WILLIAM CARPENTER, deced., was returned into Court and ordered to be recorded

- An Inventory and Appraisment of the Estate of JOHN NEWPORT, deced., was returned into Court and ordered to be recorded

- On motion of HENRY FIELD, Gent., Guardian of WILLIAM STANTON, the mark of the said STANTON being a staple in the left ear and a nick in the under part of the right ear is ordered to be recorded

- ALEXANDER WAUGH's, ROBERT TERRIL's, ANTHONY GARNETT's and THOMAS FOSTER's Hands are exempted from working on the High Way whereof THOMAS JONES, Gent., is Overseer

- JAMES COOK made Oath that he was imported immediately into this Colony from Great Britain and that this is the first time of his doing the same in order to intitle him to fifty acres of land in this Colony, which in open Court he assigned over to JAMES HERNDON

p.   Orange County Court 27th of August 1747
30   - An Indenture of Bargain and Sale between RICHARD BRADFORD of the
      one part and JAMES MITCHEL of the other part was acknowledged by the
said RICHARD and ordered to be recorded, and RACHEL, the Wife of said RICHARD appeared in Court and being privately examined as the Law directs, voluntarily relinquished her Right of Dower to the Estate conveyed by the said Indenture

- JONATHAN PRATT and ROBERT LEVILL, two of the persons appointed to view the Way from the OLD GERMANNA ROAD by JOHN WILHITE's to the Church at TENNANT's Old Field, returning that it is the most convenient way for a Road. It is ordered that the said Way be established a Public Road and that AMBROSE POWELL be Surveyor of the same and that HENRY SPARKS, JOHN HOLCOM, JOHN THORNTON, WILLIAM CLARK's male labouring Tithables, JOHN LATON, THOMAS PETTY, JUNR., STOKELY TOWLES, RUSSELL HILL, TOBIAS WILHITE, JOHN WILHITE, ISAAC MEDLEY and their respective labouring Tithables and those belonging to AMBROSE POWELL do attend the said POWELL and obey his directions in clearing and keeping the said Road in repair according to Law and that the said POWELL cause Posts of Directions to be erected where necessary

    - Upon the Attachment brought by ELIZABETH POLLARD against the Estate of JOHN CLAYTON, JUNR., said ELIZABETH made Oath to her Account of eight pounds, thirteen shillings against the said CLAYTON, and GEORGE LIVINGSTON being sworn saith that he hath nothing in his hands, wherefore he is discharged

    - A Bill of Sale from JAMES MAXWELL to LAWRENCE GARR was proved by the Oaths of TULLY CHOICE and ISAAC SMITH, two of the witnesses thereto and ordered to be recorded

    - An Instrument of Writing purporting a Mortgage from JAMES MAXWELL to ANDREW GARR was proved by the Oaths of TULLY CHOICE and ISAAC SMITH, two of the witnesses thereto, and ordered to be recorded

    - Indentures of Lease and Release between WILLIAM DEATHERAGE of one part and CHARLES DEWITT, JUNR. of other part and a Receipt on the Release was proved by the Oaths of ROBERT EASTHAM, JAMES PENDLETON and ROBERT FREEMAN, the witnesses thereto, and ordered to be recorded

    - Indentures of Lease and Release between FRANCIS THORNTON, Gent., and FRANCES his Wife and HANDCOCK LEE, Gent., and MARY his Wife of one part and JOHN FROGG and MICHAEL WALLACE, Gentleman of the other part were proved by the Oath of GEORGE TAYLOR, Gent., another witness thereto, and the same having been before proved by two other witnesses thereto, were ordered to be recorded

    - An Indenture of Feoffment between NATHANIEL HILLING and KEZIAH his Wife of one part and MICHAEL LAWLER of other part and a Memorandum of Livery of Seisen and Receipt thereon indorsed were acknowledged by said NATHANIEL & KEZIAH and ordered to be recorded, she being first privately examined as the Law directs

    - Upon the Attachment brought by ANTHONY GHOLSTON against the Estate of JOHN CLAYTON, JUNR., the said GHOLSTON made Oath to his Account for three pounds, twelve shillings against the said CLAYTON

p.   <u>Orange County Court 27th of August 1747</u>
31   - Upon the Petition of WILLIAM RAWSON, he is exempted from paying County Levies

    - WILLIAM RUSSELL, Gent., Plt. agst THOMAS DOWDE, Deft. In Debt This day came as well Plt. by GEORGE WYTHE, Gent., his Attorney as Deft. by ZACHARY LEWIS Gent., his Attorney, and Deft. defends the force and injury when

&c., and says that he does not owe the Debt in the Declaratiion mentioned in manner and form as Plt. against him hath supposed and of this he puts himself upon the Country, and Plt. likewise; therefore the Trial of the issue is referred til the next Court

    - The Attachment of GEORGE BUCHANNAN and COMPANY against WILLIAM PETTY is continued

    - Our Lord the King, agst. JOHN WILSON   On an Information

The former Process not being served, another is awarded against Deft. returnable to next Court

    - Our Lord the King, agst. JOSEPH CAVE,   On an Information

The Attachment not being served, another is awarded against the Deft. returnable to next Court

    - The Petition of WILLIAM RUSSELL, Gent., against WALTER LEONARD is dismissed

    - RICHARD SHIP, Admr. &c. of THOMAS SHIP, deced., Plt. agst.
    CHRISTOPHER STROTHER, Deft.   On Scire Facias

This day came Plt. by his Attorney and Deft. in his proper person, and thereupon came also a Jury, to wit

JAMES HERNDON	MATHEW TOOL	STOKELY TOWLES
AMBROSE POWELL	EDWARD WATTS	WILLIAM McDONAUGH
JOHN BARNETT	BRYANT SYSON	JOELL WATTS
FRANCIS MOOR	JOHN DILLARD &	JAMES SUGGITT

who being elected tried and sworn the truth to speak upon the issue joined, upon their Oath do say that Deft. did assume upon himself in manner and form as Plt. against him in this suit hath complained and they do assess Plt.'s damages by occasion of the non performance of that assumption to five pounds, fifteen shillings and five pence besides his costs. Therefore it is considered by the Court that Plt. recover against Deft. his damages aforesaid in form aforesaid assessed and his costs by him about his suit in this behalf expended, and Deft. in mercy, &c.

    - THOMAS CHEW, Gent., Plt. agst JACOB STOVER, Admr. &c. of
    JACOB STOVER, deced., Deft.   In Chancery

Continued til the next Court

p.   Orange County Court 27th of August 1747

32   - CHARLES DEWITT, Plt. agst THOMAS BURK, Deft.   In Case
    Continued til next Court at motion and costs of Deft.

    - WILLIAM BEVERLEY, Gent., Plt. agst GEORGE HOME, Deft.   In Case

The Deft. not appearing, on motion of Plt. by his Attorney, an Attachment is awarded him against Deft.'s Estate returnable to next Court

    - The Petition of WILLIAM KELLY against WILLIAM CLARK is continued til the next Court

    - RICHARD WINSLOW, Gent., Plt. agst WILLIAM RUSSELL, Gent., Deft.
    In Case

The Auditors having not yet made their report of their Proceedings, this suit is continued til next Court for them to make their return

    - The Attachment of JAMES HUNTER against VALLENTINE BOSTICK is continued til next Court

    - The Attachment of ROBERT SEAYRES against the Estate of WILLIAM JONES is continued til next Court

        - ROBERT RAE & DANIEL CAMPBELL, Merchants, Plts. agst.
        GEORGE HOME, Deft.   In Case
The Deft. not appearing, on motion of Plts. by their Attorney, an Attachment is
awarded them against Deft.'s Estate returnable to next Court
        - JOHN SMITH, JUNR., Plt. agst THOMAS YATES, Deft.   In Debt
Continued til next Court for Plt. to give security for costs
        - Our Lord the King, agst. MICHAEL COOK,   On an Information
Continued til next Court
        - An Inventory and Appraisment of the Estate of WILLIAM SKILLION,
deced., was returned and ordered to be recorded

p.   Orange County Court 27th of August 1747
33   - Upon the Presentment of the Grandjury against MARY THORNTON, the
        former Attachment not being served, another is awarded against her return-
able to next Court
        - JOHN GRYMES & FRANCIS WILLIS, Esqrs., Exrs. &c. of HENRY
        WILLIS, Gent., deced., Plts. agst. GEORGE HOME, Deft. In Case
Continued til next Court
        - EDWARD TEAL, Plt. agst JOHN MICHAEL, WILLIAM BEVERLEY
        and PHILLIP CLAYTON, Gent., Defts.   In Chancery
Continued for Plt. to give security for costs
        - On motion of BENJAMIN PORTER, it is ordered that JOHN CHRISTO-
PHER pay said PORTER all such costs as have hitherto and will hereafter accrue on
the Petition of said PORTER against said CHRISTOPHER and his Wife for counter
security on a Bond for the administration of EDWARD SOUTHALL's Estate
        - RICHARD WINSLOW, Gent., Plt. agst DENNIS BYRNE,
        EDWARD SPENCER & ISAAC SMITH, Defts.   In Debt
Continued til next Court at motion and costs of Plt.
        - ISAAC SMITH, Plt. agst ROBERT BOHANNON, Deft.   In Chancery
Continued til next Court
        - BENJAMIN BORDEN, Plt. agst. JAMES ARMSTRONG, Deft.   In Debt
Continued til next Court
        - JAMES BELL, Plt. agst GEORGE HOME, Deft.   In Case
The Sherif returning on the last Attachment nothing found, ordered on motion of
Plt. by his Attorney another Attachment issue against Deft.'s Estate returnable to
next Court
        - JAMES PENDLETON & PHILLIP CLAYTON, Plts. agst
        JOHN RAY, Deft. In Debt
    The Sherif returning on the last Attachment noting found, ordered on motion of
Plts. that another Attachment issue against Deft.'s Estate returnable to next Court

p.   Orange County Court 27th of August 1747
34   - The Attachment of PHILLIP CLAYTON and JAMES PENDLETON
        against the Estate of THOMAS HANNON, is continued til the next Court
        - HUMPHREY BELL, Plt. agst WILLIAM COX, Deft.   In Debt
The Deft. not being yet arrested, on motion of Plt. by his Attorney, another Plurius

Capias is awarded him against Deft. returnable to next Court

- JOHN BELFIELD & WILLIAM JORDAN, Gent., Exrs. &c. of THOMAS WRIGHT BELFIELD, deced., Plts. agst WILLIAM MORTON, Deft. In Chancery

The Auditors having not yet made their Report of their Proceedings, this suit is continued til the next Court for them to make return

- DANIEL HORNBY, Gent., Plt. agst. WILLIAM MORTON, Deft. In Debt

The Auditors having not yet made Report of their Proceedigns, this suit is continued til the next Court for them to make return

- WILLIAM WROE, Exr. &c. of WILLIAM BRIDGES, deced., Plt. agst WILLIAM WHITE, Deft.   On a Scire Facias on a Judgment of this Court obtained the 30th day of July 1743 by the Testator against the Deft. for one pound, sixteen shillings and five pence currentmoney for Debt., forty nine pounds of nett tobacco and seven shillings and six pence for costs

The Deft. having been warned and not appearing, on motion of Plt. by his Attorney it is ordered that Judgment be entered for Plt., that he have Execution according to the force form and effect of the recovery aforesaid, and for his costs in suing forth and prosecuting this Writ

- JOHN WHARTON, Plt. agst JANE WHARTON, Admrx. &c. of THOMAS WHARTON, deced., Deft.   In Case

This day came Plt. by ZACHARY LEWIS, Gent., his Attorney and Deft. in her proper person and Deft. defends the force and injury when, &c., and saith that the Intestate did not assume upon himself in manner and form as Plt. against him hath declared and of this she puts herself upon the Country, and Plt. likewise, Therefore the Trial of the issue is referred til the next Court

p. 35   Orange County Court 27th of August 1747

- RICHARD DOGGETT by GEORGE DOGGETT, his next Friend, Plt. agst WILLIAM BUNTON, Deft.   In Assault & Battery

Dismissed being agreed by the parties

- MARTIN DUETT, Plt. agst MICAJAH PICKETT, Deft. In Assault & Battery

This day came as well Plt. by ZACHARY LEWIS, Gent., his Attorney as Deft. by GEORGE WYTHE, Gent., his Attorney, and Deft. prays and has leave to imparl thereof til next Court and then to plead

- KEENE FIELD, quitam &c., Plt. agst. WILLIAM RUSSELL, Gent., Deft. In Debt for Retailing Liquors without a Licence

This day came as well Plt. who as well &c., by ZACHARY LEWIS, Gent., his Attorney, as Deft. by GEORGE WYTHE, Gent., his Attorney, and Deft. defends the force and injury when, &c., and says that he is not Guilty in manner and form as Plt. against him hath complained and of this he puts himself upon the Country, and Plt. likewise, Therefore the Trial of the issue is referred til next Court

- Ordered that the male labouring Tithables belonging to ROBERT JACKSON, Gent., do work under the Overseer of the Road from the Mill of ROBERT SLAUGHTER, Gent., to the Main Road by WILLIAM JOHNSTON's

- DIANNA WHEELER, Exrx. &c. of JOHN WHEELER, deced., Plt. agst DAVID KINKEAD, Admr. &c. of JOHN HOBSON, deced. Deft.

On a Writ of Scire Facias

On motion of Plt. another Scire Facias is awarded him against Deft. returnable to next Court

    - An Instrument of Writing from JAMES SUGGITT to ELIZABETH SUG-GITT his Daughter was proved by the Oath of ERASMUS TAYLOR, FRANCIS TYLER and AMBROSE POWELL, witnesses thereto, and ordered to be recorded

    - HUMPHREY BELL of London, Merchant, Plt. agst.
      WILLIAM NASH, Deft.   In Case

This day came Plt. by his Attorney and Deft. being again called came not, therefore it is ordered that Judgment be entered for Plt. against Deft. and JAMES POLLARD his Security for the Debt in the Declaration mentioned and costs to be ascertained on Inquiry by a Jury at next Court

p.   Culpeper County Court 27th of August 1747
36   JOHN ALLAN, Merchant, Plt. agst WILLIAM McDONAUGH, Deft. In Debt
    This day came Plt. by his Attorney and Deft. being again solemnly called came not. Therefore it is considered by the Court that Plt. recover against Deft. and WILLIAM CRAWFORD, his Security, and THOMAS CHEW, Gent., Sherif of Orange County, twenty seven pounds, seventeen shillings and two pence, the Debt in the Declaration mentioned, and his costs by him about his suit in this behalf expended, and Deft. in mercy, &c., But this Judgment, the costs excepted, is to be discharged by paiment of thirteen pounds, eighteen shillings and seven pence with Interest thereon at the rate of five percent per annum to be computed from the twenty sixth day of May 1746 to the time of paiment and costs

    - JOHN COBOURN, Plt. agst. WILLIAM LONG, Deft.   In Case

This day came as well Plt. by his Attorney as GEORGE LIVINGSTON, Security for Deft.'s appearance, by his Attorney and said Security saith that the Deft. did not assume upon himself in manner and form as Plt. against him hath complained and of this he puts himself upon the Country, and Plt. likewise, therefore the Trial of the issue is referred til next Court

    - ANDREW HARRISON who was fined at the last Court for not appearing as an Evidence on behalf of EDWARD WARE, Plt. against WILLIAM STEPHENS, Deft., unless he should shew cause to the contrary, at this Court appeared and being heard, it is ordered that he be discharged from the same

    - Ordered that the Court be adjourned til tomorrow morning 8 o'clock

    - The Minutes of these Proceedings were signed
                                    ROBERT SLAUGHTER

p.   - At a Court continued and held for Orange County on Fryday the 28th day
37   of August, 1747   Present
       FRANCIS SLAUGHTER   GEORGE TAYLOR
       WILLIAM RUSSELL   GOODRICH LIGHTFOOT   Gentlemen
                                  JAMES PENDLETON

    - Upon the Attachment brought by CHRISTOPHER HOMES and others against the Estate of RICHARD YARBROUGH, AMBROSE POWELL one of the Garnishees being sworn saith that he has an old Dish, a Plate and a Saw in which the

the said YARBROUGH has a fourth part and that said YARBROUGH is indebted to him in twenty shillings. Whereupon it is ordered that the said POWELL deliver the said things to the Sherif who is ordered to make sale of them according to Law and the money arising from such sale to pay to said POWELL in discharge of the said twenty shillings and the residue, if any, to the Plts.

    - RICHARD WINSLOW, Gent., Plt. agst DENNIS BYRNE,
    EDWARD SPENCER & ISAAC SMITH, Deft.   On a Scire Facias
Continued til next Court

    - Upon the Presentment of the Grandjury against THOMAS FOX, this day came as well ZACHARY LEWIS, Gent., Attorney for our Lord the King, as Deft. by GEORGE WYTHE, Gent, his Attorney and thereupon came also a Jury, to wit

AMBROSE POWELL	SPENCER BOBO		ISAAC SMITH
ZACHARIA GIBBS	ELI GRIFFIN		ALEXANDER WAUGH
JOHN MORTON	HENRY BOURN		THOMAS NEWMAN
MATHEW TOOLE	THOMAS DAVIS	&	SAMUEL RICE

who being elected tried and sworn the truth to speak upon the issue joined bought in a Special Verdict in these words; "We of the Jury do find that Deft. did make a Stone Stop across part of the RIVER RAPPAHANNOCK in this County which the course and passage of the River was obstructed in greatest part; We find that the River where the Stop was made is not navigable and that there is no Bridge over the same in any part thereof. If upon the whole matter the Court shall adjudge that the Deft. is Guilty of the Presentment, we find him Guilty and otherwise we find him Not Guilty" and the Cause is continued till next Court for the matters of Law arising thereupon to be argued

    - Upon the Presentment of the Grandjury against JOHN INGRAM, this day came as well ZACHARY LEWIS, Gent., Attorney for our Lord the King, as the Deft. by GEORGE WYTHE, Gent., his Attorney, and thereupon came also a Jury, to wit

AMBROSE POWELL	SPENCER BOBO		ISAAC SMITH
ZACHARIA GIBBS	ELI GRIFFIN		ALEXANDER WAUGH
JOHN MORTON	HENRY BOURN		THOMAS NEWMAN
MATHEW TOOLE	THOMAS DAVIS	&	SAMUEL RICE

who being elected tried and sworn the truth to speak upon the issue joined, brought in a Special Verdict in these words, "We the Jury do find that the Deft. did make a Stone Stop across the RIVER RAPPAHANNOCK in this County by which the course and passage of the said River was obstructed in greatest part; We do find that the River where the said Stop was made was not navigable and that there is no Bridge over the

p.   <u>Culpeper County Court 27th of August 1747</u>
38   same in any part thereof, If upon the whole matter, the Court shall adjudge that the Deft. is Guilty of the Presentment, we find him Guilty, otherwise we find him Not Guilty." and the Cause is continued til next Court for the mattes of Law arising thereupn to be argued

    - Upon the Presentment of the Grandjury against JOHN WILLIS, this day came as well ZACHARY LEWIS, Gent., Attorney for our Lord the King as the Deft. by GEORGE WYTHE, Gent., his Attorney and thereupon came also a Jury, to wit

| AMBROSE POWELL | SPENCER BOBO | ISAAC SMITH |
| ZACHARIA GIBBS | ELI GRIFFIN | ALEXANDER WAUGH |

| THOMAS MORTON | HENRY BOURN | | THOMAS NEWMAN |
| MATHEW TOOLE | THOMAS DAVIS | & | SAMUEL RICE |

who being elected tried and sworn the truth to speak upon the issue joined, brought in a Special Verdict in these words, "We of the Jury do find that the Deft. did make a Stone Stop across part of the RIVER RAPPAHANNOCK in this County by which the Course of the River was obstructed in greatest part; We find that the River where the Stop was made is not navigable and that there was no Bridge over the same in any part thereof. If upon the whole matter the Court shall adjudge that the Deft. is Guilty of the Presentment, we find him Guilty, and otherwise we find him Not Guilty,: and the Cause is continued till the next Court for the matter of Law arising therefrom to be argued

    - WILLIAM RUSSELL, Gent., Plt. agst. CAIN FIELD, Deft.   In Deft.
This day came the parties by their Attornies and Deft. puts in his Plea in abatement of Plt.'s Writ, and the Cause is continued til next Court

    - SPENCER THADEUS BRAMHAM and WILLIAM POUND being brought before the Court for a misbehaviour; whereupon witnesses being sworn and examined touching the premises and said BRAMHAM and POUND heard in their own defence, in consideration whereof it is ordered that they be committed to the custody of the Sherif there to remain until they shall fine two Securities each. Whereupon the said SPENCER THADEUS BRAMHAM with CHRISTOPHER HOMES and HENRY BOURN his Securities and the said WILLIAM POUND with JOHN BRAMHAM, WILLIAM NASH and JOHN CHRISTOPHER his Securities, came into Court and acknowledged themselves indebted to our Sovereign Lord George the Second, King of Great Britain, &c., in the sums following, that is to say, SPENCER THADEUS BRAMHAM and WILLIAM POUND in the sum of Twenty pounds each, and every one of their Securities in the sum of ten pounds each, to our said Lord the King his heirs and Successors rendered upon condition that SPENCER THADEUS BRAMHAM and WILLIAM POUND shall be of good behaviour towards his Majesty and all his liege people for the space of one year and a day and then this Recognizance to be void

    - Present ROBERT GREEN, Gent.

p.   Orange County Court 27th of August 1747
39   - The Attachment brought by PHILLIP CLAYTON and JAMES PENDLETON against THOMAS HANNON is dismissed

    - ROBERT HARRIS, Gent., Plt. agst JOSEPH WALSH, Deft.   In Case
This day came the parties by their Attornies and thereupon came a Jury to wit,

AMBROSE POWELL	ERASMUS TAYLOR		SPENCER BOBO
ZACHARIAH GIBBS	ELI GRIFFIN		ALEXANDER WAUGH
JOHN MORTON	HENRY BOURN		MATHEW TOOLE
THOMAS DAVIS	WILLIAM BELL	&	SAMUEL RICE

who being elected tried and sworn the truth to speak upon the issue joined, upon their Oath do say that Deft. did assume upon himself in manner and form as Plt. against him hath complained and they do assess Plt.'s damages by occasion of the non performace of that assumption to two thousand one hundred pounds of tobacco besides his costs; Therefore it is considered by the Court that Plt. recover against Deft. his damages aforesaid in form aforesaid assessed and his costs by him about his suit in this behalf expended, and the Deft. in mercy, &c.

- ISAAC SMITH, Plt. agst TIMOTHY CROSTHWAIT, Admr. of
WILLIAM CROSTHWAIT, deced., Deft.   In Case
This day came the parties by their Attornies and thereupon came a Jury, to wit

AMBROSE POWELL	ERASMUS TAYLOR	SPENCER BOBO
ZACHARY GIBBS	ELI GRIFFIN	ALEXANDER WAUGH
JOHN WOOTON	HENRY BOURN	MATHEW TOOL
THOMAS DAVIS	WILLIAM BELL &	SAMUEL RICE

who being elected tried and sworn the truth to speak upon the issue joined, upon their
Oath do say the the Intestate, WILLIAM, did assume upon himself in manner and
form as Plt. against him hath declared, and they do assess Plt.'s damages by occasion
of the non performance of that assumption to three pounds, fourteen shillings and
eleven pence current money. Therefore it is considered by the Court that Plt. recover
against Deft. his damages aforesaid in form aforesaid assessed and his costs by him
about his suit in this behalf expended, to be levied of the goods and chattels of the said
Decedent in the hands of the Deft. to be administered if so much thereof he hath, but
if not that then the costs to be levied of his own proper goods and chattels, and Deft.
in mercy, &c.
       - ROBERT HILL, Plt. agst ALEXANDER WAUGH, Deft.   In Case
This day came the parties by their Attornies and thereupon the Deft.'s Plea in
award of Judgment being argued and adjudged good, it is ordered that the Verdict
given in this Cause be set aside and a new Trial to be had between the parties
       - JOHN MORTON having made Oath to his Majesty's Person and Govern-
ment and took the Abjuration Oath and subscribed the Test was sworn CON-
STABLE in the room of JOHN SMITH, JUNR. and took the Oath appointed by the
Tobacco Law

p.   Orange County Court 27th of August 1747
40   - JANE WHARTON, Admrx., &c. of THOMAS WHARTON, deced., Plt.
       agst THOMAS CHEW, Gent., Deft.   In Case
The Deft. not appearing and the Coroner returning that he could find no effects in
his Bailiwick, on motion of Plt. by her Attorney, another Attachment is awarded her
against the said Deft.'s Estate returnable to the next Court
       - THOMAS THORNTON, Plt. agst JOHN CHRISTOPHER, Deft. In Debt
This day came as well Plt. by ZACHARY LEWIS, Gent., his Attorney as Deft. in
custody of the Sherif of this County and Deft. by GEORGE WYTHE, Gent., his Attorney prayed and had oyer of the Writing Obligatory in the Declaration mentioned and
of the Condition thereof to imparl thereof til the next Court and then to plead
       - HUMPHREY BELL of London, Merchant, Plt. agst.
       RICHARD WINSLOW, Gent., Deft.   In Case
This day came as well Plt. by ZACHARY LEWIS, Gent., his Attorney as Deft. by
GEORGE WYTHE, Gent., his Attorney, and Deft. defends the force and injury when,
&c., and saith that he did not assume upon himself in manner and for as Plt. against
him hath complained, and of this he puts himself upon the Country, and Plt. likewise,
therefore the Trial of the issue is referred til the next Court
       - The Petition of HUMPHREY BELL against JOHN SMITH, JUNR. is con-
tinued til next Court
       - JOHN LEWIS, BEVERLEY WHITING & WARNER WASHINGTON,
       Gent. Executors &c. of JOHN WASHINGTON, deced., Plts. agst

ROBERT FREEMAN, Deft.   In Case

Ths day came Plts. by their Attorney and Deft. being again solemnly called came
not. ThereforeJudgment is entered for Plts. against the Deft. and THOMAS CHEW,
Gent., Sherif of Orange County, for the Debt in the Declaration mentioned and costs
to be ascertained on Inquiry by a Jury at next Court

p.   Orange County Court 27th of August 1747
41   - JOHN BEVERLEY, Plt. agst SPENCER BRAMHAM, Deft.
        In Assault and Battery

This day came the parties by their Attornies and Deft. again saving and reserving
to himself all advantages as well to the Writ as to the Declaration prays and has further leave to imparl thereof til the next Court and then to plead

        - Upon Petition of WILLIAM FRAZIER against ISAAC SMITH for a Debt
therein supposed to be due, this day came the parties by their Attornies, who being
fully heard, it is considered by the Court that the Petition be dismissed and that Plt.
pay unto Deft. his costs

                - Present JOHN FINLESON,   )
                - Absent   WILLIAM RUSSELL,   ) Gentleman
        - WILLIAM RUSSELL, Gent., Plt. agst. JANE WHARTON, Admrx. &c. of
        THOMAS WHARTON, deced., Deft.   In Case

This day came Plt. by his Attorney and Deft. in his proper person and Deft. defends
the force and injury when, &c. and saith that the Intestate did not assume upon himself in manner and form as Plt. against her hath complained and of this she puts herself upon the Country, and Plt. likewise, Therefore the Trial of the issue is referred til
next Court

        - JOHN BLANTON, Plt. agst. GEORGE DOGGETT, Deft.   In Debt

This day came Plt. by ZACHARY LEWIS, Gent., his Attorney and Deft. being
returned arrested was solemnly called but came not. Therefore on the motion of Plt.,
it is ordered that unless he appears at next Court and answers the Plt.'s action,
Judgment shall then be entered for Plt. against him, the Deft., and LEONARD ZIG-
LAR, his Security, for the Debt in the Declaration mentioned and costs

        - The Attachment of ROBERT RAE and DANIEL CAMPBELL against
NATHANIEL HEDGMAN is continued til next Court

        - The Attachment of ANDREW ROSS against NATHANIEL HEDGMAN is
continued til next Court

        - The Petition of GEORGE BUCHANNAN & CO. against THOMAS PETTY is
continued til next Court at Plt.s's costs

        - On motion of SAMUEL LOCKHART, a witness for WILLIAM FRAZIER,
Plt. against ISAAC SMITH, Deft., it is ordered that said WILLIAM pay him two
hundred sixty pounds of tobacco for two days attendance at this Court and for coming
seventy miles from AUGUSTA County and returning according to Law

p.   Orange County Court 27th of August 1747
42   - The Petition of RICHARD WINSLOW, Gent., against ISAAC SMITH is
        continued til next Court
        - The Petition of GEORGE BUCHANNON &c. against ROBERT HILL is
continued till next Court at Plts.'s costs

- THOMAS CHEW, Gent., Plt. agst SUSANNA RUCKER, Exrx. &c.
of PETER RUCKER, Exr. &c. of JOHN RUCKER, deced., Deft.   In Case
Continued til next Court
- RICHARD WINSLOW, Gent., Plt. agst THOMAS WHARTON, Deft. In Case
This suit is dismissed and it is ordered that Plt. pay Deft. his costs
- Upon Presentment of the Grandjury against ANNE BRIDGES, another
summons is awarded against her returnable to next Court
- The Petition of EDWARD WARE against WILLIAM STEPHENS is con-
tinued til next Court at Plt.'s costs
- ROBERT GREEN, Gent., Plt. agst GABRIEL LOVING, Deft.   In Case
Dismissed being agreed by the parties and the Deft. is to pay Plt. his costs
- JOHN MORGAN & MARY his Wife, Plts. agst WILLIAM LIGHTFOOT,
Deft.   In Case
By consent of the partied by their Attorneys and by their mutual agreement, the
matters in difference is referred to the determination of FRANCIS MOOR and
BRYANT SYSON whose award thereupon is to be made the Judgment of this Court
- THOMAS GRAVES, Plt. agst ANDREW BOURN, Deft.   In Case
This day came Plt. by his Attorney and Deft. being again solemnly called came not,
therefore on motion of Plt., Judgment is entered against Deft. and JOHN BOURN, his
Security, for the Debt in the Declaration mentioned and costs to be ascertained on
Inquiry by a Jury at next Court

p.   Orange County Court 27th of August 1747\
43   - WILLIAM HUGHES, Plt. agst THOMAS SANDERS, Deft.   In Debt
This day came Plt. by GEORGE WYTHE, Gent., his attorney and Deft. being
returned arrested was solemnly called but came not. Therefore on motion of Plt. it is
ordered that unless he appears here at the next Court and answers Plt.'s action,
Judgment shall then be entered for Plt. against him, the Deft., and JOSEPH EVE, his
Security, for the Debt in the Declaration mentioned
- THOMAS BURK, Plt. agst JOHN ASHER, ROBERT LYON and
JOSEPH PHILLIPS, Defts.   In Trespass
This day came the parties by their Attornies and Defs. say that they are Not
Guilty in manner and form as Plt. against them hath complained, and of this they put
themselves upon the Country, and Plt. likewise,, therefore the Trial of the issue is
referred til the next Court
- HENRY PICKETT, Plt. agst THOMAS COLEMAN, Deft.   In Case
This day came the parties by their Attornies and Deft. saith tht he is Not Guilty of
the Trover and Conversion in manner and form as Plt. against him hath complained,
and of this he puts himself upon the Country, and Plt. likewise; therefore the Trial of
the issue is referred til the next Court
- JAMES DUN, Plt. agst JOHN SMITH, JUNR., Deft.   In Debt
Continued til next Court
- JOHN SPOTSWOOD, Gent, Plt. agst FRANCIS KIRTLEY, JUNR. and
JAMES EARLEY, Defts.   In Trespass
On motion of Plt. by his Attorney, the Deft., EARLEY, is struck out of the Record,
and Deft., KIRTLEY, being again solemnly called and not appearing, Judgment is
granted Plt. against him, the Deft., and FRANCIS KIRTLEY, his Security for the

Debt in the Declaration mentioned to be ascertained on Inquiry by a Jury at next Court

p.   Orange County Court 27th of August 1747
44   - MATHEW TOOLE, Plt. agst. MARTIN WALLOCK, Deft.   In Trespass
        This day came the parties by their Attornies and thereupon came a Jury, to
wit   AMBROSE POWELL   RICHARD VERNON   ISAAC SMITH
        SAMUEL RICE   JEREMIAH MORTON   WILLIAM BELL
        WILLIAM CRAWFORD   ALEXANDER WAUGH   ELI GRIFFIN
        CHRISTOPHER HOMES   ZACHARY GIBBS   &   JAMES SUGGITT

who being elected tried and sworn the truth to speak upon the issue joined, upon their Oath do say that Deft. is Guilty of the Trespass in the Declaration mentioned and they do assess Plt.'s damages by occasion thereto to fifty shillings current money besides his costs; Therefore it is considered by the Court that Plt. recover against Deft. his damages aforesaid in form aforesaid assessed and his costs by him about his suit in this behalf expended, and Deft. may be taken, &c.

        - PHILEMON HAWKINS having obtained an Attachment against the Estate of JOHN CLAYTON, JUNR., who hath privately removed himself out of this County or so absconds that Process cant be served on him for twenty one pounds, fifteen shillings and six pence current moneny due from the said CLAYTON to said HAWKINS by Bill and Account, and the Sherif of this County making return tht he hath attached a Chairm two Horses, four Cows and Calves, this day came Plt. by his Attorney and Deft. not appearing to replevy the attached effects, the Plt. produced the Bill and proved his Account by his own Oath. Therefore it is considered by the Court that Plt. recover against Deft. forty two pounds, nine shillings and six pence and his costs by him about his suit in this behalf expended, But this Judgment to be discharged by paiment of the said twenty one pounds, fifteen shillings and six pence with Interest on twenty one pounds, four shillings and three pence at the rate of five percent per annum to be computed from the first day of July last past to the time of paiment and costs, and it is ordered that the Sherif make sale of the attached effects according to Law and the money arising from such sale to pay to Plt. in discharge of this Judgment, and the residue if any to keep in his hands till further Orders from this Court, and that he make return of such sale to the next Court

        - ERASMUS TAYLOR having obtained an Attachment against the Estate of JOHN CLAYTON, JUNR., who hath privately removed himself out of this County or so absconds that Process cant be served on him for six pounds, nine shillings current money due from the said CLAYTON to the said TAYLOR and the Sherif of this County making return that he had attached a Chair, two Horses, four Cows & Calves, this day came Plt. and Deft. not appearing to replevy the attached effects, the Plt. proved his demand to be just by his own

p.   Orange County Court 27th of August 1747
45   Oath. Therefore it is considered by the Court that Plt. recover against Deft.
        the six pounds, nine shillings and his costs by him about his suit in this behalf expended, and it is ordered that the Sherif make sale of the attached effects and the money arising from such sale after discharging the Judgment of PHILEMON HAWKINS against the said Deft., to pay to Plt. in discharge of this Judgment, and the residue if any to keep in his hands til further Orders from this Court and that he make

return of such sale to next Court

      - JOHN WILLIS having obtained an Attachment against the Estate of JOHN CLAYTON, JUNR. who has privately removed himself out of this County or so absconds that Process cant be served on him and the Sherif returning that he hath attached a Chair, two Horses and four Cows and Calves, which he is ordered to sell according to Law

      - ELIZABETH POLLARD having obtained an Attachment against the Estate of JOHN CLAYTON, JUNR. who hath privately removed himself out of this County or so absconds that Process cant be served on him for eight pounds, thirteen shillings due from said CLAYTON to said POLLARD by Account, the Sherif of this County returning that he hath attached three Horses and an Old Chest, this day came Plt. by her Attorney and Deft. not appearing to replevy the attached effects, the Plt. having proved her demand to be just by her own Oath, therefore it is considered by the Court that Plt. recover against Deft. the eight pounds, thirteen shillings and her costs by her about her suit in this behalf expended, and it is ordered that the Sherif make sale of the attached effects according to Law and pay the money arising from such sale to the Plt. in discharge of this Judgment and the residue if any restore to the Deft. and that he make return of the said sale to the next Court

      - ANTHONY GHOLSTON having obtained an Attachment against the Estate of JOHN CLAYTON, JUNR., who hath privately removed himself out of this County or so obsconds that Process cannot be served on him for three pounds, ten shillings due from said CLAYTON to said GHOLSTON on Account, the Sherif having returned that he hath attached four Cowers and Calves; this day came Plt. by his Attorney and Deft. not appearing to replevy the attached effects, the Plt. having proved his demand to be just by his own Oath; thereupon it is considered by the Court that Plt. recover against Deft. the three pounds, ten shillings and his costs by him about his suit in this behalf expended, and it is ordered that the Sherif make sale of the attached effects according to Law and pay the money arising from such sale if any remain after discharging the Attachments obtained before this to thePlt. in discharge of this Judgment and restore the residue if any to the Deft. and that he make return of such sale to the next Court

      - ROBERT HILL, Plt., agst   DANIEL CARTER and WILLIAM NASH,
      Defts. In Assault and Battery

The Deft., CARTER, not being arrested, on motion of Plt. by his Attorney a Plurius Capias is awarded against Deft. returnable to the next Court

p.   <u>Orange County Court 27th of August 1747</u>
46   - ARCHIBALD GORDON & ALEXANDER SCOTT, Plts. agst.
      WILLIAM PETTY, Deft. In Debt
        Dismissed
      - JOHN SPOTSWOOD, Gent., Plt. agst JOHN CHRISTOPHER, Deft.
      In Debt

This day came as well Plt. by ZACHARY LEWIS, Gent., his Attorney as Deft. by GEORGE WYTHE, Gent., his Attorney and Deft. prays and has oyer of the Writing Obligatory in the Declaration mentioned and to imparl thereof til the next Court and then to plead

- ANTHONY STROTHER, Gent., Plt. agst ELLIS MARCUS, Deft.   In Case
This day came Plt. by GEORGE WYTHE, Gent., his Attorney, and Deft. being
returned arrested was solemnly called but came not. Therefore on motion of Plt., it is
ordered that unless he appears here at the next Court and answers Plt.'s action,
Judgment shall be entered for Plt. against him and WILLIAM ANDERSON and
DANIEL BROWN, his Securitys, for the Debt in the Declaration mentioned and costs
    - ANTHONY STROTHER, Gent., Plt. agst MICHAEL WHATLEY, Deft.
    In Case
This day came Plt. by GEORGE WYTHE, Gent., his Attorney, and Deft. being returned arrested was solemnly called but came not. Therefore on motion of Plt. it is
ordered that unless he appears here at the next Court and answers Plt.'s action,
Judgment shall be entered for Plt. against him and THOMAS RUCKER, his Security,
for the Debt in the Declaration mentioned and costs
    - RICHARD VERNON, Plt. agst. HONOURIAS POWELL, Deft.   In Debt
This day came the parties in their proper persons and Deft. confesseth the Plt.'s
action. Therefore it is considered by the Court that Plt. recover against Deft. four
pounds, ten shillings, the ballance of the Bill to be paid in good merchantable Deer
Skins at one shilling by the pound and summer skins at one shilling and three pence
by the pound and his costs by him about his suit in this behalf expended, and Deft. in
mercy, &c. and Plt. agrees

p.   Orange County Court 27th of August 1747
47   that the execution of this Judgment shall be stayed till the next Court to be
        held for this County
    - On the motion of MATTHIAS SELSER, a witness for MATHEW TOOLE,
Plt. against MARTIN WALLOCK, Deft., ordered that said TOOLE pay him two
hundred pounds of tobacco for two days attendance at this Court and coming fifty
miles from AUGUSTA County and returning according to Law
    - ZACHARY GIBBS as a Lieutenant of a Company of Foot in this County
took the usual Oaths to his Majesties Person and Government and took the Abjuration Oath and subscribed the Test
    - The Petition of MARGARET GIBSON against JOHN SMITH is continued til
next Court
    - ELIZABETH HARDIN, Plt. agst MICHAEL WHATLEY, Deft.   In Debt
This day came as well Plt. by his Attorney as the Security for the Deft.'s appearance by his Attorney, and said Security saith that Deft. hath paid the Debt in the
Declaration mentioned and of this he puts himself upon the Country and Plt. likewise,
therefore the Trial of the issue is referred til next Court
    - RICHARD BRIDGES, Plt. agst THOMAS CHEW, Gent., Deft.   In Debt
Continued till next Court
    - The Petition of THOMAS CHEW, Gent. against ROBERT GREEN, Gent., is
continued til next Court
    - RANDAL FUGITT, Plt. agst JOHN BRAMHAM, Deft. In Case
This day came as well Plt. by GEORGE WYTHE, Gent., his Attorney as Deft. by
ZACHARY LEWIS, Gent., his Attorney and Deft. prays and has leave to imparl
thereof til the next Court and then to plead

- WILLIAM RUSSELL, Gent., Plt. agst CHRISTOPHER ZIMMERMAN, Admr. &c. of JOHN NEWPORT, deced., Deft.   In Case
This day came as well Plt. by GEORGE WYTHE, Gent., his Attorney, as Deft. by ZACHARY LEWIS, Gent., his Attorney and Deft. prays and has leave to imparl thereof til the next Court and then to plead

- ANTHONY STROTHER, Merchant, Plt. agst CHRISTOPER ZIMMERMAN, Admr. &c. of JOHN NEWPORT, deced., Deft.   In Case
This day came as well Plt. by GEORGE WYTHE, Gent., his Attorney as Deft. by ZACHARY LEWIS, Gent., his Attorney and Plt. prays and has leave to imparl thereof til next Court and then to plead

p.   Orange County Court 27th of August 1747
48   - ANTHONY FLINCH, Plt. agst ELI GRIFFIN, Deft.   In Debt
This day came as well Plt. by GEORGE WYTHE, Gent., his Attorney as Deft. by ZACHARY LEWIS, Gent., his Attorney and Deft. prays and has leave to imparl thereof til next Court and then to plead

- WILLIAM BELL, Plt. agst ROBERT JACKSON, Gent., Deft.   In Case
This day came as well GEORGE WYTHE, Gent. his Attorney as Deft. by ZACHARY LEWIS, Gent., his Attorney and Deft prays and has leave to imparl thereof til next Court and then to plead

- ROBERT SHEDDEN, Plt. agst THOMAS CHEW, Gent., Sherif of Orange County, Deft.   In Debt
This day came as well Plt. by GEORGE WYTHE, Gent., his Attorney as Deft. by ZACHARY LEWIS, Gent., his Attorney and Deft. prays and has leave to imparl thereof til next Court and then to plead

- WILLIAM KELLY, Plt. agst ROBERT EASTHAM, Gent., Admrx. &c. of JOHN LATHAM, deced., Deft.   In Case
This day came as well Plt. by GEORGE WYTHE, Gent., his Attorney as Deft. by ZACHARY LEWIS, Gent., his Attorney, and Deft. prays and has leave to imparl thereof til next Court and then to plead

- EDWARD PRICE, Plt. agst PATRICK LEONARD, Deft.   In Case
Ths day came as well Plt. by ZACHARY LEWIS, Gent., his Attorney as Deft. by GEORGE WYTHE, Gent., his Attorney and Deft. prays and has leave to imparl thereof til next Court and then to plead

- WILLIAM JACKSON and ELIZABETH his Wife, Plts. agst. MICAJAH PICKETT, Deft.   In Case
This day came as well Plts. by GEORGE WYTHE, Gent., their Attorney as Deft. in his proper person and Deft. prays and further leave to imparl thereof til next Court and then to plead

p.   Orange County Court 27th of August 1747
49   - JOHN SMITH, Plt. agst CHRISTOPHER ZIMMERMAN, Admr. &c. of JOHN NEWPORT, deced., Deft.   On a Scire Facias on a Judgment of this Court obtained by the said SMITH against the said NEWPORT the 20th day of July 1746 for two thousand four hundred pounds of tobacco to be paid in three casks for Debt and thirty seven pounds nett tobacco and fifteen shillings or one hundred fifty pounds of tobacco for Costs

This day came Plt. by his Attorney an Deft. being duly summoned and not appearing, ordered that Judgment be entered for Plt. that he have execution against the Deft. for the sums aforesaid and for his costs in suing forth and prosecuting this Writ to be levied of the goods and chattels of the Decedent in the hands of the Deft. to be administered if so much thereof he hath but if not that then the costs of this suit to be levied of the proper goods of the said Deft.

    - MARGARET RICE, Admrx. &c. of HENRY RICE, deced., Plt. agst
    ELI GRIFFIN, Deft.   In Case

This day came the parties by their Attornies and by their Council all matters and Accounts in difference are refered to Mr. LEWIS and Mr. WYTHE

    - FRANCIS THORNTON of SPOTSYLVANIA County, Gent., Plt. agst
    SAMUEL POUND otherwise called SAMUEL POUND of Orange County Deft.

This day came Plt. by ZACHARY LEWIS, Gent., his Attorney and Deft. in custody of the Sherif of this County and Deft. confesseth Plt.'s action. Therefore it is considered by the Court that Plt. recover against Deft. twenty nine pounds, seventeen shillings and nine pence, the Debt in the Declaration mentioned, and his costs by him about his suit in this behalf expended, and Deft. in mercy, &c., but this Judgment, the costs excepted, is to be discharged by paiment of fourteen pounds, eighteen shillings and ten pence half penny with Interest thereon at the rate of five percent per annum to be computed from the first day of October 1746 to the time of paiment and costs, and on the prayer of the Plt., the Deft. is committed to the custody of the Keeper of the Common Goal of this County for Debtors there to remin until he shall satisfy this Judgment

    - FRANCIS THORNTON, Gent., Plt. agst JOSEPH THOMAS, Gent., Deft.
    In Debt

This day came Plt. by ZACHARY LEWIS, Gent., his Attorney and Deft. being returned arrested was solemnly called but came not. Therefore on motion of Plt. it is ordered that unless he appears at the next Court and answers Plt.'s action, Judgment shall then be entered for Plt. against him, the Deft., and THOMAS CHEW, Gent., Sherif of Orange County, for the Debt in the Declaration mentioned and costs

p.   Orange County Court 27th of August 1747
50   - JOHN SPOTSWOOD, Gent., Plt. agst JOHN EARLEY, Deft.   In Trespass

    The Deft. not being arrested, on motion of Plt. by his Attorney, an Alias Capias is awarded him against the Deft. returnable to the next Court

    - ISAAC SMITH, Plt. agst FRANCIS WILLIAMS, Deft.   In Chancery

The Deft. not appearing to answer Plt.'s Bill, on motion of Plt. by his Council, and Attachment is awarded him against Deft. for his Contempt returnable to next Court

    - Upon Petition of JAMES PORTEUS against JOHN GARHART for one pound, ten shillings, this day came Plt. by his Attorney and Deft. having been served with a copy of the Petition and summoned to appear was called but came not; therefore it is considered by the Court that Plt. recover against Deft. the one pound, ten shillings and his costs by him about his suit in this behalf expended

    - FRANCIS BROWN, Plt. agst. EDWARD SPENCER, Gent., Deft. In Debt

This day came as well Plt. by ZACHARY LEWIS, Gent., his Attorney ad Deft. by GEORGE WYTHE, Gent., his Attorney and Deft. prays and has oyer of the Writing Obligatory in the Declaration mentined and to imparl thereof til next Court and then

to plead
          - ROBERT HILL, Plt. agst ALEXANDER WAUGH, Deft. In Case
     The parties came into Court and entered into the following agreement; vizt. the Plt.
on his part doth agree that if Deft. will pay him seven Pistoles and the costs of this
suit, the suit shall be dismissed, which Deft. doth agree to pay, whereupon the suit is
dismissed
          - WILLIAM McDONAUGH, Plt. agst JOANNA SIMS, Admrx. &c. of
          RICHARD SIMS, deced., Deft. In Debt
     This day came Plt. by ZACHARY LEWIS, Gent., his Attorney, and Deft. being
returned arrested was solemnly called but came not. Therefore on motion of Plt., it is
ordered that unless Deft. appears here at the next Court and answers Plt.'s action,
Judgment shall be entered for Plt. against her, the Deft., for the Debt in the
Declaration mentioned and costs

p.   Orange County Court 27th of August 1747
51   - MARGARET GIBSON, Admrx., &c. of JONATHAN GIBSON, Gent., Plt.
          agst WILLIAM RUSSELL, Gent., Deft.   In Case
     By consent of the parties all matters and Accounts in difference between them are
referred to HENRY DOWNES, JOSEPH THOMAS and JOHN NICHOLAS or any
two of them to settle
          - The Churchwardens of Saint Mark's Parish, Plts. agst. ANNE BRIDGES,
          Deft. In Debt
Dismissed
          - On motion of CHRISTOPHER ZIMMERMAN, a witness for JAMES
PORTEUS, Plt. against JOHN GARHART, Deft., it is ordered that said JAMES pay
him fifty pounds of tobacco for two days attendance at this Court according to Law
          - EDWARD SPENCER, Gent., Plt. agst SHEM COOK, Deft.   In Debt
     This day came Plt. by GEORGE WYTHE, Gent., his Attorney, and Deft. being re-
turned arrested was solemnly called but came not; Therefore on motion of Plt., it is
ordered that unless he appears here at next Court and answers Plt.'s action, Judgment shall then be entered for Plt. against him, the Deft. and MICAJAH PICKETT,
his Security, for the Debt in the Declaration mentioned and costs
          - EDWARD SPENCER, Gent., Plt. agst DAVID GRIFFIN Deft.   In Debt
     This day came Plt. by GEORGE WYTHE, Gent., his Attorney and Deft. being re-
turned arrested was solemnly called but came not. Therefore on motion of Plt. it is
ordered that unless he appears here at next Court and answers Plt.'s action, Judgment shall be entered for Plt. against him, the Deft. and WILLIAM STROTHER, his
Security, for the Debt in the Declaration mentioned, and costs
          - EDWARD SPENCER, Gent.,Plt. agst JOHN WILLIS, Gent., Deft. In Debt
     This day came Plt. by GEORGE WYTHE, Gent., his Attorney and Deft. being re-
turned arrested was solemnly called but came not. Therefore on motion of Plt., it is
ordered that unless he appears here at next Court and answers Plt.'s action, Judgment shall be entered for Plt. against him, the Deft., ad THOMAS CHEW, Gent.,
Sherif of Orange County, for the Debt in the Declaration mentioned and costs

p.   Orange County Court 27th of August 1747
52   - The Petition of TIMOTHY CROSTHWAIT, Admr. &c. of WILLIAM

CROSTHWAIT, deced., against EDWARD SPENCER, Gent., is continued til next Court

- Upon Petition of EDWARD SPENCER, Gent. against JOSEPH PHILLIPS for three pounds, nine shillings and three pence said to be due by Promissory Note, this day came Plt. by his Attorney and Deft. having been served with a copy of the Petition and summoned to appear was called but came not. Therefore it is considered that Plt. recover against Deft. the three pounds, nine shillings and three pence and his costs by him about his suit in this behalf expended

- Upon Petition of EDWARD SPENCER, Gent., against CHARLES DEWITT for three pounds, fifteen shillings and eight pence said to be due by Promissory Note, this day came Plt. by his Attorney and Deft. having been served with a copy of the Petition and summoned to appear was called but came not. Therefore it is considered that Plt. recover against Deft. the three pounds, fifteen shillings and eight pence and his costs by him about his suit in this behalf expended, But this Judgment, the costs excepted, is to be discharged by the paiment of one pound, seventeen shillings and ten pence with Interest thereon at the rate of five percent per annum to be computed from the twenty seventh day of March 1747 to the time of paiment and costs

- RICHARD VERNON, Plt. agst HONORIAS POWELL, Deft.
In Assault and Battery
The parties mutually agree to submit all matters in difference between them to the determination of WILLIAM RUSSELL and PHILLIP CLAYTON, Gent., and agree that their award be made the Judgment of the Court and the same is ordered accordingly

- JOHN LINCH, Plt. agst ROBERT FREEMAN, Deft.   In Case
Dismissed

- The Petition of DANIEL HORNBY against JOHN BRAMHAM is continued til next Court at the Plt.'s costs

- The Petition of JOHN BELFIELD and WILLIAM JOURDAN, Gent, Exrs. &c. of THOMAS WRIGHT BELFIELD, Gent., deced. against JOHN BRAMHAM is continued til next Court at Plt.'s costs

- The Attachment of HENRY DOWNES against RICHARD McGRAUGH is continued til next Court

- WILLIAM RUSSELL, Gent., Plt. agst THOMAS WRIGHT, Deft.   In Case
Continued til next Court

p.   Orange County Court 27th of August 1747
53   - WILLIAM CATLETT, Plt. agst FINDLEY McCOLLESTER, Deft. In Case
Dismissed

- Upon the Attachment brought by JOHN SMITH against the Estate JOHN SMITH, JUNR., JOHN WILLIAMS, one of the Garnishees being sworn saith that he hadth five sheep and seale weights belonging to said SMITH and JOHN SMITH, being sworn saith that he hath a Rum Cask, a small do., a pair of old Cart Wheels, a Gun, an old Gun Barril and Lock, a broad ax, a cross cut tennent saw, a small ironpot and hooks, two iron basons, a small brass kettle, a Table, two Horse Bells, an old Bridle, a slate, account books, some old iron, five pewter plates, a small pewter bason, six earthen plates, two funnells and half pint pot, a jill pot, a coffey pot, a tea pot, two iron candlesticks, a gridiron, a flesh fork, a skimmer, two plates, a piggin, a Bed, a Rug two bedsteads, an iron pestle, nine spoons, a spinning Wheel, five old chairs, a chest, a small box, five case knives, three forks, some flax and a common prayer book, which he is ordered to deliver up to the Sherif to be by him sold according to Law and the money arising from such sale to keep in his hand til further orders

- Upon Petition of JAMES PENDLETON and PHILLIP CLAYTON, Gent. against WILLIAM KIRTLEY, WILLIAM CLIFT and ROGER ABBIT for a Debt therein supposed to be due; the former Process not being served, another summons is awarded the Plts. against the Defts. returnable to next Court

- Upon Attachment brought by JOHN ALLAN against the Estate of JOHN SMITH, JUNR., the Sherif returned that he had attached some hoggs which he is ordered to sell according to Law and the money arising for such sale to keep in his hands til further orders

- RICHARD VERNON having obtained an Attachment against the Estate of RICHARD McGRAW, JOHN HUGHES, one of the Garnishees being sworn saith he owes the Deft. fourteen shillings and ten pence, this day came Plt. and Deft. not appearing, the Plt. proved his demand to be just by his Account. Therefore it is considered by the Court that Plt. recover against Deft. three pounds, sixteen shilings and four pence and his costs by him about his suit in this behalf expended, and THOMAS THORNTON, LAWRENCE BRADLEY and GEORGE HOME, the other Garnishees not appearing, it is ordered that an Attachment issue against them returnable to the next Court and that the said HUGHES pay the fourteen shillings and ten pence to the Plt. towards discharge of part of this Judgment

p.   Orange County Court 27th of August 1747
54   - Upon an Attachment brought by CHRISTOPHER HOMES, GEORGE
        HOME, JEREMIAH ROSSON & RUSSELL HILL against the Estate of
RICHARD YARBROUGH, this day came the parties by their Attornies and Deft. not appearing to replevy the effects condemned in the several Garnishee's hands, whereupon the Plts. produced in Court a transcript of a Judgment of this Court obtained by DANIEL HORNBY, Gent., against them in a Recognizance and Bail. Therefore it is considered by the Court that Plts. recover against Deft. thirty nine pounds, seventeen shillings and five pence to be discharged by the paiment of thirteen pounds, eighteen shillings and eight pence with Interest thereon after the rate of five percent per annum to be computed from the 29th day of September 1743 to the time the same shall be paid to DANIEL HORNBY, and one hundred and eighty two pounds of nett tobacco and fifteen shillings or one hundred fifty pounds of tobacco, the costs of the said Judgment, together with their costs by them about their suit in this behalf expended

        - Ordered that the Court be adjourned til the fourth Thursday in next month
        - The Minutes of these proceedings were signed
                                        ROBERT GREEN

- At a Court held for Orange County on Thursday the twenty second day of October in the twenty first year of the Reign of our Sovereign Lord George the Second by the grace of God, King of Great Britain, &c., MDCCXLVII before his Majesties Justices of the Peace for the said County, (to wit)
ROBERT SLAUGHTER   JOHN FINLESON   HENRY FIELD

ABRAHAM FIELD   FRANCIS SLAUGHTER
GEORGE TAYLOR   and   PHILIP CLAYTON   Gentlemen

- Ordered that the Sherif summon twenty four of the most capable Freeholders of this County to appear at next Court as a Grandjury of Inquest for the body of this County

- Ordered that BENJAMIN ROBERTS, WILLIAM PEYTON and WILLIAM CLIFT, or any two of them do sometime between this and the next Court go and view the Bridge over the WILDERNESS RUN and report to the Court the condition they shall find the same to be in and whether the same is according to the Condition of a Bond given by THEOPHILUS EDDINS and JONATHAN GIBSON, Gentleman, Security for the said EDDINS building the Bridge, a copy of which Bond the Clerk of the Court is ordered to convey to the said Viewers

- Ordered that the Sherif give public notice that the County Levy will be laid at the next Court held for this County

p.   Orange County Court 22d of October 1747
55   - A Bond from JOHN CHRISTOPHER, EDWARD SPENCER and
         ALEXANDER WAUGH to MARY TALIAFERRO, LAWRENCE TALIA-
FERRO and WILLIAM HUNTER, Executors of JOHN TALIAFERRO, deced., FRANCIS CONWAY, Son and heir of FRANCIS CONWAY, deced., and BENJAMIN PORTER with a Condition thereunder written was acknowledged by the said CHRISTOPHER, SPENCER and WAUGH and ordered to be recorded

- An Indenture between JOHN CHRISTOPHER and ANNE his Wife of the one part and EDWARD SPENCER and ALEXANDER WAUGH, of the other part was acknowledged by said JOHN & ANNE and ordered to be recorded, she being first privily examined as the Law directs

- EDWARD SPENCER, Gent. having produced a Commission under the hand of the Honble, the Lieutenant Governor of this Colony and Seal of said Colony, appointing him SHERIF of this County. Whereupon he entered into and acknowledged Bond with JOHN WILLIS, ALEXANDER WAUGH and JAMES SUGGITT his Securities in the sum of one thousand pounds sterling for the faithfull performance of all things pertaining to said Office. Thereupon EDWARD SPENCER and JOHN BRAMHAM, JUNR., having took the usual Oaths to his Majesties Person and Governemtn and taken the Abjuration Oath and subscribed the Test said SPENCER was sworn into is said Office and on the motion of the said SPENCER the said BRAMHAM was sworn UNDER SHERIF under him

- An Assignment of Lease from THOMAS CHAMBERS to RICHARD NALLE was acknowledged by said THOMAS and ordered to be recorded

- An Indenture of Feoffment between ROBERT COLEMAN and SARAH his Wife of one part and JOSEPH ABELL of the other part and a Memorandum of Livery of Seisen thereon indorsed were acknowedged by the said ROBERT and SARAH and ordered to be recorded, she being first privily examined as the Law directs

- ANNE, the Wife of THOMAS FOSTER, being privily examined touching the conveyance made by JOHN & THOMAS FOSTER to JAMES GARNETT acknowledged the same to be her act and deed which is ordered to be certified

- Ordered that WILLIAM KELLY, PATRICK BRADLEY, CHRISTOPHER

BOWEN, THOMAS GODFREY and SYLVESTER FARRELL, being the said
KELLY'S Tythables be added to the List in Saint Mark's Parish in this County
    - Ordered that ROBERT GREEN and HENRY FIELD, Gent., do petition the
County Court of KING GEORGE to have a Road cleared from THOMAS HORD's
Quarter the most convenient way in that County to the Town of FALMOUTH
    - Ordered that WILLIAM BLEDSOE, JUNR. be added to the Lists of Tith-
ables in Saint Thomas's Parish in this County
    - Ordered that JAMES CHISSUM & WILLIAM CHISSUM be added to the
Lists of Tithables in Saint Thomas's Parish in this County
    - Upon Petition of ALEXANDER CLEVELAND, he is exempted from paying
County Levy for the future
    - The Attachment brought by GEORGE BUCHANNON & COMPANY
against WILLIAM PETTY is continued till next Court
    - The King agst JOHN WILSON   On an Information
The former Process not being served, another is awarded against the Deft. return-
able to the next Court

p.   Orange County Court 22d October 1747
56   - The King agst JOSEPH CAVE   On an Information
The Deft. not appearing, another Attachment is awarded against him returnable to the next Court
    - The King agst JAMES HEMPHILL,   On an Information
Continued till next Court
    - WILLIAM BEVERLEY, Gent., Plt. agst GEORGE HOME, Deft.   In Case
The Deft. not appearing, on motion of Plt. by his Attorney, another Attachment is
awarded him against Deft.'s Estate returnable to next Court
    - The Petition of WILLIAM KELLY against WILLIAM CLARK is continued til
next Court
    - The Attachment brought by ROBERT SEAYRES against WILLIAM
JONES is continued til the next Court
    - The Attachment brought by JAMES HUNTER against VALENTINE
BOSTICK is continued til next Court
    - ROBERT RAE & DANIEL CAMPBELL, Plts. agst GEORGE HOME, Deft.
    In Case
The Deft. not appearing, on motion of Plts. by their Attorney, another Attachment
is awarded them against Deft.'s Estate returnable to next Court
    - JOHN SMITH, JUNR., Plt. agst THOMAS YATES, Deft.   In Debt
ThePlt. having been ruled to give Security for costs in case he should be cast in this
suit, and failing therein, this suit abates
    - The Presentment of the Grandjury against MARY THORNTON is dismssed
    - The Executors of HENRY WILLIS, Gent., deced:, Plts. agst
    GEORGE HOME, Deft. In Case
Continued til next Court

p.   Orange County Court 22d of October 1747
57   - EDWARD TEAL, Plt. agst JOHN MICAL, PHILIP CLAYTON &
    WILLIAM BEVERLEY, Gent., Defts. In Chancery

The Plt. having been ruled to give Security for costs in case he be cast in this suit, and failing therein, this suit abates

    - RICHARD WINSLOW, Gent., Plt. agst WILLIAM RUSSELL, Gent., Deft. In Case

Continued til the next Court

    - BENJAMIN BORDEN, Plt. agst JAMES ARMSTRONG, Deft. In Debt

Continued til the next Court

    - JAMES BELL, Plt. agst GEORGE HOME, Deft. In Case

The Deft. not appearing, on motion of Plt., another Attachment is awarded him against Deft.'s Estate returnable to next Court

    - HUMPHREY BELL, Plt. agst. WILLIAM COX, Deft. In Debt

The Deft. not being arrested on the former Process, on motion of Plt. another Plurius Capias is awarded against the Deft. returnable to next Court

    - JOHN BELFIELD and WILLIAM JOURDAN, Gent., Exrs. &c. of
    THOMAS WRIGHT BELFIELD, Gent., deced., Plts agst
    WILLIAM MORTON, Deft.   In Chancery

Continued til next Court for the Auditors to make their Report of their Proceedings in this Cause

    - DANIEL HORNBY, Plt. agst WILLIAM MORTON, Deft. In Debt

Continued til next Court for the Auditors to make their Report of their Proceedings in this Cause

p.   Orange County Court 22d of October 1747
58   - MARTIN DUETT, Plt. agst MACAJAH PICKETT, Deft.
    In Assault and Battery

This day came the parties by their Attornies and Deft. defends the force and injury when, &c., and saith that he is Not Guilty in manner and form as Plt. against him hath complained and of this he puts himself upon the Country and Plt. likewise. Therefore the Trial of this issue is referred til next Court

    - DIANNAH WHEELER, Exrx. &c. of JOHN WHEELER, deced., Plt. agst
    DAVID KINKEAD, Admr. &c. of JOHN HOBSON, deced., Deft.
    In a Scire Facias on a Judgment of this Court obtained the 24th day of August
    1744 by JOHN WHEELER in his life time against the Deft. whereby he re-
    covered fourteen pounds, three shillings and one penny current money for his
    damages in a certain action of Trespass upon the Case and one hundred forty
    pounds of tobacco for his costs of that suit to be levied of the goods and
    chattels of the Intestate, JOHN HOBSON, in the hands of the Deft. to be ad-
    ministered if so much thereof he hath, if not then the costs to be levied of the
    proper goods and chattels of said Deft.

This day came Plt. by her Attorney and the Sherif having returned that the Deft. hath nothing in his Bailiwick whereby he could cause him to know neither is he found in the same. Therefore it is ordered that Judgment be entered for Plt., that she have execution according to the force form and effect of the recovery aforesaid and for her costs of suing forth and prosecuting this suit

    - JANE WHARTON, Admrx. &c. of THOMAS WHARTON, dece., Plt. agst
    THOMAS CHEW, Gent., Deft. In Case

The Deft. not appearing, on motion of Plt., another Attachment is awarded her

against Deft.'s Estate returnable to the next Court
    - Upon the Attachment brought by ANTHONY GHOLSTON against the Estate of JOHN CLAYTON, JUNR. ELIZABETH POLLARD being sworn saith that she hath three shirts, two pair of stockings, about half a yard of fine linnen and some fine thread belonging to said CLAYTON which she is ordered to deliver to the Sherif who is ordered to make sale thereof according to Law and pay the money arising by such sale to the Plt. in discharge of this Judgment formerly obtained and restore the residue if any to the Deft.
    - Then the Court adjourned til tomorrow morning 8 o'clock
    - The Minutes of these Proceedings were signed
                              ABRA: FIELD

p.   _- At a Court continued and held for Orange County on Friday the 23d day_
59   of October 1747   Present
    THOMAS CHEW   FRANCIS SLAUGHTER
    ABRAHAM FIELD   and   HENRY FIELD   Gentlemen

    - Ordered that ANDREW HARRISON, JOHN MALLORY and JEREMIAH DEAR or any two of them being first sworn before a Justice of the Peace of this County, do some time between this and the next Court view and value the improvements made on two hundred acres of land in this County belonging to JAMES GAINES being part of a thousand acres granted to JOSEPH HAWKINS, Gent., by Pattent bearing date the 28th day of September 1738, having a regard to all accounts of expences made to them by the said GAINES and make report thereof to the Court
    - Indentures of Apprenticeship between ALLAN WYLIE, an Infant, of one part and FREDERICK FISHBACK of the other part were acknowledged by the said ALLAN and FREDERICK and being approved of by the Court ordered to be certified
    - JOHN BRAMHAM, Plt. agst WILLIAM RUSSELL, Gent., Deft.
    In Covenant
By consent of the parties by their Attornies, it is ordered that this Cause be tried the first at the next Court to be held for this County and that the suit do not abate by the death of either party and by the further consent of the parties by their Attorneys a Commission is awarded to examine and take the Deposition of JOHN WHARTON, an infirm witness in this Cause, for the Plt. de bene esse the Plt. giving the other legal notice of the time and place of executing the same
    - JOHN BRAMHAM, Plt. agst WILLIAM RUSSELL, Gent., Deft.   In Case
By consent of the parties by their Attornies, it is ordered that this Cause be tried the first the next Court to be held for this County and that the suit do not abate by the death of either party and by the further consent of the parties by their Attornies a Commission is awarded to examined and take the Deposition of JOHN WHARTON, an infirm witness in this Cause, for the Plt. de bene esse, the Plt. giving the other legal notice of the time and place of executing the same
    - Ordered that JOSEPH PHILLIPS's mark being a crop in the right ear and a slit be recorded
    - RICHARD WINSLOW, Gent., Plt. agst ROERT SEAYRES and JOHN SEAYRES, Defts.   In Case

Continued till next Court

60   - WILLIAM RUSSELL, Gent., Plt. agst THOMAS DOWDE, Deft.   In Debt
Continued till next Court
         - CHARLES DEWITT, Plt. agst THOMAS BURK, Deft.   In Case
This day came the parties by their Attornies and thereupon came a Jury to wit,

JOHN CHRISTOPHER	JAMES SUGGITT	JOHN BOWEN
ANDREW HARRISON	THOMAS DILLARD	GEORGE ROBERTS
MUMFORD STEVENS	JOHN BRAMHAM	ISAAC SMITH
BRYANT SYSON	JOHN TRIPLETT &	SAMUEL POUND

who being elected tried and sworn the truth to speak upon the issue joined, upon their
Oath do say that the Deft. is Guilty of the Slander in the Declaration specified and
they do assess Plt.'s damages by occasion thereof to forty shillings sterling besides his
costs; Therefore it is considered by the Court that Plt. recover against Deft. his
damages aforesaid in form aforesaid assessed and his costs by him abouthis suit in
this behalf expended, and Deft. in mercy, &c.
         - Ordered that GEORGE PARSONS's mark being a crop in the right ear and
two slits and an underkeel in the left be recorded
         - WILLIAM RUSSELL, Gent., Plt. agst CAIN FIELD, Deft.   In Debt
This day came the parties by their Attornies and Plt. put in his Replication to
Deft.'s Plea in abatement. Thereupon the Deft. prays and has time til the next Court
to consider of it
         - THOMAS THORNTON, Plt. agst JOHN CHRISTOPHER, Deft.   In Debt
This day came the parties by their Attornies and thereupon the Deft. saith he had
performed the condition in the Writing Obligatory mentioned which on his part ought
to have been performed and of this he puts himself upon the Country, and Plt. likewise. Therefore the Trial of the issue is referrred til the next Court
         - The Presentments of the Grandjury against THOMAS FOX, JOHN
INGRAM and JOHN WILLIS are continued til next Court
         - The Petiton of HUMPHREY BELL against JOHN SMITH, JUNR. is con-
tinued til next Court

61   - JOHN BEAZLEY, Plt. agst SPENCER BRAMHAM, Deft.
         In Assault and Battery
This day came the parties by their Attornies, and Deft. defends the force and injury
when, &c., and saith that he is Not Guilty in manner and form as Plt. against him
hath complained, and of this he puts himself upon the Country, and Plt. likewise,
Therefore the Trial of the issue is referred til next Court and Plt. and Deft. may give
what special matters he pleases in evidence at the Trial
         - JOHN BLANTON, Plt. agst. GEORGE DOGGETT, otherwise called I
         GEORGE DOGGETT of SPOTSYLVANIA, Deft.   In Debt
This day came Plt. by his Attorney and Deft. being again solemnly called came not.
Therefore it is considered by the Court tht Plt. recover against Deft. and LEONARD
ZIGLER, his Security, ten pounds current money of Virginia, the Debt in the Declaration mentoned and his costs by him about his suit in this behalf expended, and Deft. in
mercy, &c.

- The Attachment of ROBERT RAE & DANIEL CAMPBELL against
NATHANIEL HEDGMAN is continued til next Court
- The Attachment of ANDREW ROSS against NATHANIEL HEDGMAN is
continued til next Court
- The Petition of GEORGE BUCHANNON &c. against THOMAS PETTY is
continued til next Court at Plt.'s costs
- The Petition of GEORGE BUCHANNON &c. against ROBERT HILL is
continued til next Court at Plt.'s costs
- THOMAS CHEW, Gent., Plt. agst SUSANNAH RUCKER and PETER
RUCKER, Exrs. &c. of JOHN RUCKER, deced., Defts.   In Case
Continued til next Court
- Upon the Presentment of the Grandjury against ANNE BRIDGES for
having a bastard Child in Saint Mark's Parish, the said ANNE being called and not
appearing, it is considered that she make her Fine with the Churchwardens of the
said Parish by the paiment of five hundred pounds of tobacco and costs or fifty
shillings for the use of the Poor of the said Parish and that she also pay the costs of
this Presentment
- WILLIAM HUGHES, Plt. agst THOMAS SANDERS, Deft.   In Debt
This suit is dismissed, the Deft. agreeing to pay Plt. his costs
- THOMAS PARK, Plt. agst JOHN ASHER, ROBERT LYNES and
JOSEPH PHILLIPS, Defts.   In Trespass
Dismissed, being agreed by the parties

p.   Orange County Court 23d October 1747
62   - JAMES DUN, Plt. agst JOHN SMITH, JUNR., Deft.   In Debt
This day came Plt. by his Attorney and Deft. being again solemnly called came
not; therefore it is considered that Plt. recover against Deft. and JOHN SMITH, his
Security twelve hundred pounds of tobacco, the Debt in the Declaration mentioned,
and his costs by him about his suit in this behalf expended, and the Deft. in mercy, &c
- JOHN SPOTSWOOD, Gent., Plt. agst FRANCIS KIRTLEY, Deft.
In Trespass
Continued til next Court
- ROBERT HILL, Plt. agst DANIEL CARTER & WILLIAM NASH, Defts.
In Assault and Battery
On motion of Plt. by his Attorney, it is ordered that the Deft., NASH, be struck out
of these Proceedings and as to the Deft., CARTER, the Sherif making no return on
the Alias Capias this suit is continued for him to do the same
- JOHN SPOTSWOOD, Gent., Plt. agst JOHN CHRISTOPHER, Deft. In Debt
This day came the parties by their Attornies, and Deft. saith he oweth Plt. nothing
of the Debt in the Declaration mentioned and of this he puts himself upon the Coun-
try, and Plt. likewise, Therefore the Trial of the issue is referred til next Court
- The Information against MICHAEL COOK is continued til next Court
- RICHARD WINSLOW, Gent., Plt. agst DENNIS BYRNE,
EDWARD SPENCER and ISAAC SMITH, Defts.   In Debt
Continued til next Court at Plt.'s costs
JOHN MORGAN & MARY his Wife, Plts. agst. WILLIAM LIGHTFOOT, Deft.
In Case

Continued for the Auditors to make their report

p.   Orange County Court 23d of October 1747
63   - JOHN WHARTON, Plt. agst JANE WHARTON, Admrx. &c. of THOMAS
      WHARTON, deced., Deft. In Case
Continued til next Court
      - On motion of WILLIAM TAPP, a witness for CHARLES DUETT, Plt.
against THOMAS BURK, Deft., who made Oath that he had attended three days as a
witness in that Cause, it is ordered that the said CHARLES pay him seventy five
pounds of tobacco for the same according to Law
      - On motion of JOSEPH WILLIAMS, a witness for CHARLES DUETT, Plt.
against THOMAS BURK, Deft., who made Oath that he had attended four days as a
witness in that Cause, it is ordered that the said CHARLES pay him one hundred
pounds of tobacco for the same according to Law
      - Ordered that the Allowance for the above attendance be not taxed in the Bill
of Costs
      - On motion of SARAH BRIDGES, a witness for CHARLES DEWITT, Plt.
against THOMAS BURK, who made Oath that she had attended three days as a witness in this Cause, it is ordered that the said CHARLES pay her seventy five pounds
of tobacco for the same according to Law
      - KEENE FIELD, quitam &c., Plt. agst WILLIAM RUSSELL, Gent. Deft.
      In Debt
Continued til next Court
      - HUMPHREY BELL, Plt. agst WILLIAM NASH, Deft.   In Case
Continued til next Court
      - JOHN COBOURN, Plt. agst WILLIAM LONG, Deft.   In Case
Continued til next Court at Plt.'s costs
      - RICHARD WINSLOW, Gent., Plt. agst DENNIS BYRNE, EDWARD
      SPENCER and ISAAC SMITH, Defts. On a Scire Facias
Continued til next Court at Plt.'s costs
      - HUMPHREY BELL, Plt. agst RICHARD WINSLOW, Gent., Deft. In Case
Continued til next Court at Plt.'s costs

p.   Orange County Court 23d of October 1747
64   - WILLIAM RUSSELL, Gent., Plt. agst JANE WHARTON, Admrx. &c. of
      THOMAS WHARTON, deced., Deft.   In Case
Continued til next Court
      - The Petition of RICHARD WINSLOW, Gent., against ISAAC SMITH is con-
tinued til next Court at Plt.'s costs
      - ISAAC SMITH, Plt. agst ROBERT BOHANNON, Deft.   In Chancery
By consent of the parties by their Council, it is ordered that this Cause be tried at
the next Court without further delay
      - HENRY PICKET, Plt. agst THOMAS COLEMAN, Deft. In Case
Continued til next Court at Plt.'s costs
      - ANTHONY STROTHER, Gent.,Plt. agst ELLIS MARCUS, Deft.   In Case
This day came Plt. by his Attorney and Deft. being again solemnly called came not.
Therefore it is ordered that Judgment be entered for Plt. against him, the Deft., and

WILLIAM ANDERSON & DANIEL BROWN, his Securities, for the Debt in the Declaration mentioned and his costs to be ascertained by Inquiry of a Jury at next Court

- ANTHONY STROTHER, Gent., Plt. agst MICHAEL WHATLEY, Deft. In Case

This day came Plt. by his Attorney and Deft. being again solemnly called came not; Therefore it is considered that Judgment be entered for Plt. against him, the Deft. and THOMAS RUCKER, his Security, for the Debt in the Declaration mentioned and costs to be ascertained by Inquiry of a Jury at the next Court

- The Petition of MARGARET GIBSON against JOHN SMITH is continued til next Court at Deft.'s costs

- ELIZABETH HARDIN, Plt. agst MICHAEL WHATLEY, Deft. In Debt
Continued til next Court at Deft.'s costs

p. 65 **Orange County Court 23d of October 1747**

- RICHARD BRIDGES, Plt. agst THOMAS CHEW, Gent., Deft. In Debt

By consent of the parties by their Attornies, a Commission is awarded Plt. to be directed to ROBERT GREEN, ROBERT EASTHAM and JAMES PENDLETON, Gent., or any two of them, to examine and take the Depositions of ELIZABETH DOWDE and MARY BOWMAN, two inform witnesses in this Cause, for the Plt. de bene esse he giving the Deft. legal notice of the time and place of executing the same

- RANDAL FUGETT, Plt. agst JOHN BRAMHAM, Deft. In Case

This day came the parties by their Attornies and Deft. defends the force and injury when, &c., and saith that he did not assume upon himself in manner and form as Plt. against him hath complained and of this he puts himself upon the Country, and Plt. likewise, Therefore the Trial of the issue is referred til the next Court

- WILLIAM RUSSELL, Gent., Plt. agst JOHN BRAMHAM, Deft. In Case

This day came the parties by their Attornies and Deft. defends the force and injury when, &c., and saith he did not assume upon himself in manner and form as Plt. against him hath complained and of this he puts himself upon the Country, and Plt. likewise, Therefore the Trial of the issue is referred til next Court

- WILLIAM RUSSELL, Gent., Plt. agst CHRISTOPHER ZIMMERMAN, Admr. &c. of JOHN NEWPORT, deced., Deft. In Case

This day came the parties by their Attornies and Deft. defends the force and injury when, &c. and saith he did not assume upon himself in manner and form as Plt. against im hath declared, and of this he puts himself upon the Country, and Plt. likewise and further Deft. saith that he had fully administered all and singular the goods and chattels of the said Intestate which had come to the hands of the said Administrator, before the exhibiting of the Plt.'s bill aforesaid, and that he hath no goods and chattles wherewith he can satisfy the same. Therefore on motion of Plt., time til the next Court is granted him to consider the Deft.'s Plea and then to reply

- ANTHONY STROTHER, Gent., Plt. agst CHRISTOPHER ZIMMERMAN, Admr. &c. of JOHN NEWPORT, Deft. In Case

Ths day came the parties by their Attornies and Deft. defends the force and injury when, &c., and saith he did not assume upon himself in manner and form as Plt against him hath declared, and of this he puts himself upon the Country, and Plt. likewise, and further the Deft. saith that he did fully administer all and singular the goods and chattels of the said Intestate which had come to the hands of said Administrator before the exhibiting of the Plt.'s Bill aforesaid, and that he hath no goods and chattels wherewith he can satisfy the same. Therefore on motion of Plt. time til the next Court is granted him to consider the Deft.'s Plea and then to reply

p.
66 <u>Orange County Court 23d of October 1747</u>
- MARGARET RICE, Admrx., &c. of HENRY RICE, deced., Plt. agst ELI GRIFFIN, Deft.   In Case
Continued for the Auditors to make their report
- JOHN LEWIS, BEVERLEY WHITING and WARNER WASHINGTON, Gent., Exors. &c. of JOHN WASHINGTON, Gent., late Sherif of GLOUCESTER County, deced., Plts. agst ROBERT FREEMAN, Deft.   In Case
This day came the Plts. by their Attornies and thereupon came a Jury, to wit

ANDREW BOURN	WILLIAM TAPP	JOHN POUND
NICHOLAS JONES	JOHN FIELD	CHRISTOPHER SUTTON
NATHAN TURNER	RANDAL FUGETT	JOSEPH PHILLIPS
THOMAS THORNTON	MATHEW HUBARD &	EDWARD WARE

who having sworn well and truly to inquire of damages in this Cause, upon their Oath do say that Plts. have sustained damages by occasion of Deft.'s breach of promise in the Declaration specified to fifteen pounds, eight shillings and four pency half penny besides their costs. Therefore it is considered by the Court that Plts. recover against the Deft. and THOMAS CHEW, Gent., late Sherif of Orange County, their damages aforesaid in form aforesaid assessed and their costs by them about their suit in this behalf expended, and Deft. in mercy, &c.
- THOMAS GRAVES, Plt. agst ANDREW BOURN, Deft.   In Case
This day came Plt. by his Attorney and Deft. in his proper person and Deft saith he cannot gainsay Plt.'s action but that he is indebted to him in seven pounds, two shillings and six pence. Therefore it is considered by the Court that Plt. recover against Deft. the seven pounds, two shillings and six pence and his costs by him about his suit in this behalf expended, and Deft. in mercy, &c.
- Upon Petition of EDWARD WARE against WILLIAM STEVENS for a Debt therein supposed to be due, this day came the parties by their Attornies who being fully heard, it is considered by the Court that this Petition be dismissed and the Deft. go thereof thence without day and recover against Plt. his costs
- ANTHONY FLINCH, Plt. agst ELI GRIFFIN, Deft.   In Debt
Continued til next Court

p.
67 <u>Orange County Court 23d of October 1747</u>
- FRANCIS THORNTON, Gent., Plt. agst JOSEPH THOMAS, Gent., Deft.   In Debt
Dismissed being agreed by the parties and it is ordered that Deft. pay to Plt. his costs
- WILLIAM BELL, Plt. agst ROBERT JACKSON, Gent., Deft.   In Case
This day came the parties by their Attornies and Deft. defends the force and injury when, &c. and saith that he did not assume upon himself in manner and form as Plt. against him hath complained, and of this he puts himself upon the Country, and Plt. likewise, and the parties agree that the Deft. may give the special matters in Evidence at the Trial which is referred til the next Court

- JOHN SPOTSWOOD, Gent., Plt. agst JOHN EARLY, Deft. In Trespass
This day came Plt. by ZACHARY LEWIS, Gent., his Attorney, and Deft. being re-
turned arrested was solemnly called but came not. Therefore on motion of Plt., it is
ordered that unless he appears at next Court and answers Plt.'s action, Judgment
shall then be entered for Plt. against him, the Deft. and JEREMIAH EARLY, his
Security, for the Debt in the Declaration mentioned and costs
- FRANCIS BROWN, Plt. agst EDWARD SPENCER, Gent., Deft. In Debt
This day came the parties by their Attornies and Deft. saith that he hath paid the
Debt in the Declaration mentioned according to the Writing Obligatory therein also
mentioned and of this he puts himself upon the Country and Plt. likewise, Therefore
the Trial of the issue is referred til next Court
- WILLIAM McDONAUGH, Plt. agst JOANNA SIMS, Admrx. &c. of
RICHARD SIMS, deced., Deft. In Debt
This day came Plt. by ZACHARY LEWIS, Gent., his Attorney and Deft. being
again solemnly called came not. Therefore it is considered by the Court that Plt.
recover against Deft. fourteen pounds, sixteen shillings and one penny, the ballance of
the Debt in the Writing Obligatory mentioned in the Declaration and his costs by hi
about his suit in this behalf expended, to be levied of the goods and chattels of the said
RICHARD in the hands of Deft. to be administered if so much thereof she hath, if not
then the costs to be levied of the Deft.'s proper goods and chattles and Deft. in mercy,
&c.

p.   Orange County Court 23d of October 1747
68   - Upon the Attachment brought by JOHN WILLIS against the Estate of
JOHN CLAYTON, JUNR., the Deft. not appearing to replevy the attached
things, it is considered that Plt. recover against Deft. one pound, seven shllings and six
pence and his costs by him about his suit in this behalf expended
- MARGARETT GIBSON, Admrx. &c. of JONATHAN GIBSON, Gent., deced.,
Plt. agst WILLIAM RUSSELL, Gent., Deft. In Case
Continued til next Court for the Auditors to make their report
- EDWARD PRICE, Plt. agst PATRICK LEONARD, Deft. In Case
This day came the parties by their Attornies and Deft. says that he is Not Guilty of
the Slander in the Declaration mentioned and of this he puts himself upon the Coun-
try, and Plt. likewise, and the parties agree that Deft. may give the special matters in
Evidence at the Trial which is referred til next Court
- ROBERT SHEDDEN, Plt. agst THOMAS CHEW, Gent., Deft. In Debt
This day came the parties by their Attornies and Deft. says he owes the Plt.
nothing of the Debt in the Declaration mentioned and of this he puts himself upon the
Country and Plt. likewise, therefore the Trial of the issue is referred til next Court
- EDWARD SPENCER, Gent., Plt. agst SHEM COOK, Deft. In Debt
Dismissed, being agreed by the parties and it is ordered that Deft. pay unto Plt. his
costs
- EDWARD SPENCER, Gent., Plt. agst DAVID GRIFFIN, Deft. In Debt
Dismissed, being agreed by the parties and it is ordered that Deft. pay unto Pl. his
costs
- EDWARD SPENCER, Gent., Plt. agst JOHN WILLIS, Gent., Deft. In Debt
Dismissed, being agreed by the parties and it is ordered that Deft. pay Plt. his costs

p.   <u>Orange County Court 23d of October 1747</u>
69   - ThePetition of TIMOTY CROSTHWAIT against EDWARD SPENCER is
dismissed
        - WILLIAM JACKSON and ELIZABETH his Wife, Plts. agst
MICAJAH PICKETT, Deft.   In Case
Dismissed
        - RICHARD VERNON, Plt. agst HONORIAS POWELL, Deft.
        In Assault and Battery
Continued til next Court
        - The Petition of DANIEL HORNBY against JOHN BRAMHAM is continued
til next Court
        - The Petition of BELFIELD's Executors against JOHN BRAMHAM is con-
tinued til next Court
        - The Attachment of HENRY DOWNES against the Estate of RICHRD
McGRAW, is continued
        - The Attachment of JOHN SMITH against the Estate of JOHN SMITH,
JUNR., is continued
                - Present.   GEORGE TAYLOR, Gent.
        - The Petition of JAMES PENDLETON and PHILLIP CLAYTON, Gent.
against WILLIAM KIRTLEY, WILLIAM CLIFT and ROGER ABBETT is continued
til next Court
        - The Attachment brought by JOHN ALLAN against the Estate of JOHN
SMITH, JUNR. is continued til next Court
        - Upon the Attachment brought by RICHARD VERNON against RICHARD
McGRAW, THOMAS THORNTON being sworn declared that he hath nothing in his
hands belong to the said McGRAW, whereupon he is discharged and the other Garnishee, LAWRENCE BRADLEY and GEORGE HOME not appearing, an Attachment is awarded against them returnable to next Court
        - WILLIAM RUSSELL, Gent., Plt. agst THOMAS WRIGHT, Deft.   In Case
Continued til next Court
        - GEORGE STUBBLEFIELD, Plt. agst EDWARD FRANKLYN, Deft. In Debt
   This day came Plt. by ZACHARY LEWIS, Gent., his Attorney and Deft. being
arrested was solemnly called but came not. Therefore on the motion of Plt., it is
ordered that unless he appears here at next Court and answers Plt.'s action, Judgment shall then be entered for Plt. against him, the Deft. and THOMAS CHEW,
Gent., late Sherif of Orange County, for the Debt in the Declaration mentioned and
costs

p.   <u>Orange County Court 23d of October 1747</u>
70   - ALEXANDER SCOTT, Plt. agst JAMES TAYLOR WHITE, Deft. In Debt
        - This day came Plt. by ZACHARY LEWIS, Gent., his Attorney and Deft.
being arrested was solemnly called but came not. Therefore on motion of Plt., it is
ordered that unless he appears at the next Court and answers Plt.'s action, Judgment shall then be entered for Plt. against him, the Deft. and THOMAS CHEW, Gent.
late Sherif of Orange County, for the Debt in the Declaration mentioned and costs
        - JOHN SPOTSWOOD, Gent. Plt. agst THOMAS THORNTON, Deft. In Debt
   This day came Plt. by ZACHARY LEWIS, Gent., his Attorney, and Deft. being

arrested was solemnly called but came not. Therefore on motion of Plt., it is ordered that unless he appears at next Court and answers Plt.'s action, Judgment shall then be entered for Plt. against him the Deft. and THOMAS CHEW, Gent., late Sherif of Orange County, for the Debt in the Declaration mentioned and costs

- WILLIAM NASH, Plt. agst JAMES POLLARD, Deft. In Assault & Battery
This day came Plt. by ZACHARY LEWIS, Gent., his Attorney and Deft. being arrested was solemnly called but came not, therefore on motion of Plt., it is ordered that unless he appears at next Court and answers Plt.'s action, Judgment shall then be entered for Plt. against him the Deft., and THOMAS CHEW, Gent., late Sherif of Orange County, for the Debt in the Declaration mentioned and costs

- JAMES HUNTER, Merchant, Plt. agst. GEORGE DOGGETT, Deft. In Case
The Deft. not being arrested, on motion of Plt. by his Attorney, an Alias Capias is awarded him against the Deft. returnable to next Court

- WILLIAM HUNTER, Gent., Plt. agst GEORGE DOGGETT, Deft. In Debt
The Deft. not being arrested, on motion of Plt. by his Attorney, an Alias Capias is awarded him against the Deft. returnable to the next Court

p.   Orange County Court 23d of October 1747
71   - RICHARD SHIP, Admr. &c. of THOMAS SHIP, deced., Plt. agst
        GEORGE DOGGETT, Deft.   In Case
The Deft. not being arrested, on motion of Plt. by his Attorney, an Alias Capias is awarded him against the Deft. returnable to next Court

- Upon the Petition of JOHN SPOTSWOOD, Gent., against EDWARD WARE for nine hundred pounds of tobacco and cask said to be due by the ballance of a Promisory Note, this day came Plt. by ZACHARY LEWIS, Gent., his Attorney, and Deft. not appearing tho warned, it is considered by the Court that Plt. recover against Deft. the nine hundred pounds of tobacco and cask and his costs by him about his suit in this behalf expended

- The Petition of ROBERT DUNLOP and THOMAS DUNLOP against JONAS JENKINS is continued til next Court

- THOMAS SCOTT, Plt. agst RICHARD MAULDIN and
THOMAS RUCKER, Defts.   In Debt
This day came Plt. by GEORGE WYTHE, Gent., his Attorney and Defts. being returned arrested were solemnly called but came not; Therefore it is ordered that unless they appear at next Court and answer Plt.'s action, Judgment shall be then entered for Plt. against them, the Defts., and REUBEN RUCKER, their Security, for the Debt in the Declaration mentioned and costs

- RICHARD WINSLOW, Gent., Plt. agst THOMAS CHEW, Gent., Deft.
In Case
This day came Plt. by GEORGE WYTHE, Gent., his Attorney, and Deft. being summoned was called but came not. Therefore on Plt.'s motion, it is ordered that unless he appears at next Court and answers Plt.'s action, Judgment shall then be entered for Plt. against him, the Deft. for the Debt in the Declaration mentioned and costs

- Upon the Petition of MARGRETT GIBSON, Admrx. of JONATHAN GIBSON, Gent., deced., against JOHN LYNCH for three pounds current money therein said to be due by a Promisory Note, this day came Plt. by ZACHARY LEWIS, Gent., his Attorney, and Deft. not appearing tho warned, it is considered by the Court that Plt. recover against Deft. the three pounds and his costs by him about his suit in this bealf expended, together with a Lawyer's fee

 - The Petition of EDWARD WATTS against MUMFORD STEVENS is continued til next Court at Deft.'s costs

p. Orange County Court 23d of October 1747
72 - Upon Petition of JAMES SUGGITT against NATHAN TURNER for three
  pounds current money said to be due by Bill, this day came Plt. and Deft. not appearing tho warned, therefore it is considered by the Court that Plt. recover against Deft. the three pounds and his costs by him about his suit in this behalf expended

 - JOHN GORDON, Plt. agst CHARLES KAVANAUGH, Deft. In Debt
This day came Plt. by GEORGE WYTHE, Gent., his Attorney and Deft. being returned arrested was solemnly called but came not. Therefore on motion of Plt. it is ordered that unlesshe appears at next Court and answers Plt.'s action, Judgment shall then be entered for Plt. against him, the Deft., and THOMAS CHEW, Gent., late Sherif of Orange County, for the Debt in the Declaration mentioned and costs

 - Upon Petition of NICHOLAS JONES against WILLIAM LONG for the Debt therein said to be due by Account, this day came Plt. and Deft. not appearing, it is considered by the Court that Plt. recover against Deft. two pounds, three shillings and six pence half penny and his costs by him about his suit in this behalf expended

 - The Petition of NICHOLAS JONES against PATRICK LEONARD is dismissed

 - The Petitin of ANNE McCULLOCK against ELI GRIFFIN is dismissed

 - CHARLES HARRISON, Plt. agst NICHOLAS JONES, Deft. In Case
The Deft. not being arrested, on motion of Plt. by his Attorney an Alias Capias is awarded him against the Deft. returnable to next Court

 - TULLY CHOICE, Plt. agst THOMAS LOCKER, Deft. In Case
Dismissed

 - WILLIAM GALE of Whitehaven, Merchant, Plt. agst.
THOMAS COVINGTON, Deft. In Case
The Under Sherif, CHRISTOPHER ZIMMERMAN, JUNR., to whom the Process was delivered not making his return, it is ordered that the Sherif summon him to appear at next Court to do the same

p. Orange County Court 23d of October 1747
73 - WILLIAM GALE of Whitehaven, Merchant, Plt. agst.
JOHN CARDER, Deft. In Case
The Under Sherif, CHRISTOPHER ZIMMERMAN, JUNR., to whom the Process was delivered not making his return, it is ordered that the Sherif summon him to appear at next Court to do the same

 - WILLIAM GALE of Whitehaven, Merchant, Plt. agst
WILLIAM MORGAN, Deft. In Case
The Under Sherif, CHRISTOPHER ZIMMERMAN, JUNR., to whom the Process was delivered not making his return, it is ordered that the Sherif summon him to appear at next Court to do the same

- JAMES MADISON, quitam &c., Plt. agst JOSEPH PHILLIPS, Deft. In Debt
Continued til next Court
- EDWARD SPENCER, Gent., Plt. agst THOMAS JONES, Deft.   In Debt
The Under Sherif, CHRISTOPHER ZIMMERMAN, JUNR., to whom the Process
was delivered not making his return, it is ordered that the Sherif summon him to
appear at next Court to do the same
- JOHN SEAYRES, Plt. agst VALENTINE MORGAN, Deft.   On a Writ of
Scire Facias on a Judgment of this Court obtained the 25th day of May 1744
by the Plt. against Deft. for one pound, fifteen shillings and five pence current
money and forty nine pounds of nett tobacco for his costs by him about his
suit in this behalf expended
This day came Plt. by ZACHARY LEWIS, Gent., his Attorney, and Deft. being
warned and not appearing, therefore it is ordered that Judgment be entered for Plt.,
that he have execution against Deft. according to the force form and effect of the recovery aforesaid, and for his costs in suing forth and prosecuting this suit
- JOHN SEAYRES, Plt. agst ROBERT ADAMS, Deft. On a Scire Facias
The Sherif returning that Deft. hath nothing in his Bailiwick by which he could
cause him to know neither is he found in the same. Therefore on motion of Plt. by his
Attorney an Alias Scire Facias is awarded him against Deft. returnable to next Court
- The Attachment brought by JOHN FINNEL against the Estate of ROBERT
SEAYRES is dismissed, being agreed by the parties
- The Attachment brought by WILLIAM GHOLSTON against the Estate of
JOHN CLAYTON, JUNR. is dismissed

p.   Orange County Court 23d of October 1747
74   - Upon the Petition of MATHEW HUBBARD against JOHN DOGAN for five
        pounds current money said to be due by a Note of Hand, this day came the
parties who being fully heard, it is considered that Plt. recover against Deft. the four
pounds and his costs by him about his suit in this behalf expended
- TULLY CHOICE having obtained an Attachment against the Estate of
ROBERT SEAYRES who hath privately removed himself out of the County or so
absconds that Process can't be served on him for three pounds, ten shillings and four
hundred fifty pounds of tobacco, the late Sherif, HENRY DOWNES, making return
that he hath attached one Horse, this day came Plt. and Deft. not appearing to
replevy the Horse, the Plt. produced a settlement of Accounts under the hand writing
of said Deft. Therefore it is considered by the Court that Plt. recover against Deft.
three hundred twelve pounds of tobacco and three shillings and ten pence, the ballance of the said Account and his costs by him about his suit in this behalf expended,
and it is ordered that the late Sherif deliver the said Horse to the present Sherif who is
ordered to make sale thereof according to Law and pay the money arising from such
sale to the Plt. in discharge of this Judgment and restore the residue if any to Deft.
and make return thereof to the Court
- Ordered that WILLIAM STROTHER, FRANCIS STROTHER, JAMES
CONNER and CHARLES CAVANAUGH or any three of them being first sworn
before a Justice of the Peace for this County, do appraise in current money the slaves
and person Estate of MILDRED WILLIS in this County and return the Appraisment
- Absent. ROBERT EASTHAM, Gent.

- WILLIAM KELLY, Plt. agst ROBERT EASTHAM, Gent., Admr. &c. of JOHN LATHAM, deced., Deft. In Case

This day came as well Plt. by GEORGE WYTHE, Gent., his Attorney as Deft. by ZACHARY LEWIS, Gent., his Attorney and Deft. defends the force and injury when, &c. and saith that the Intestate did not assume upon himself in manner and form as Plt. against him hath complained and of this he puts himself upon the Country and the Plt. likewise, Therefore the Trial of the issue is referred til the next Court

- ROBERT RAE & DANIEL CAMPBELL, Plts. agst JONAS JENKINS, Deft. In Debt

This day came Plt. by GEORGE WYTHE, Gent., his Attorney and Deft. returned arrested was solemnly called but came not. Therefore on motion of Plt. it is ordered that unless he appears at next Court and answers Plt.'s action, Judmgnet shall then be entered for Plt. against him, the Deft. and ROBERT TREEWICK his Security, for the Debt in the Declaration mentioned and costs

p. 75   Orange County Court 23d of October 1747

- JAMES PENDLETON and PHILLIP CLAYTON, Gent., Plts. agst JOHN RAY, Deft. In Case

The Sherif having returned on the Attachment that the Deft. hath no goods or chattels in his Bailiwick, on Plt.'s motion, another Attachment is awarded against the Deft.'s Estate returnable to next Court

- Upon motion of GEORGE TAYLOR, Gent., Security of TIMOTHY CROSTHWAIT's administration of the Estate of WILLIAM CROSTHWAIT, deced., it is ordered that ZACHARY TAYLOR, JOSEPH THOMAS, TAVERNER BEALE and JOHN NICHOLAS or any three of them do examine state and settle the said TIMOTHY's Accounts of the administration of the Decedent's Estate and make report thereof to the Court

- ISAAC SMITH, Plt. agst FRANCIS WILLIAMS, Deft. In Chancery

The Deft. having stood out Process of Contempt without putting in his Answer to Plt.'s Bill, on motion of Plt. by his Council, his Bill is taken for confessed. Therefore it is ordered and decreed that the Deft. his heirs, Executors and Administrators do deliver the Negro woman slave named Bess and the Negro boy slave named Wiggon in the Bill mentioned and the increase of the said Negro woman to the Plt. his heirs Executors, Administrators or assigns.upon his, the said Plt., his heirs Executors, Administrators or assigns paying Deft. his heirs Executors, Administrators or assigns forty two pounds, ten shillings and six pence current money according to the Agreement in the Bill also mentioned, which sum is to be paid on or before the twenty first day of December next, and upon paiment thereof the absolute property of the said Negroes is vested in the Plt. And it is further ordered that Deft. pay unto Plt. his costs by him in this behalf expended

- Ordered that the Court be adjourned til the fourth Thursday in next month
- The Minutes of these Proceedings were signed

THOS: CHEW

p. 76   - At a Court held for Orange County on Thursday the 26th day of November in the twenty first year of the Reign of our Sovereign Lord George the Second by the grace of God of Great Britain, France and Ireland, &c.,

Annoq. Domini MDCCXLVII before his Majesties Justices of the Peace
for the said County, to wit

THOMAS CHEW   JOHN FINLESON
WILLIAM RUSSELL   JAMES PENDLETON
ROBERT SLAUGHTER   ROBERT GREEN
GOODRICH LIGHTFOOT   PHILLIP CLAYTON, Gentlemen

- JAMES SUGGITT, Foreman,   ANDREW HARRISON   JOHN UNDERWOOD
BRYANT SYSON   JOHN BOURN   BRYANT THORNHILL
JAMES CONNER   MATTHEW TOOL   FRANCIS MICHAEL
THOMAS SIMS   JOHN INGRAM   BENJAMIN HAWKINS
THOMAS THORNTON   CHARLES MORGAN   ROBERT TREEWICK
JOHN MALLORY   PETER RUCKER   DANIEL SINGLETON
EDWARD WARE   THOMAS GAHAGAN &   SAMUEL FARGUSON

were sworn a Grandjury of Inquest for the body of this County and having received
their charge withdrew and returning into Court made the following Presentments, to
wit;

We of the Grandjury do present WILLIAM POUND of Saint Thomas Parish for
not making of Corn

We likewise do present LAWRENCE BRADLEY for swearing two profance
Oaths living in Saint Mark's Parish

We likewise do present JOHN McCENNY for swearing two profane Oaths
living in Saint Mark's Parish

We likewise do present GEORGE COOK for swearing two profane Oaths living
in Saint Thomas's Parish

We likewise do present the Overseer of the Road from the Raccoon to the Sum-
merduck Forest keeping the same in repair

We likewise do present CHARLES HOLSFORD for swearing two profane
Oaths living in St. Mark's Parish

We likewise do present BENJAMIN HENSLEY for not tending of Corn linving
in Saint Thomas's Parish

We likewise do present JOHN HENSLEY for not tending Corn living in the said
Parish

We likewise do present JOHN GILBERT for a Vagabond living in Saint
Thomas's

An Indictment against JOHN MORGAN and MARY his Wife for an Assault
and Battery, not a true Bill

An Indictment against MICHAEL O'NEAL and MARGARET his Wife for an
Assault, a true Bill

An Indictment against JOHN GOUGH and ROBERT BICKERS for an
Assault and Battery, a true Bill

And having nothing further to present were discharged

- Ordered that Process issue against the severall persons this day presented
by the Grandjury to cause them to come to the next Court to answer the severall Presentments against them

- An Indenture of Feoffment between WILLIAM JOHNSTON and ELIZA-
BETH his Wife of one part and BRADLEY KIMBROW of other part was acknowledged by the said WILLIAM & ELIZABETH, and ordered to be recorded, she being

first privily examined as the Law directs

p.   <u>Orange County Court 26th of November 1747</u>
77   - An Indenture of Feoffment between MATHEW DAVIS and JOSEPH
DAVIS of one part and JOHN NOEL of other part was acknowledged by the
said JOSEPH and proved to be the act and deed of MATHEW DAVIS by the Oaths of
WILLIAM (blank) ELIZABETH BELL and HENRY PICKETT, the witnesses thereto
and ordered to be recorded
         - An Indenture of Feoffment between LEONARD PHILLIPS and JEMIMA his
Wife of one part and JOHN NOEL of the other part was proved by the Oaths of
WILLIAM BELL, ELIZABETH BELL and JOSEPH DAVIS, the witnesses thereto
and ordered to be recorded
         - An Indenture of Feoffment between THOMAS RUCKER of one part and
WILLIAM RUCKER of other part and a Memorandum of Livery of Seisen thereon
indorsed were acknowledged by the said THOMAS and ordered to be recorded
         - An Indenture of Feoffment between THOMAS RUCKER of one part and
THOMAS COFER of other part and a Memorandum of Livery of Seisen thereon
indorsed were acknowledged by the said THOMAS and ordered to be recorded
         - ANTHONY STROTHER, Gent., Plt. agst ELLIS MARCUS, Deft. In Case
The Plt. this day proved his Account against Deft., the ballance whereof is three
pounds, eighteen shillings and three pence half penny, which is ordered to be certified
         - ANTHONY STROTHER, Gent.,Plt. agst MICHAEL WHATLEY, Deft.
         In Case
The Plt. this day in open Court proved his Account against Deft. the ballance
whereof is seven pounds, nine shillings and six pence which is ordered to be certified
         - ANTHONY STROTHER, Gent., Plt. agst CHRISTOPHER ZIMMERMAN,
         Admr., &c. of JOHN NEWPORT, deced., Deft.   In Case
The Plt. this day in open Court proved his Account against Deft. the ballance
whereof is five pounds, three shillings and four pence half penny which is ordered to be
certified
         - An Indenture of Bargain and Sale between ERASMUS TAYLOR of one part
and JOHN NICHOLAS of other part was acknowledged by ERASMUS TAYLOR and
ordered to be recorded
         - Ordered that DAVID ZACHARY, the male labouring Tithables belonging to
HARRY BEVERLEY at his upper Quarter, RICHARD DURRETT's male labouring
Tithables, JAMES BEAZLEY, WILLIAM WATKINS and GEORGE ANDERSON,
JUNR. his male labouring Tithables be added to the gang to work on the Road under
JOHN BLACKEY, Overseer of the same

p.   <u>Orange County Court 26th of November 1747</u>
78   - Indentures of Lease and Release between JOHN WISDOM & ANN his
         Wife of one part and ABRAHAM MAYFIELD, JUNR., of other part and a
Receipt endorsed on the Release were acknowledged by said JOHN & ANN and
ordered to be recorded, she being first privately examined as the Law directs
         - An Indenture of Bargain and Sale between THOMAS SMITH of one part and
FRANCIS TALIAFERRO, Gent., of other part and a Receipt thereon endorsed were
proved by the Oaths of ALEXANDER WAUGH, JOHN FINNELL and WILLIAM

TALIAFERRO, the witnesses thereto and ordered to be recorded
        - A Bond from THOMAS SMITH to FRANCIS TALIAFERRO, Gent., was
proved by the Oaths of ALEXANDER WAUGH, JOHN FINNELL and WILLIAM
TALIAFERRO, witnesses thereto, and ordered to be recorded
        - ROBERT EASTHAM, Gent., having obtained an Attachment against the
Estate of FRANCIS GARDINER who hath privately removed himself out of the
County or so absconds that Process cannot be served on him for six pounds current
money due from the said FRANCIS to said ROBERT by Account, the late Sherif of
this County making return that he hath attached one bay Horse, a pair of leather
Breeches, two old Shirts, chequ'd handkerchief, one cloth Jackett not made, one old
pair of Trowzers, this day came Plt. and Deft. not appearing to relevy the attached
effects, the Plt. proved his Account by his own Oath, the ballance whereof is four
pounds, one shilling and his costs by him about his suit in this behalf expended, and it
is ordered that the late Sherif deliver the said things to the present Sherif who is
ordered to make sale thereof according to Law and the money arising from such sale
to pay to Plt. in discharge of this Judgment and restore the residue, if any, to Deft.
and that he make return of such sale to the next Court
        - Ordered that MARK FINX be added to the List of Tithables in Saint Mark's
Parish
        - Ordered that MUMFORD STEVENS, THOMAS WEATHERBY and
GEORGE (blank), Tithables belonging to the said MUMFORD, be added to the Lists
in Saint Thomas's Parish
        - Ordered that two Tithables belonging to RICHARD TUTT, Gent., be added to
the Lists in Saint Mark's Parish
        - An Indenture of Feoffment between CHARLES CAVANAUGH and ANNE
his Wife of one part and WILLIAM ROANE, Gent., of other part and Memorandum of
Livery of Seisen and a Receipt from the said CHARLES thereon endorsed were acknowledged by said CHARLES & ANN and ordered to be recorded, she being first
privately examined as the Law directs
        - A Bond from CHARLES KAVANAUGH to WILLIAM ROANE was acknow-
ledged by the said CHARLES and ordered to be recorded

p.   Orange County Court 26th of November 1747
79   - An Indenture of Feoffment between ROBERT GREEN, Gent. and
        ELEANOR his Wife of one part and the Revd. JOHN THOMPSON , Clk. of the
other part and a Memorandum of Livery of Seizen thereon endorsed were acknowledged by ROBERT GREEN, and ordered to be recorded
        - An Indenture of Feoffment between JAMES GAINES and MARY his Wife of
one part and TIMOTHY CHANDLER of other part and a Memorandum of Livery of
Seizen thereon endorsed were acknowledged by the said JAMES and MARY and
ordered to be recorded, she being first privily examined as the Law directs
        - THOMAS McGEE is by the Court appointed Surveyor of the Road from
SOUTHWEST MOUNTAIN ROAD near HARDING's Quarter to the County Line in
the room of EDWARD HALEY and it is ordered that the gang which worked under the
said HALEY do attend and obey the directions of said McGEE in keeping the Road in
repair and that said McGEE cause Posts of Directions to be erected where necessary
        - An Indenture of Feoffment between EDWARD WARE and LUCY his Wife of

one part and HENRY WARE of the other part and a Memorandum of Livery of Seisen from said EDWARD thereon endorsed were acknowledged by the said EDWARD and LUCY and ordered to be recorded, she being first privily examined as the Law directs

- It appearing to the Court that an Order made last Court whereby persons were apointed to value the improvements made by JAMES GAINES on two hundred acres of land said to be part of the said thousand acres of land granted to JOSEPH HAWKINS, Gent., by Pattent dated the 28th of September 1728, is erroneous, the said two hundred acres being part of a Pattent for four hundred acres which Pattent dated 10th September 1735. It is ordered that the said Order be amended by the Clerk and the persons making their Report the same is ordered to be recorded

- The the Court proceeded to lay the Levy

	Orange County	DR.	Tobo,
To	The Clerk of the Court for public services		1240
To	WILLIAM DUNCAN for an old Wolf's head certified by ROBERT EASTHAM, Gent.		140
To	LEWIS DAVIS YANCEY for six young Wolves heads certified by JAMES PENDLETON, Gent.		420
To	WILLIAM RUSSELL, Gent., for an old Wolf head certified by ROBERT EASTHAM, Gent.		140
To	DANIEL SINGLETON for an old Wolfs head certified by EDWARD SPENCER, Gent.		140
To	BENJAMIN CAVE, assignee of JOHN BLEDSOE, for an old Wolf's head certified by EDWARD SPENCER, Gent.		140
To	MUMFORD STEVENS for an old Wolf's head certified by GEORGE TAYLOR, Gent.		140
To	JOHN WASHBOURN for an old Wolf's head certified by ROBERT EASTHAM, Gent.		140
To	JOHN BRAMHAM, Goaler, by his Account		2260
			4760

- A Deed Poll from MARY BEARBACK to JOHN JONES was acknowledged by the said MARY and ordered to be recorded

p. 80   Orange County Court 26th of November 1747
- It appearing to the Court that Indentures of Lease and Release between ROBERT GREEN, Gent. of one part and SAMUEL FARGUSON of other part which were acknoweldged by the said GREEN 26th day of March last past and by the Court ordered to be recorded, were not dated and by the consent of said ROBERT GREEN It is orderd that the Deeds be dated the day they were admitted to Record
- Then the Court adjourned til tomorrow morning 8 o'clock
- The Minutes of these Proceedings were signed
THOS: CHEW

- At a Court continued and held for Orange County on Friday the 27th day of November 1747   Present
THOMAS CHEW   HENRY FIELD
ABRAHAM FIELD   GEORGE TAYLOR   Gentlemen
                   &   PHILIP CLAYTON

- Ordered that JOHN BRAMHAM, JEREMIAH MORTON, FRANCIS

MOOR and GEORGE WELLS or any three of them do sometime between this and
the next Court go to and view the Road from the SOUTH WEST MOUNTAINS to the
Courthosue and the Rolling Road from up the River to the Road leading to
FREDERICKSBURG ROAD, the land of BRIANT SYSON and report a more convenient way if it can be found

- Ordered that JOHN BRANHAM, JEREMIAH MORTON, FRANCIS
MOOR and GEORGE WELLS or any three of them do sometime between this and
the next Court go to and view the Way from the upper end of BRYANT SYSON's Lott
to the Courthouse and report the most convenient way

- PHILIP EASTIN is by the Court appointed Overseer of the Road from Mr.
ZACHARY TAYLOR's Old Ordinary to CAVE's Ford in the room of RICHARD
WINSLOW, Gent. and AMBROSE BULLARD

- An Indenture of Bargain and Sale between HENRY DOWNES of one part
and ANDREW HARRISON of other part was acknowledged by the said HENRY and
ordered to be recorded

p. 81	Orange County Court 27th of November 1747		
	- Then the Court proceeded again to lay the Levy		
	Orange County	DR	Tobo.
	Brought forward		4760
To	JOHN BRAMHAM for the Rent of the Courthouse		144
To	JOHN REYNOLDS, Constable, for viewing tobacco fields		200
To	ditto for setting Posts of Directions on a Road		100
To	BRYANT SYSON for repairing the MOUNTAIN RUN Bridge		750
To	JOHN NIX for an old Wolf's head certified by JAMES PENDLETON, Gent.		140
To	JOHN ASKEW, Assignee of WILLIAM LAND for an old Wolf's head certified by GEORGE TAYLOR, Gent.		140
To	GEORGE TAYLOR, Gent., Assignee of GEORGE DOUGLASS, for an old Wolf's head certified by he said TAYLOR		140
To	THOMAS STANTON, Assignee of FRANCIS HARVIE, for five young wolves heads certified by GOODRICH LIGHTFOOT, Gent.		353
To	ROBERT SLAUGHTER, Gent., for taking Coroner's Inquest		94
To	TULLY CHOICE by his Account for services as Undersherif		525
To	JANE WHARTON, Admrx. &c. of THOMAS WHARTON, deced., for summoning a Coroner's Jury		35
To	MARGARETT GIBSON, Admrx. &c. of JONATHAN GIBSON, deced. for two Record presses for the Office		1000
To	WILLIAM WHITE, Constable for viewing tobacco Fields		281
To	ZACHARIAH BLANKENBEKER for viewing tobacco Fields		99
To	THOMAS GAHAGAN for viewing tobacco Fields		133
To	WILLIAM HENDERSON for viewing tobacco Field		366
To	EDWARD SPENCER, Gent., for Smith's Work about the Prison		354
To	The Clerk of the Court for three Called Courts		420
To	ZACHARY LEWIS, Gent. for being King's Attorney		2080
To	HENRY DOWNES, late Undersheif, for summoning three Called Courts		420
To	JOHN SPOTSWOOD, Gent., for his FERRY at GERMANNA		3000
To	HENRY DOWNES for public services as Undersherif		1240
To	ditto as Collector for 22 Delinquents at 13 per Poll		286
To	ditto for Expences in going to the Clerk of the House of Burgess's Office to know what tobacco was levied for this County at laying the last Public Levy		250
To	THOMAS FOX for guarding Prison four nights		100

To	WILLIAM POUND for guarding Prison four nights	100
To	JOHN CLEVELAND for Levies for the years 1744, 1745 & 1746 he being	
	Constable during that time	46
To	6 per cent for Collection of 18753 lbs tobo.	1053
To	A Fraction in the Collector's hands	137
		18753

p.   Orange County Court 27th of November 1747
82   By 2679 Tithables at 7 lbs. tobo per poll   18753

    - Ordered that each Tithable person in this County pay the Sherif or Collector seven pounds of tobacco, it being the County Levy for the year 1747 and that the Sherif or Collector pay the same to the severall persons for whom it is proportioned

    - Ordered that ROBERT SLAUGHTER and GEORGE TAYLOR, Gent., do treat with two Gentlemen in the Commission of the Peace for SPOTSYLVANIA County to employ workmen to repair the Bridge over the WILDERNESS RUN, being the Dividing Line between that County and this, the Bridge being found out of order upon view thereof pursuance to an Order of this Court

    - RICHARD WINSLOW, Gent., came into Court and undertook to mend two of the Windows of the Courthouse by glazing them before next February Court for which he is to be paid when the money shall be received for the tobacco due to this County from ESSEX and KING & QUEEN

    - Upon motion of ANDREW HARRISON, a witness for EDWARD WARE Plt. against WILLIAM STEVENS, Deft., it is ordered that said EDWARD pay him fifty pounds of tobacco for two days attendance at last Court according to Law

    - Upon the Attachment of THOMAS DILLARD against GEORGE HOME, WILLIAM TAP being sworn declared he hath forty three shillings in his hands belonging to the said HOME

    - WILLIAM HENDERSON is by the Court continued in the Office of Constable in that part of the Little Fork lying in Parish of Saint Thomas and WILLIAM RICE is appointed CONSTABLE of the other part of the said Fork and it is ordered that he be sworn into the said Office at the next Court

    - An Indenture of Mortgage between THOMAS FOX of the one part and EDWARD SPENCER of the other part was acknowledged by the parties and ordered to be recorded

    - JOHN BRAMHAM, Plt. agst. WILLIAM RUSSELL, Gent.,   In Covenant
  This day came the parties by their Attornies and thereupon came a Jury, to wit;

PETER RUCKER	GEORGE ROBERTS	JAMES RUCKER
THOMAS ALLEN	RUSH HUDSON	RICHARD VERNON
TAVERNER BEALE	FRANCIS WILLIAMS	JOHN SMITH
GEORGE ANDERSON	MARTIN DUETT &	HENRY BOURN

who being elected tried and sworn the truth to speak upon the issue joined, went out of the Court to consult of their Verdict

    - The Minutes of these Proceedings were signed
                          THOS: CHEW

    - At a Court continued and held for Orange County on Saturday the 28th day of November 1747   Present
      THOMAS CHEW   HENRY FIELD

ABRAHAM FIELD   GEORGE TAYLOR   Gentlemen
                          & PHILIP CLAYTON

- ISAAC SMITH, Plt. agst ROBERT BOHANNON, Deft. In Chancery
This Cause was this day heard upon the Bill, Answer and Replication and the argu-
ments of the Council on both sides. In consideration thereof, it is ordered and decreed
that Deft. convey the two hundred acres of land in the Bill and Answer mentioned to
the Plt. in fee simple by good and sufficient conveyance upon said Plt. paying him
twenty pounds current money with Interest thereon after the rate of five percent per
annum to be computed on ten pounds part thereof from the thirteenth day of June
1741 and on ten pounds, the other part thereof, from the tenth day of June 1742 to
the time of payment of the same which is to be on or before the Court day for this
County in June next
          - Present. ROBERT SLAUGHTER, Gent.
- THOMAS CHEW, Gent., Plt. agst JACOB STOVER, Admr. &c. of JACOB
STOVER, deced.,, HENRY DOWNES and JACOB CASSELL, Defts.
In Chancery
This day came the parties by their Council and thereupon the Deft., DOWNES's,
Demurrer put into Plt.'s Bill of Complaint being argued, it seems to the Court here
that the same in insufficient. Therefore it is ordered that said Deft. answer Plt.'s said
Bill further and that he pay the Plt. his costs by him in this behalf expended
          - ALEXANDER SCOTT, Plt. agst JAMES TAYLOR WHITE, Deft. In Debt
This day came Plt. by his Attorney and Deft. in his proper person and Deft. confesseth the Plt.'s action. Therefore it is considered by the Court that Plt. recover
against Deft. five pounds, four shillings current money, the Debt in the Declaration
mentioned, and his costs by him about his suit in this behalf expended, and Deft. in
mercy, &c., but this Judgment, the costs excepted, is to be discharged by payment of
two pounds, twelve shillings with Interest thereon at the rate of five percent per
annum from the first day of January 1746 to the time of paiment and costs
          - The Petition of EDWARD WATTS against MUMFORD STEVENS is dis-
missed

p.   Orange County Court 28th of November 1747
84   - DAVID ROSS came into Court and made Oath that he was imported
      immediately into this Colony from Great Britain and that this is the first time
of his making Oath to the same in order to intitle him to fifty acres of land within this
Colony, which right is in open Court assigned to HENRY NIXON
      - BENJAMIN CAVE, one of the Gentlemen named in the Commission of the
Peace for this County, took the Oaths to his Majesties Person and Government and
took and subscribed the Abjuration Oath and the Test was sworn a Justice of the
Peace for this County and then took the Oath of a Judge of the County Court in
Chancery
          - Present. BENJAMIN CAVE, Gent.
      - ELIJAH MORTON is by the Court appointed CONSTABLE in this County
in the room of JOHN BOOTEN and it is ordered that he be sworn into his said Office
at the next Court
          - An Assignment of a Lease for Lives made by ALEXANDER SPOTSWOOD,

Esqr., deced., to SAMUEL POUND, from SAMUEL POUND to THOMAS JAME-
SON was acknowledged by said SAMUEL to the recording of which said Assignment
JOHN BRAMHAM, JUNR. by ZACHARY LEWIS, Gent. his Attorney, objected by
reason that said BRAMHAM hath filed a Bill in Chancery against the said POUND
and JAMESON to establish an agreement made between said POUND and BRAM-
HAM for the said Lease, but the same being overruled, the said Assignment is ordered
to be recorded

    - On motion of FRANCIS WILLIAMS by GEORGE WYTHE, Gent., his Coun-
sel, to set aside a Decree in Chancery made at the last Court in favour of ISAAC
SMITH against him said FRANCIS, which was opposed by said ISAAC by
ZACHARY LEWIS, Gent., his Counsel, and upon hearing the parties by their said
Counsels, it is ordered that the Decree be set aside upon FRANCIS WILLIAMS
finding Security to abide by such Order or Decree as shall be hereafter made in this
Cause, and that he shall not remove the Negroe's in the said former Decree mentioned out of this County so that said ISAAC in case he shall recover them may have
the effect of such Order or Decree which shall be made in this Cause nor abuse them
in the meantime. Whereupon THOMAS SIMS, RUSH HUDSON and JOHN
CHRISTOPHER came into Court and became Securities for the said WILLIAMS
accordingly

    - EDWARD SPENCER, Gent., came into court and undertook the collection of
the County Levy for this present year. Whereupon he entered into and acknowledged
Bond with WILLIAM RUSSELL, Gent., HENRY DOWNES and EDWARD WATTS
his Securities accordingly

    - It appearing to the Court that RICHARD LAMB hath neglected the Educa-
tion of his Children; whereupon it is ordered that the Churchwardens of Saint Thomas Parish do bind out the said Children according to Law

p.   Orange County Court 28th of November 1747
85   - It appearing to the Court that JOHN JONES hath neglected the Education
    of his Children, whereupon it is ordered that the Churchwardens of Saint Mark
Parish do bind out the Children according to Law

    - BENJAMIN CAVE, Gent., is by the Court appointed Overseer of the Road
from the TOMBSTONE to the TRAPP

    - DANIEL CARTER is by the Court appointed CONSTABLE in this County
from MUDDY RUN to the upper end of MOUNT PONEY and from thence to the
Courthouse and all the lower end of Saint Mark Parish and he having taken the Oaths
to his Majesties Person and Government and took and subscribed the Abjuration
Oath and the Test is sworn in to his said Office and then took the Oath appointed by
the Tobacco Law

    - Upon the Attachment brought by TULLY CHOICE against the Estate of
JOHN MORGAN, GEORGE COOK came into Court and undertook the said MOR-
GAN that in case he shall be cast in this suit he shall pay the condemnation of the
Court or render his body to Prison or that he the said GEORGE COOK, will do it for
him

    - The Attachment of GEORGE BUCHANNON &c. against WILLIAM PETTY
is continued til next Court

- The King agst JOHN WILSON, Deft.,   On an Information
The said WILSON not appearing, another summons is awarded against him re-
turnable to the next Court
- The King agst JOSEPH CAVE, Deft.   On an Information
The Deft. not appearing, another Attachment is awarded against him returnable to
the next Court
- The Indictment against JAMES HEMPHILL is continued til next Court
- WILLIAM BEVERLEY, Gent., Plt. agst GEORGE HOME, Deft. In Case
The Sherif returning that Deft. hath nothing in his Bailiwick, on Plt.'s motion the
Attachment is continued against the Deft.'s Estate returnable to the next Court
- The Petition of WILLIAM KELLY against WILLIAM CLARK is continued til
next Court
- JOHN BRAMHAM, Plt. agst WILLIAM RUSSELL, Gent. Deft. In Covenant
The Jury sworn yesterday to try the issue joined in this Cause came into Court and
returned a Special Verdict in these words, to wit, "We of the Jury do find that Deft.
hath not performed his Covenant

p.   Orange County Court 28th of November 1747
86   in repairing the Ordinary House to the value of four pounds current money and
      for the non payment of the Rents for the said Ordinary five years at thirty
pounds per year one hundred and fifty pounds current money.
"We likewise find that one McKAY, a Merchant, holding a Storehouse under the Plt.
on the land lett to the Deft. sold duirng the time and before the expiration of the said
Lease one quart of Rum to one JOHN WHARTON; to one SYSON severall gallons of
Rum, and to one CROUCHER two gallons of Rum, they all persons trading and
dealing with said McKAY's Store. Now upon the whole matter if the Law be for the
Plt. we find for him four pounds for the charge of repairing the Ordinary and the Rents
above, if not we find for the Deft." and the Cause is continued till next Court for the
matters of Law arising thereupon to be argued
- Upon motion of JOHN BOURN, a witness for JOHN BRAMHAM, Plt.
against WILLIAM RUSSELL, Gent., Deft., who made Oath that he had attended ten
days as a witness in that Cause, it is ordered that said BRAMHAM pay him two
hundred fifty pounds of tobacco for the said attendance according to Law
- Upon motion of JOHN WHARTON, a witness for JOHN BRAMHAM, Plt.
against WILLIAM RUSSELL, Gent., Deft. who made Oath that he had attended
twelve days as an Evidence in that Cause, it is ordered that said BRAMHAM pay
him three hundred pounds of tobacco for his said Attendance according to Law
- Upon Petition of WILLIAM JOHNSTON against JOHN WINELL
SANDERS this day came Plt. by his Attorney and Deft. confesseth the Plt.'s Petition.
Therefore it is considered by the Court that Plt. recover against Deft. one pound,
nineteen shillings and five pence farthing and his costs by him about his suit in this
behalf expended, together with a Lawyer's fee
- Ordered that the Court be adjourned to the fourth Thursday in next month
- The Minutes of thes Proceeding were signed
                              (no signature recorded)

p.
87
   - At a Court held for Orange County on Thursday the 25th day of February in the twenty first year of the Reign of our Sovereign Lord George the Second by the grace of God King of Great Britain, France and Ireland, &c., Annoq Domini MDCCXLVII before his Majesties Justices of the Peace for the said County (to wit)

ROBERT SLAUGHTER		WILLIAM RUSSELL	
JAMES PENDLETON		BENJAMIN CAVE	
GEORGE TAYLOR	&	PHILIP CLAYTON	Gentlemen

- An Indenture of Feoffment between JAMES PENDLETON and ELIZABETH his Wife of one part and SAMUEL FARGUSON of the other part and a Memorandum of Livery of Seisen and Receipt thereon endorsed were acknowledged by the said JAMES and ordered to be recorded

- Indentures of Lease and Release between THOMAS WILLIAMS and KATHERINE his Wife of one part and LAWRENCE BATTAILE of other part were proved by the Oaths of WILLIAM CARTER, WILLIAM STEVENS and JOHN HIATT, the witnesses thereto, and ordered to be recorded

- Upon Petition of MARGARET RUSH against MATHEW TOOL setting forth the said MATHEW's misusage to her Child, it is ordered that the Sherif summon the said MATHEW to appear at the next Court and answer the said Petition

- An Indenture of Bargain and Sale between WILLIAM LUCAS, SENR. of one part and THOMAS JARMAN of other part was acknowledged by the said WILLIAM and ordered to be recorded

- Tom, a Negro man slave belonging to WILLIAM HUNTER, was brought into Court and examined concerning the felonious burning of a fodder stack with a quantity of Corn therein, the property of RICHARD THOMAS , deced., and denied the fact. Whereupon it is ordered that the said Tom receive thirty nine lashes on his bare back well laid on and it is ordered that the Sherif cause immediate execution hereof to be done

- JOHN LACY brought his servant woman, ANNE SMITH, into Court for having a bastard Child, whereupon it is ordered that she serve her said Master one whole year after present servitude is expired and said LACY doth agree to satisfy and pay the Parish of Saint Mark the fine for the said Offence for which the said ANNE doth agree to serve the said LACY seven months and a half over and above the said one year

- Ordered that the Sherif take the Estate of WILLIAM LUCAS, JUNR. (who is said deceased above three months ago intestate leaving so small an Estate that no one hath administered thereon) into his possession and make sale thereof according to Law and make return of such sale to the next Court

- Upon Petition of TIMOTHY CROSTHWAIT, he is allowed to keep an ORDINARY at his House in this County for one year from this time on his giving security, whereupon he with EDWARD SPENCER and RICHARD WINSLOW entered into and acknowledged his Bond for his keeping the said ORDINARY according to Law and it is ordered that the Clerk of the Court prepare a Licence for him accordingly

p.
88
Orange County Court 25th of February 1747/48
- An Indenture of Bargain and Sale between WILLIAM HENDERSON of

one part and CHARLES WALKER of the other part was acknowledged by the said WILLIAM and ordered to be recorded

 - A Bond from CHARLES WALKER to WILLIAM HENDERSON was acknowledged by the said CHARLES and ordered to be recorded

 - ISAAC SMITH, Plt. agst FRANCIS WILLIAMS, Deft.   In Chancery
The Deft. this day filed his Answer to Plt.'s Bill to which he made Oath in open Court

 - PATRICK RICHEE was brought into Court to answer the Complaint of MICHAEL (HAN-----------) for a breach of the Peace in wounding him; whereupon witnesses were sworn and examined touching the premises and said PATRICK heard in his own Defence and it appearing to the Court that said MICHAEL lies dangerously ill of the said wound, it is ordered that said PATRICK be committed to the Common Goal of this County there to remain without Bail until further Order from this Court

 - A Deed of Gift from SAMUEL RICE to MICHAEL RICE was acknowledged by said SAMUEL and ordered to be recorded

 - A Deed of Gift from SAMUEL RICE to FISHER RICE was acknowledged by said SAMUEL and ordered to be recorded

 - a Deed of Gift from SAMUEL RICE to AMON BOHANNON RICE was acknowledged by the said SAMUEL and ordered to be recorded

 - A Deed of Gift from SAMUEL RICE to WILLIAM RICE was acknowledged by said SAMUEL and ordered to be recorded

 - JOHN SAMPSON who stood bound over to this Court to answer the Complaint of FINDLY McCOLLESTER, appeared and the said FINDLEY not appearing the Complaint is dismissed

 - THOMAS DILLARD having obtained an Attachment against the Estate of GEORGE HOME, who hath privately removed himself out of this County or so absconds that Process cannot be served on him for two pounds, four shillings and nine pence and eighty three pounds of nett tobacco due from GEORGE HOME to said THOMAS upon a Judgment of this Court, this day came Plt. by his Attorney and Deft. not appearing to replevy the effects condemned in the hands of the Garnishee, it is considered that Plt. recover against Deft. the two pounds, four shillings and nine pence and eighty three pounds of nett tobacco and his costs by him about his suit in this behalf expended, and LEWIS DAVIS YANCEY, JAMES TUTT and WILLIAM TUTT, the other Garnishees, being sworn, said LEWIS DAVIS YANCEY saith that he oweth

p.   Orange County Court 26th of February 1747/48
89   the Deft. eleven shillings and six pence, the said JAMES TUTT saith that he owes the said HOME seventeen shillings and three pence, which they are ordered to pay the Plt. togther with the two pounds, three shillings condemned in the hands of WILLIAM TAPP, the other Garnishee, which he is ordered to pay to Plt. is to go in satisfaction of part of this Judgment and costs, and WILLIAM TUTT saith tht hath nothing in his hands and the Attachment is ordered to be further served

 - Upon Complaint of JOHN LATHAM against PHILIP EDWARD JONES, his Master, it is ordered that the Sherif summon the said JONES to appear at next Court to answer the Complaint

 - Ordered that the Court be adjourned til tomorrow morning 8 o'clock

- The Minutes of these Proceedings were signed

                         ROBERT SLAUGHTER

- At a Court continued and held for Orange County on Friday the 26th of February 1747   Present

THOMAS CHEW	ABRAHAM FIELD
GEORGE TAYLOR	ROBERT SLAUGHTER Gentlemen
BENJAMIN CAVE	GOODRICH LIGHTFOOT

- Upon the motion of PETER JOHNSTON it is ordered that his mark being a whole in each ear be recorded

- JOHN BRAMHAM, Plt. agst WILLIAM RUSSELL, Gent., Deft. In Case

Dismissed being agreed by the parties

- ROBERT RAE and DANIEL CAMPBELL, Plts. agst.
GEORGE HOME, Deft.   In Case

The Attachment not being served, on motion of Plts. another Attachment is awarded against Deft.'s Estate returnable to the next Court

- JOHN GRYMES & FRANCIS WILLIS, Esqr., Executors &c. of HENRY
WILLIS, Gent., deced., Plts. agst GEORGE HOME, Deft. In Case

The former Order for settling the Accounts in difference between the parties not being complied

p.   <u>Orange County Court 26th of February 1747/48</u>
90   with, it is ordered that FRANCIS THORNTON, HANCOCK LEE and
        ANTHONY STROTHER, Gent., the persons in the former Order or any two of them do examine state and settle all matters and Accounts in difference between the parties and make return thereof to the next Court

- RICHARD WINSLOW, Gent., Plt. agst WILLIAM RUSSELL, Gent., Deft.
In Case

Continued for the Auditors to make their report

- BENJAMIN BORDEN, Plt. agst JAMES ARMSTRONG, Deft.   In Debt

Continued til the next Court

- JAMES BELL, Plt. agst GEORGE HOME, Deft.   In Case

The Attachment not being served, on motion of Plt, another Attachment is awarded against the Deft.'s Estate returnable to the next Court

- HUMPHREY BELL, Plt. agst WILLIAM COX, Deft.   In Debt

The Deft. not being yet arrested, on motion of Plt. another Plurius Capias is awarded him against Deft. returnable to next Court

- JOHN BELFIELD & WILLIAM JORDAN, Executors, &c. of THOMAS
WRIGHT BELFIELD, Gent., deced, Plts. a gst WILLIAM MORTON, Deft.
In Chancery

The persons appointed to settle the Accounts between the parties this day made their return and by consent of the parties by their Counsel, it is ordered that this suit do not abate by the death of either party

- DANIEL HORNBY, Gent., Plt. agst WLLIAM MORTON, Deft. In Debt
The persons appointed to settle the Accounts between the parties this day made return and by consent of the parties by their Attornies, it is ordered that this suit not abate by the death of either party

p.   Orange County Court 26th of February 1747/48
91   - MARTIN DEWITT, Plt. agst MICAJAH PICKET, Deft.
         In Trespass Assault and Battery
       Dismissed, being agreed by the parties
                - Absent. THOMAS CHEW & GEORGE TAYLOR, Gent.
        - JANE WHARTON, Admrx. &c. of THOMAS WHARTON, deced., Plt. agst.
       THOMAS CHEW, Gent., Deft.   In Case
GEORGE TAYLOR, Gent., undertook for Deft. that in case he shall be cast in this suit he shall pay the condemnation of the Court or render his body to Prison in discharge thereof, or that he the said GEORGE TAYLOR will do it for him; and Deft. prays and has leave to imparl thereo til the next Court and then to plead
                - Present. THOMAS CHEW & GEORGE TAYLOR, Gent.
        - RICHARD WINSLOW, Gent., Plt. agst ROBERT SEAYRES and
       JOHN SEAYRES, Defts. In Case
This day came Plt. by his Attorney and thereupon came also a Jury, to wit;

JOSEPH REYNOLDS	JOHN CHRISTOPHER	STOKELY TOWLES
BRYANT SYSON	ISAAC SMITH	JOHN SMITH
ALEXANDER WAUGH	GEORGE WELLS	JOHN
WILLIAM JACKSON	FRANCIS MOOR &	WILLIAM POUND

who being sworn well and truly to inquire of damages in this suit, the Plt. offered in evidence an Account against Deft. signed by one of them which was objected to by ZACHARY LEWIS, Gent., on the Deft.'s behalf but the same was allowed by the Court to go as evidence to the Jury. Whereupon the said LEWIS put in a Bill of Exceptions to the same with the leave of the Court and the Jury returning into Court, upon their Oaths do say that Plt. hath sustained damages by occasion of the non performance of the premises and assumption in the Declaration specified to thirteen pounds, one shilling and ten pence current money besides his costs and the Cause is continued til the next Court for the matters of Law arising on the Bill of Exceptions to be argued
        - WILLIAM RUSSELL, Gent., Plt. agst THOMAS DOWDE, Deft.   In Debt
This day came the parties by their Attornies and thereupon came a Jury, to wit,

WILLIAM MORGAN	ROBERT TREEWICK	PETER MORGAN
THOMAS JAMESON	WILLIAM PANNILL	HARBIN MOOR
ROBERT	JOHN GOUGH	HENRY BOURN
THOMAS THORNTON	THOMAS WOOTON &	RICHARD BRIDGES

who being elected tried and sworn the truth to speak upon the issue joined, upon their Oaths do say that the

p.   Orange County Court 26th of February 1747/48
92   Deft. doth not owe the Debt in the Declaration mentioned as in pleading he
         hath alledged; Therefore it is considered that the Plt. take nothing by his Bill but for his false clamour be in mercy &c, & that Deft. go thereof thence without day and recover against Plt. his costs by him about his defence in this behalf expended

- HUMPHREY BELL of London, Merchant, Plt. agst
RICHARD WINSLOW, Gent., Deft.   In Case
This day came the parties by their Attornies and Deft. relinquishing his former Plea saith he cannot gainsay Plt.'s action. Therefore it is considered by the Court that Plt. recover against Deft. seven pounds, sixteen shillings and eleven pence half penny, the Debt in the Declaration mentioned, and his costs by him about his suit in this behalf expended, and Deft. in mercy, &c.

- WILLIAM RUSSELL, Gent., Plt. agst CAIN FIELD, Deft.   In Debt
By agreement of the parties, this suit is dismissed and it is ordered that Deft. pay unto Plt. his costs by him about his suit in this behalf expended

- KANE FIELD quitam &c., Plt. agst WILLIAM RUSSELL, Gent., Deft.
By agreement of the parties, this suit is dismissed, and it is ordered that Deft. pay unto Plt. his costs by him about his suit in this behalf expended

- On motion of WILLIAM (? Cowne) a witness for HUMPHREY BELL, Plt. against RICHARD WINSLOW, Gent., Deft., it is ordered that said BELL pay him two hundred ninety pounds of tobacco for two days attendance at this court and coming eighty miles from KING WILLIAM County and returning according to law

- On motion of HUMPHREY WALLIS, a witness for HUMPHREY BELL, Plt. against RICHARD WINSLOW, Gent., Deft. it is ordered that said BELL pay him three hundred ten pounds of tobacco for four days attendance in that suit, for coming thirty five miles from SPOTSYLVANIA county and returning according to Law

- On motion of CHARLES ASHER, a witness for WILLIAM RUSSELL, Gent. Plt. against THOMAS DOWDE, Deft., who made Oath that he had attended eight days as a witness in that suit, it is ordered that said WILLIAM pay him two hundred pounds of tobacco according to Law

p.   Orange County Court 26th of February 1747/48
93   - On motion of ROBERT LINES, a witness for WILLIAM RUSSELL, Gent.
       against THOMAS DOWDE Deft., who made Oath that he had attended six days as an evidence in that suit, it is ordered that said WILLIAM pay him one hundred fifty pounds of tobacco according to Law

- On motion of CORNELIUS REYNOLDS, a witness for WILLIAM RUS-SELL, Gent., against THOMAS DOWDE, Deft., who made Oath that he had attended four days as a witness in that sit, it is ordered that said WILLIAM pay him one hundred pounds of tobacco according to Law

- On motion of WILLIAM MORGAN, a witness for KEENE FIELD at the suit of WILLIAM RUSSELL, Gent., who made Oath that he had attended four days as an evidence in that suit, it is ordered that said KEENE pay him one hundred pounds of tobacco according to Law

- On motion of SAMUEL HOWELL, a witness for KEENE FIELD at the suit of WILLIAM RUSSELL, Gent., who made Oath that he had attended five days as an evidence in that suit, it is ordered that said KEENE pay him one hundred twenty five pounds of tobacco according to Law

- Upon Petition of HUMPHREY BELL against JOHN SMITH, JUNR., this day came Plt. by his Attoeney and Deft. not appearing tho summoned, it is considered by the Court that Plt. recover against Deft. one pound, eighteen shillings and eight pence and his costs by him about his suit in this behalf expended, together with a

Lawyer's fee
    - JOHN BEAZLEY, Plt. agst SPENCE BRAMHAM, Deft.
    In Assault and Battery
Continued til next Court at motion and costs of Plt.
    - The Petition of NEIL BUCHANNON's Executors against THOMAS PETTY
is continued til next Court
    - The Petition of NEIL BUCHANNON's Executors against ROBERT HILL is
continued til next Court at Plt.'s costs
    - JOHN SPOTSWOOD, Gent., Plt. agst FRANCIS KIRTLEY, Deft.
    In Trespass
Dismissed
    - ROBERT HILL, Plt. agst DANIEL CARTER, Deft. In Assasult & Battery
The Deft. not being arrested, on motion of Plt. by his Attorney, a Plurius Capias is
awarded against the Deft. returnable to next Court

p.   Orange County Court 26th of February 1747/48
94   - JOHN SPOTSWOOD, Gent., Plt. agst JOHN CHRISTOPHER, Deft.
        In Debt
This day came the parties by their Attornies and Plt. saith that Deft. doth owe the
debt in the Declaration mentioned and this he prays may be enquired of by the
Country and Deft. likewise. Therefore the Trial of the issue is referred til next Court
    - RICHARD BARDINE, who was summoned as an evidence for our Lord the
King against MICHAEL COOK not appearing, it is ordered that he make his Fine
with our said Lord the King by the payment of three hundred fifty pounds of tobacco
unless he shew cause to the contrary at next Court
    - JOHN MORGAN & MARY his Wife, Plts. agst WILLIAM LIGHTFOOT,
    Deft.   In Case
By agreement of the parties, this suit is dismissed and it is ordered that Deft. pay
unto Plt. his costs by him about his suit in this behalf expended and Deft. came into
Court and acknowledged that the Slander in the Declaration is false and altogether
groundless
    - HUMPHREY BELL of London, Merchant, Plt. agst
WILLIAM NASH, Deft.   In Case
This day came Plt. by his Attorney and thereupon came also a Jury to wit,
    RICHARD VERNON   ISAAC SMITH   SAMUEL POUND
    JOSEPH REYNOLDS   THOMAS THORNTON   JOHN SMITH
    THOMAS WOOTON   JOHN POUND   BRYANT SYSON
    JEREMIAH MORTON   HENRY BOURN   &   DANIEL BROWN
who being sworn well and truly to Enquire of damages in this suit, upon their Oath do
say that Plt. hath sustained damages by occasion of the breach of promise in the
Declaration specifyed to sixteen hundred pounds of tobacco besides his costs. Therefore it is considered by the Court that Plt. recover against Deft. and JAMES
POLLARD his Security his damages aforesaid in form aforesaid assessed and his
costs by him about his suit in this behalf expended, and Deft. in mercy, &c.

p.   Orange County Court 26th of February 1747/48
95   - JOHN WHARTON, Plt. agst JANE WHARTON, Admrx. &c. of THOMAS
        WHARTON, deced., Deft.   In Case

This day came Plt. by his Attorney and Deft. in her proper person and thereupon came also a Jury, to wit

RICHARD VERNON	ISAAC SMITH	SAMUEL POUND
JOSEPH REYNOLDS	THOMAS THORNTON	JOHN SMITH
THOMAS WOOTON	JOHN POUND	JEREMIAH MORTON
BRYANT SYSON	HENRY BOURN &	DANIEL BROWN

who being elected tried and sworn the truth to speak upon the issue joined, upon their Oath do say that the Intestate dif assume upon himself in manner and form as Plt. against him hath complained and they do assess Plt.'s damages by occasion of the non performance of that assumption to eighteen pounds, ten shillings besides his costs. Therefore it is considered by the Court that Plt. recover against Deft. his damages aforesaid in form aforesaid assessed and his costs by him about his suit in this behalf expended, and Deft. in mercy, &c., to be levied of the goods and chattels of the Intestate in the hands of the Administratrix to administer if so much she hath and if not then the costs to be levied of the proper goods and chattels of the Deft.

- JOHN COBURN, Plt. agst WILLIAM LONG, Deft.   In Case
Continued til next Court at motion and costs of Plt.

- WILLIAM RUSSELL, Gent., Plt. agst JANE WHARTON, Admrx.&c. of THOMAS WHARTON, deced., Deft.   In Case
By consent of the parties, it is ordered that EDWARD SPENCER, Gent., JEREMIAH MORTON and JOHN BRAMHAM or any two of them do examine state and settle all matters and Accounts in difference between the parties and make return thereof to next Court

- Upon motion of RICHARD WINSLOW, Gent., against ISAAC SMITH, by consent of the parties it is ordered that JOHN NICHOLAS do examined state and settle all matters and Accounts in difference between the parties and make return thereof to next Court

- JOHN SPOTSWOOD, Gent., Plt. agst JOHN EARLEY, Deft. In Trespass
Dismissed

- The Petition of THOMAS CHEW, Gent. against ROBERT GREEN, Gent., is dismissed

p.   Orange County Court 26th of February 1747/48
96   - HENRY PICKETT, Plt. agst THOMAS COLEMAN, Deft.   In Case
This day came the parties by their Attornies and thereupon came a Jury to wit

RICHARD VERNON	ISAAC SMITH	JOHN GOUGH
JOSEPH REYNOLD	THOMAS THORNTON	JOHN SMITH
THOMAS WOOTON	JOHN POUND	BRYANT SYSON
JEREMIAH MORTON	HENRY BOURN &	DANIEL BROWN

who being elected tried and sworn the truth to speak upon the issue joined, upon their Oath do say that Deft. is Guilty in manner and form as Plt. against him hath complained and they do assess Plt.'s damages by occasion thereof to eleven pounds besides his costs; Therefore it is considered by the Court that Plt. recover against Deft. his damages aforesaid in form aforesaid assessed and his costs by him about his suit in this behalf expended, and Deft. in mercy, &c.

- On motion of WILLIAM HENDERSON, a witness for THOMAS COLEMAN at the suit of HENRY PICKETT, who made Oath that he had attended six days as an Evidence in that suit, it is ordered that said THOMAS pay him one hundred fifty

pounds of tobacco for his said attendance according to Law
    - On motion of JAMES RUCKER, a witness for THOMAS COLEMAN at the
suit of HENRY PICKETT, who made Oath that he had attended five days as an
Evidence in that suit, it is ordered that said THOMAS pay him one hundred twenty
five pounds of tobacco for his said attendance according to Law
    - Upon motion of JOHN FORRESTER, a witness for THOMAS COLEMAN at
the suit of HENRY PICKETT, it is ordered that said THOMAS pay him fifty pounds
of tobacco for two days attendance at this Court according to Law
    - Upon motion of WILLIAM JACKSON, a witness for HENRY PICKETT, Plt.
against THOMAS COLEMAN, Deft., who made Oath that he had attended five days
as an Evidence in that suit, it is ordered that said HENRY pay him one hundred and
twenty five pounds of tobacco for his said attendance according to Law
    - On motion of SUSANNAH ADAMS, a witness for HENRY PICKETT, Plt.
against THOMAS COLEMAN, Deft., who made Oath that she had attended six days
as an Evidence in that suit, it is ordered that said HENRY pay her one hundred fifty
pounds of tobacco for her said attenance according to Law
    - On motion of SAMUEL BIRD, a witness for HENRY PICKETT, Plt. against
THOMAS COLEMAN, Deft., it is ordered that said HENRY pay him fifty pounds of
tobacco for two days attendance at this Court according to Law

p.   Orange County Court 26th of February 1747/48
97   - THOMAS THORNTON, Plt. agst JOHN CHRISTOPHER, Deft. In Debt
    This day came the parties by their Attornies and the Defendant relinquishing is
former Plea saith he cannot gainsay Plt.'s action.   Therefore it is considered by the
Court that Plt. recover against Deft. one thousand pounds of tobacco and cask and
his costs by him about his suit in this behalf expended, and Deft. in mercy, &c.
    - Upon the Presentment of the Grandjury against THOMAS FOX, the Special
Verdict was this day argued. It is the opinion of the Court that THOMAS FOX is
Guilty of the offence in the Presentment against him set forth. Therefore it is considered that he make his Fine with our Lord the King by the paiment of five hundred
pounds of tobacco and that he pay the costs of this Presentment and that he be
taken, &c.
    - Upon the Presentment of the Grandjury against JOHN INGRAM, the
Special Verdict was this day argued. It is the opinion of the Court that JOHN IN-
GRAM is Guilty of the offence in the Presentment against him set forth. Therefore it
is considered that he make his Fine with our Lord the King by the paiment of five
hundred pounds of tobacco and that he pay the costs of this Presentment and that he
be taken, &c.
    - Upon the Presentment of the Grandjury against JOHN WILLIS, the Special
Verdict being argued, it is the opinion of the Court that JOHN WILLIS is Guilty of the
offence in the Presentment against him set forth. Therefore it is considered that he
make his Fine with our Lord the King by the paiment of five hundred pounds of
tobacco and that he pay the costs of this presentment and that he be taken, &c.
    - Ordered that the Court be adjourned to the fourth Thursday in March next
    - The Minutes of these Proceedings were signed
                                 THOS: CHEW

- At a Court held for Orange County on Thursday the twenty fourth day of March in the twenty first year of the Reign of our Sovereign Lord George the Second by the grace of God of Great Britain, &c., King, Defender of the faith, &c., Annoq: Domini one thousand seven hundred and forty seven; Before his Majesty's Justices of the Peace for the said County (to wit)

ROBERT SLAUGHTER   WILLIAM RUSSELL
ROBERT GREEN   HENRY FIELD
          GEORGE TAYLOR, Gentlemen

- Pursuant to Law, the Court doth set and rate the following Prices of Liquors, Diet, Fodder, Provender, Stabling and Pasturage at and for which the several Ordinary Keepers in this County are to sell and entertain the ensuing year, to wit

Barbados Rum by the gallon	L	10...0
New England Rum by the gallon		2...6
Virginia Brandy distilled from Cyder or Mobby without the Peach		
or Stone a gallon		8...0
Peach Brandy distilled with the Peach & Stone by the gallon		6...0
Whiskey by the gallon		6...0
Punch of Flip the quart with three jills of Rum and white Sugar		1...3
The same with Brown Sugar		1...0
Good Brandy Punch the quart with three jills of Brandy and white Sugar		1...0
The same with Brown Sugar		9
Whiskey Punch the quart with three jills of Whiskey and white Sugar		9
The same with Brown Sugar		9 1/2
New England Rum Punch the quart		3 3/4
Wired Strong Beer the bottle		1...3
Cask Strong Beer the quart		1...0
English Cyder the quart		1...3

p. ## Orange County Court 24th of March 1747/48
98   The Rate of Liquors &c. continued

Virginia Cyder the quart	4 1/2
Virginia Ale the quart	6
French Brandy the gallon	16...0
French Brandy Punch the quart with three jills	2...6
Madeira Wine the quart	2...6
Fiall Wine the quart	2
White Wine, Sack or Claret by the quart	4
A hot Diet	1
A cold Diet	6
Lodging with clean sheets	6
Stableage one night with Fodder	6
Pasturage twenty four hours	6
Indian Corn & Oats the gallon dry measure	6

- An Indenture of Bargain and Sale between EDWARD FRANKLYN of one part and JOSEPH EDMONDS of other part was acknowledged by said EDWARD and ordered to be recorded

- An Indenture of Bargain and Sale between EDWARD FRANKLYN of one part and JOHN EUBANK of other part was acknowledged by said EDWARD and ordered to be recorded

- An Indenture of Feoffment between GEORGE SLAUGHTER of one part and WILLIAM RICE of other part and a Memorandum of Livery of Seisen thereon endorsed were acknowledged by said GEORGE and ordered to be recorded

- An Indenture of Feoffment between HENRY DOWNS of one part and RICHARD DOWNS of other part and a Memorandum of Livery of Seisen thereon endorsed were acknowledged by said HENRY and ordered to be recorded

- Present. FRANCIS SLAUGHTER & PHILIP CLAYTON, Gent.

- A Negro man slave belonging to MUMFORD STEVENS was led to the Bar under the custody of the Sherif on suspicion of his being Guilty of stealing three hogs, the property of BENJAMIN CAVE, Gent., and upon examination denied the fact wherewith he stood charged. Whereupon divers witnesses were examined touching the premises and he heard in his defence. In consideration whereof it is the opinion of the Court that he is Guilty of stealing hogs the propery of a person unknown. Therefore it is considered that he receive thirty nine lashes on his bare back well laid on at the Common Whipping Post of this County, and it is said to the Sherif that he cause immediate execution hereof to be done

- Indentures of Lease and Release between JOHN THOMAS of one part and HENRY AYLER of the other part and a Receipt endorsed on the Release was acknowledged by said JOHN and ordered to be recorded, And MARY, Wife of said JOHN, personally appeared in Court and being first privately examined as the Law directs voluntarily relinquished her Right of Dower in the Estate conveyed the the Indenture

- Ordered that ROBERT CAVE, WILLIAM RICE and JOHN BUFORD or any two of them do between this and the next Court go to and view the Way from GARTH's FORD to the lower ELK RUN and make report to the Court of the most convenient way for a Road

- WILLIAM KELLY brought his Servant, THOMAS GODFREY, before the Court for running away and absenting himself from his service eighteen days. It is ordered that said GODFREY serve his Master two days for every day he was absent from his Master after the time of his present servitude is expired and further that he serve his Master for two hundred ten pounds of nett tobacco expended in apprehending him according to Law

- JEREMIAH YEARLY is by the Court appointed Overseer of the Road from GARTH's FORD to the Plantation of HENRY DOWNS's Gent., in the room of MICHAEL PEARSON who is discharged from that Office; And it is ordered that the gang formerly under said PEARSON do attend and obey the directions of said YEARLY in clearing and keeping the Road in repair

p.   Orange County Court 24th of March 1747/48
99   - A Deed of Gift from RICHARD MAULDIN to JOHN WILSON was acknowledged by said RICHARD and ordered to be recorded

- JOHN BRAMHAM and JEREMIAH MORTON, two of the persons appointed to view the Way from the SOUTHWEST MOUNTAINS to the Courthouse and the Rolling Road from up the River to the Road leading to FREDERICKSBURG thro' the land of BRYANT SYSON this day made their report that they have viewed the ways and find the new road now laid off to be convenient. Whereupon it is ordered that the said new Roads be kept open and that the Old Roads with their gangs do clear and keep the said road in repair according to Law

- Present. JAMES PENDLETON, Gent.

- An Indenture of Feoffment between WILLIAM DEATHERAGE and ANNA his Wife of one part and HENRY HUFFMAN of other part with a Memorandum of Livery of Seisen and Receipt thereon endorsed were acknowledged by the said WILLIAM and ordered to be recorded

- CHARLES DEWITT, JUNR. having taken the Oaths to his Majesty's Person and Government and subscribed the Abjuration Oath and the Test, was sworn UNDERSHERIF under EDWARD SPENCER, Gent., Sherif of this County

- Upon Petition of MARGARET RUSH against MATTHEW TOOL, this day came the parties by their Attornies who being fully heard, it is considered that the Petition be dismissed

- SOLOMON WATKINS was brought before the Court and nothing appearing against him he is discharged

- Upon Petition of JOSEPH REYNOLDS he is allowed to keep ORDINARY at the place where HENRY RICE formrly kept Ordinary. Whereupon he with RICHARD WINSLOW and JOHN CHRISTOPHER, his Securities entered into and acknowledged his Bond for keeping his said Ordinary according to Law

- ALEXANDER ROSSE and EDWARD ROWLAND from Great Britain and THOMAS GAHAGAN from Ireland, came into Court and made Oath that they were imported immediately into this Colony and that this is the first time of their making Oath to the same in order to intitle each of them to fifty acres of land in this Colony, which Rights they severally assigned over to JAMES HERNDON

- Upon the Attachment brought by THOMAS DILLARD against the Estate of GEORGE HOME, JOHN YANCEY being sworn declares that he hath no Estate of the said HOME, therefore he is discharged

- Ordered that the Sherif summon twenty four of the most capable Freeholders of this County to appear at the Court to be held for this County in May next to serve as a Grandjury of Inquest for the body of the County

- WILLIAM KELLY, EDWARD STUBBLEFIELD and THOMAS RUCKER being summoned to attend this Court this day as Jurymen were solemnly called but came not. Therefore it is considered by the Court that for their contempt therein they severally make their Fine with our Lord the King by the paiment of four hundred pounds of tobacco to his Majesty's use and that they be taken, &c.

- ANTHONY STROTHER, Gent., Plt. agst ELLIS MARCUS, Deft. In Case
This day came Plt. by his Attorney and thereupon came a Jury, to wit,

ROBERT MARSH	WILLIAM JONES	THOMAS THORNTON
AMBROSE POWELL	GEORGE HOME	SPENCER BOBO
LEWIS TOONE	JONATHAN PRATT	JOHN CARDER
WILLIAM MORGAN	JOHN MORGAN and	RICHARD PINION

who being sworn well and truly to inquire of damages in this Cause, upon their Oath do say that Plt. hath sustained damages by occasion of the Breach of Promise in the Declaration specified to three pounds, eight shillings and three pence half penny besides his costs. Therefore it is considered by the Court that Plt. recover against Deft. and WILLIAM ANDERSON and DANIEL BROWN, his Securities, his damages aforesaid in form aforesaid assessed and his costs by him in this behalf expended, and the Defendant in mercy, &c.

- ANTHONY STROTHER, Gent., Plt. agst MICHAEL WHATLEY, Deft. In Case
This day came Plt. by his Attorney and thereupon came a Jury, to wit,

ROBERT MARSH	WILLIAM JONES	THOMAS THORNTON
AMBROSE POWELL	GEORGE HOME	SPENCER BOBO
LEWIS TOONE	JONATHAN PRATT	JOHN CARDER
WILLIAM MORGAN	JOHN MORGAN &	RICHARD PINION

who being sworn well and truly to inquire of damages in this Cause, upon their Oath do say that Plt. hath sustained damages by occasion of the Breach of Promise in the Declaration specified to seven pounds, nine shillings and six pence besides his costs. Therefore it is considered

p. <u>Orange County Court 24th of March 1747/48</u>
100   by the Court that Plt. recover against Deft. and THOMAS RUCKER, his
        Security, his damages aforesaid in form aforesaid assessed and his costs by
him about his suit in this behalf expended, And Deft. in mercy, &c.
        - RICHARD WINSLOW, Gent., Plt. agst DENNIS BYRNE, EDWARD
        SPENCER and ISAAC SMITH, Defts.   In Debt
    This day came the parties by their Attornies and thereupon came also a Jury to

wit		
CHRISTOPHER HOOMES	DANIEL BROWN	THOMAS BROWN
EVIN MOOR	CHARLES DEWITT	BENJAMIN ROBERTS
ELLIOTT BOHANNON	JOHN HACKLEY	FRANCIS KIRTLEY
FRANCIS MOOR	THOMAS STUBBLEFIELD	JEREMIAH MORTON

who being elected tried and sworn the truth to speak upon the issue joined upon went out of the Court to consult of their Verdict
        - Upon the Petition of MARGARET GIBSON, Widow, against JOHN SMITH, the Deft. confesseth that he is indebted to Plt. five pounds. Therefore it is considered by the Court that Plt. recover against Deft. the five pounds and her costs by her about her suit in this behalf expended
        - JOHN LEWIS & FIELDING LEWIS, Plts. against WILLIAM MINOR,
        Deft.   In Case
    By Agreement of the parties, this suit is dismissed and it is ordered that Deft. pay Plts. their costs
        - ROBERT RAE & DANIEL CAMPBELL, Plts. agst
        JONAS JENKINS, Deft. In Case
ROBERT TREWICK and WILLIAM WHITE came into Court and undertook for Deft. that in case he shall be cast in this suit he shall pay the condemnation of the Court or render his body to Prison in discharge thereof, or that they or either of them will do it for him
        - THOMAS SCOTT, Plt. agst RICHARD MAULDIN &
        THOMAS RUCKER, Defts.   In Debt
    Dismissed, the Plt. acknowledged to have received satisfaction for the Bond
        - RICHARD PRYER having neglected the Education of his Children, it is ordered that the Churchwardens of Saint Mark's Parish do bind out the said Children according to Law
        - SAMUEL FARGUSON is by the Court appointed Overseer of the Road from the River at EASTHAM's FORD to ANTHONY SCOTT's, also from BELL ISLAND FORD into the aforesaid Road, and it is ordered that the male labouring Tithables that formerly worked on the said Roads do attend and obey the directions of the said SAMUEL in keeping the Roads in repair and that said SAMUEL cause Posts of Directions to be erected where necessary

- Ordered that the Court be adjourned til tomorrow morning 8 o'clock
- The Minutes of these Proceedings were signed
                                        ROBT: GREEN

- At a Court continued and held for Orange County on Friday the 25th of
March 1747   Present
         ROBERT SLAUGHTER   WILLIAM RUSSELL
         ABRAHAM FIELD   HENRY FIELD   &
                                    GEORGE TAYLOR,   Gentlemen

- THOMAS CHEW, Gent., Plt. agst SUSANNAH RUCKER & PETER
RUCKER, Exrs. &c. of JOHN RUCKER, deced., Defts.   In Case
This day came the parties by their Attornies and Defts. say that their Testator did
not assume upon himself in manner and form as Plt. against them hath complained
and of this they put themselves upon the Country, and Plt. likewise. Therefore the
Trial of the issue is referred til next Court

p.   Orange County Court 25th of March 1747/48
101   - MARGARET RICE, Admrx. &c. of HENRY RICE, deced., Plt. agst
ELI GRIFFIN, Deft.   In Case
Continued for the Auditors to make their report, and it is ordered that they proceed
ex parte to the settling and determining the matter in difference between the parties
       - ANTHONY FLINCHBACK, Plt. agst ELI GRIFFIN, Deft.   In Debt
This day came Plt. by his Attorney and Deft. saith nothing in bar or preclusion of
Plt.'s action by which the Plt. remains against the Deft. undefended. Therefore it is
considered by the Court that Plt. recover against Deft. twelve pounds, two shillings
current money, the Debt in the Declaration mentioned, and his costs by him about his
suit in this behalf expended, and Deft. in mercy, &c., But this Judgment, the costs excepted, is to be discharged by paiment of six pounds, one shilling with Interest thereon
after the rate of five percent per annum from the twenty sixth day of June 1747 to
the time of paiment and costs
       - WILLIAM BELL, Plt. agst ROBERT JACKSON, Deft.   In Case
Dismissed being agreed by the parties
       - MARGARET GIBSON, Admrx., &c. of JONATHAN GIBSON, Gent., deced.
Plt. agst WILLIAM RUSSELL, Gent., Deft.   In Case
Continued til the next Court for the Auditors to make their report
       - RICHARD VERNON, Plt. agst HONORIAS POWELL, Deft.
       In Assault and Battery
Dismissed being agreed by the parties
       - Upon the Petition of DANIEL HORNBY, Gent., against JOHN BRAMHAM,
this day came the parties by their Attornies who being fully heard, it is considered by
the Court that Plt. recover against Deft. four pounds, seven shillings and eight pence
half penny and his costs by him about his suit in this behalf expended
       - Upon the Petition of JOHN BELFIELD & WILLIAM JORDAN, Gent., Exrs.
&c. of THOMAS WRIGHT BELFIELD, Gent., deced., against JOHN BRANHAM,
this day came the parties by their Attornies who being fully heard, it is considered by
the Court that Plts. recover against Deft. one pound, ten shillings and ten pence and

their costs by them about their suit in this behalf expended
- The Petition of RICHARD VERNON against GEORGE EASTHAM is dismissed
- Present. GOODRICH LIGHTFOOT, Gent.
- Upon the Attachment of RICHARD VERNON against the Estate of RICHARD McGRAW, it is ordered that the Sherif attach LAWRENCE BRADLEY, Garnishee, to declare what of the Estate of said McGRAW he hath in his hands
- Upon the Attachment brought by JOHN SMITH against the Estate of JOHN SMITH, JUNR., this day came the Plt. and Deft. not appearing to replevy the attached effects, and the Plt. proved his Account against the Deft. by his own Oath the ballance whereof is fifteen pounds, six shillings and six pence. Therefore it is considered by the Court that Plt. recover against Deft. the fifteen pounds, six shillings and six pence and his costs by him about his suit in this behalf expended, And it is ordered that the Sherif pay the money arising from the sale of the goods he was directed by a former Order of this Court in discharge of this Judgment and restore the residue, if any, to the Deft.
- The Attachment of HENRY DOWNS against the Estate of RICHARD McGRAW is dismissed

p.   Orange County Court 25th of March 1747/48
102 - WILLIAM PICKET having obtained an Attachment against the Estate of JAMES McDANIEL who hath absconded himself so that Process can't be served on him for eight pounds due from said JAMES to said WILLIAM by Account and the Sherif making return that he hath attached one old Desk, the Drawers all nailed up said to be full of Joiner's tools, this day came Plt. by his Attorney and Deft. not appearing to replevy the attached effects and Plt. proved his Account to be just by his own Oath, the ballance whereof is five pounds, two shillings and four pence, Therefore it is considered by the Court that Plt. recover against Deft. the five pounds, two shillings and four pence and his costs by him about his suit in this behalf expended, And it is ordered that the Sherif make sale of the attached effects according to Law and pay the money arising from such sale to Plt. in discharge of this Judgment and restore the residue, if any, to the Deft. and make report thereof to next Court
- The Attachment brought by JOHN ALLAN against JOHN SMITH, JUNR. is continued til next Court
- GEORGE STUBBLEFIELD, Plt. agst EDWARD FRANKLYN, Deft. In Debt This day came Plt. by his Attorney and Deft. being again solemnly called came not. Therefore it is considered by the Court that Plt. recover against Deft. and THOMAS CHEW, Gent., late Sherif of this County, twelve pounds, ten shillings current money, the Debt in the Declaration mentioned and his costs by him about his suit in this behalf expended, and Deft. in mercy, &c.
- JAMES HUNTER, Merchant, Plt. agst. GEORGE DOGGETT, Deft. In Case This day came Plt. by ZACHARY LEWIS, Gent., his Attorney and Deft. in his proper person and Deft. prays and has leave to imparl thereof til next Court and then to plead
- WILLIAM HUNTER, Gent., Plt. agst GEORGE DOGGETT, Deft. In Debt This day came Plt. by ZACHARY LEWIS, Gent., his Attorney and Deft. in his proper person, and Defendant confesseth the Plt.'s action. Therefore it is considered by

the Court that Plt. recover against Deft. fifteen pounds, fourteen shillings current money, the Debt in the Declaration mentioned and his costs by him about his suit in this behalf expended and Deft. in mercy, &c.

  - JOHN SPOTSWOOD, Gent., Plt. agst THOMAS THORNTON, Deft. In Debt
This day came Plt. by his Attorney and Deft. being again solemnly called came not. Therefore it is considered by the Court that Plt. recover against Deft. and THOMAS CHEW, Gent., late Sherif of this County, nine hundred sixty six pounds of tobacco and cask, the ballance of the Debt in the Declaration mentioned, and is costs by him about his suit in this behalf expended, and Deft. in mercy, &c.

   Present. THOMAS CHEW & ROBERT EASTHAM, Gentlemen
  - RICHARD SHIP, Admr. &c. of THOMAS SHIP, deced., Plt. agst
  GEORGE DOGGETT, Deft. In Case
This day came Plt. by ZACHARY LEWIS, Gent., his Attorney, and Deft. in his proper person and Deft. prays and has leave to imparl thereof til next Court and then to plead

  - WILLIAM NASH, Plt. agst JAMES POLLARD, Gent., Deft.
  In Assault and Battery
This day came Plt. by his Attorney and Deft. being again solemnly called came not. Therefore it is considered by the Court that Judgment be entered for Plt. against Deft. and THOMAS CHEW, Gent., late Sherif of this County, for the Debt in the Declaration mentioned and costs to be ascertained on Inquiry by a Jury at next Court

p. <u>Orange County Court 25th of March 1747/48</u>
103 - Upon Petition of ROBERT DUNLOP and THOMAS DUNLOP, against
  JONAS JENKINS for a Debt therein said to be due, this day came the parties by their Attornies who being fully heard, it is considered that the Petition be dismissed and that Deft. recover against Plts. his costs by him about his suit in this behalf expended

  - On motion of ROBERT TREWICK, a witness for ROBERT DUNLOP and THOMAS DUNLOP, Plts. against JONAS JENKINS, Deft. who made Oath that he had attended seven days as a witness in that Cause. It is ordered that the said DUNLOPs pay him one hundred seventy five pounds of tobacco for his said attendance according to Law

  - On motion of MARGERY TREWICK, a witness for ROBERT DUNLOP and THOMAS DUNLOP, Plts. against JONAS JENKINS, Deft. who made Oath that she had attended seven days as a witness in that Cause, it is ordered that the said DUNLOPs pay her one hundred seventy five pounds of tobacco for her said attendance according to Law

  - JOHN GORDON, Plt. agst CHARLES KAVANAUGH, Deft. In Debt
This day came Plt. by his Attorney and Deft. being again solemnly called came not. Therefore it is considered by the Court that Plt. recover against Deft. and THOMAS CHEW, Gent., late Sherif of this County, eight pounds, seventeen shillings current money, the Debt in the Declaration mentioned and his costs by him about his suit in this behalf expended, and Deft. in mercy, &c., But this Judgment, the costs excepted, is to be discharged by paiment of four pounds, eight shillings and six pence with Interest thereon after the rate of five percent per annum to be computed from the sixth day of october 1746 to the time of paiment and costs

- CHARLES HARRISON, Plt. agst NICHOLAS JONES, Deft.   In Case
Continued til next Court
- WILLIAM GALE, Plt. agst WILLIAM MORGAN, Deft. In Case
Dismissed
- WILLIAM GALE, Plt. agst JOHN CARDER, Deft.   In Case
Dismissed
- WILLIAM GALE, Plt. agst THOMAS COVINGTON, Deft.   In Case
This day came Plt. by ZACHARY LEWIS, Gent., his Attorney and Deft. not being
arrested, on motion of Plt. an Alias Capias is awarded him against Deft. returnable to
next Court
- JAMES MADISON, quitam &c., Plt. agst JOSEPH PHILLIPS, Deft. In Debt
This day came Plt. who as well, &c., by GEORGE WYTHE, Gent., his Attorney and
Deft. being returned arrested was solemnly called but came not. Therefore on motion
of Plt. who as well, &c., it is ordered that unless he appears at next Court and
answers Plt.'s action, Judgment shall then be entered for Plt. against him, the Deft.,
for the Debt in the Declaration mentioned and costs
- EDWARD SPENCER, Gent., Plt. agst THOMAS JONES, Deft. In Debt
This day came Plt. by GEORGE WYTHE, Gent., his Attorney and Deft. not being
arrested, on motion of Plt. an Alias Capias is awarded him against Deft. returnable to
next Court

p.   Orange County Court 25th of March 1747/48
104   - The Attachment of JAMES HUNTER against VALENTINE BOSTICK is
        continued til next Court
        - JOHN SEAYRES, Plt. agst ROBERT ADAMS, Deft.   On a Scire Facias
        on a Judgment of this Court obtained by Plt. against Deft. the twenty ninth
        day of March 1745, for one pound, seventeen shillings and four pence current
        money for Debt., also forty nine pounds of nett tobacco for costs
The Sherif returning on the Scire Facias that the Deft. hath nothing in his Bailiwick by which he could cause him to know nor is he found in the same; therefore on
motion of Plt., it is ordered that Judgment be entered for him against Deft., that he
have execution according to the force form and effect of the Recovery aforesaid and
his costs expended in suing forth and prosecuting this Writ
        - JAMES PENDLETON & PHILIP CLAYTON, Gent., Plts. agst
        JOHN RAY, Deft. In Debt
This day came Plts. by their Attorney and the Sherif making return on this Attachment that he had attached of Deft.'s Estate one Gun and Deft. not appearing to
replevy the same, therefore it is considered by the Court that Plts. recover against
Deft. twenty seven pounds, six shillings and six pence and sixty pounds of nett tobacco and seven shillings and six pence the Debt in the Declaration mentioned, and their
costs by them about their suit in this behalf expended, and Deft. in mercy, &c., But
this Judgment, the costs excepted, is to be discharged by paiment of thirteen pounds,
thirteen shillings and three pence and sixty pounds of nett tobacco and seven shillings
and six pence with Interest on the thirteen pounds, thirteen shillings and three pence
after the rate of five percent per annum to be computed from the seventeenth day of
July 1744 to the time of paiment and costs; And it is ordered that the Sherif make
sale of the Gun according to L aw and pay the money arising from such sale to Plt.

- JOHN BRAMHAM, JUNR., by JOHN BRAMHAM, his next Friend, Plt. agst SAMUEL POUND and THOMAS JAMESON, Defts   In Chancery

This day came the parties by their Counsel and on motion of Deft. time til next Court is granted them to consider Plt.'s Bill and then to answer it

- ROBERT RAE & DANIEL CAMPBELL, Plts. agst JONAS JENKINS, Deft.   In Debt

This day came Plts. by their Attorney and Deft. not appearing tho solemnly called, therefore it is considered that Plt. recover against Deft. twenty nine pounds, fifteen shillings and three pence current money, the ballance of a Debt in the Declaration mentioned, and their costs by them about their suit in this behalf expended and Deft. in mercy, &c.

- WILLIAM MORRIS came into Court and made Oath that he was imported from Great Britain immediately into this Colony and that this is the first time he hath made Oath to the same in order to intitle him to fifty acres of land in this Colony which Right he assigned over to JAMES HERNDON

- JOHN FIELD & JOHN BRAMHAM, JUNR., having appealed from a Warrant under the hand of ROBERT SLAUGHTER, Gent., directed to the Sherif commanding him to levy five pounds of the goods of each of them for gaming within the view of the said SLAUGHTER, and they being heard, the said Warrant is reversed

- RUSSELL HILL took the Oaths to his Majesty's Person and Government and took and subscribed the Abjuration oath and the Test was sworn CONSTABLE in this County in the room of DANIEL BROWN and then took the Oath appointed by the Tobacco Law

- RICHARD WINSLOW, Gent., Plt. agst DENNIS BYRNE, EDWARD SPENCER and ISAAC SMITH, Defts

The Jury sworn yesterdy to try the issue in this Cause returned into Court and upon their Oath do say that Deft., DENNIS BYRNE, did not suffer GEORGE FOSTER to escape as Plt. in his Replication alledged. Therefore it is considered by the Court that the Plt. take

p.   Orange County Court 25th of March 1747/48
105   nothing by his Bill but for his clamour be in mercy, &c., and that Defts. go thereof hence without day and recover against Plt. their costs by them about their suit in this behalf expended, And thereupon Plt. prayed an Appeal from the Proceedings in this Cause to the tenth day of the next General Court which is granted him on his giving Bond with Security for prosecuting the Appeal to the Clerk of the Court in his Office

- ISAAC SMITH, Plt. agst FRANCIS WILLIAMS, Deft.   In Chancery

This day came the parties by their Counsel and on motion of Plt. time is allowed him til next Court to consider the Deft.'s Answer and then to reply to it

- ROBERT SHEDDEN, Plt. agst WILLIAM MORGAN, Deft.   In Debt

This day came Plt. by GEORGE WYTHE, Gent., his Attorney and Plt. moved that Deft. should give Special Bail, which being overruled, the Deft. prays and has oyer of the Writing Obligatory in the Declaration mentioned and to imparl thereof til next Court and then to plead

- ELIZABETH HARDIN, Plt. agst MICHAEL WHATLEY, Deft.   In Debt

This day came Plt. by her Attorney, and JOHN CHRISTOPHER, Security for

Deft.'s appearance by his Attorney, and thereupon came also a Jury, to wit

RANDAL FUGETT	RICHARD VERNON	GEORGE DOGGETT
SAMUEL SCRATCHWELL	ROBERT MASH	JAMES RUCKER
BRYANT SYSON	EDWARD PRICE	WILLIAM MORGAN
JOHN MARKS	LAWRENCE STROTHER &	WILLIAM PANNEL

who being elected tried and sworn the truth to speak upon the issue joined, (the Deft. offered Evidence to the Jury to which Plt. excepted which was allowed, upon their Oath do say that Deft. hath paid the Debt in the Declaration mentioned as in pleading he hath alledged and the Cause is continued til next Court for Plt. to file a Bill of Exceptions to the opinion of the Court as to allowing the Evidence

- ROBERT RAE & DANIEL CAMPBELL, Plts. agt.
ROBERT FREEMAN, Deft.   In Debt

The Deft. not being arrested, on motion of Plt., an Attachment is awarded him against Deft.'s Estate returnable to next Court

- JOHN MARKS, Plt. agst EDWARD WARE &
JOHN LYNCH, Defts.   In Debt

Dismissed

- RICHARD WINSLOW, Plt. agst DENNIS BRYNE, EDWARD
SPENCER & ISAAC SMITH, Deft.   Scire Facias

On motion of Plt. a Commission is awarded him to examine and take the Deposition of MARY ROWLAND, a witness in this Cause de bene esse, giving Deft. legal notice of the time and place for executing the same

- THOMAS DILLARD is by the Court appointed Overseer of the Road in the room of ROBERT EASTHAM, Gent., and it is ordered that the gang that was under the said EASTHAM do attend and obey the directions of said DILLARD in keeping the Road in repair

- Ordered that the Court be adjourned til tomorrow morning 8 o'clock

- The Minutes of these Proceedings were signed
THOS: CHEW

p. 106   - At a Court continued & held for Orange County on Saturday the 26th of March 1748   Present

ABRAHAM FIELD	HENRY FIELD &
WILLIAM RUSSELL	GEORGE TAYLOR Gent.

- RICHARD WINSLOW, Gent., Plt. agst THOMAS CHEW, Gent., Deft.
In Case

This day came as well Plt. by GEORGE WYTHE, Gent., his Attorney as Deft. in his proper person and Deft. prays and has leave to imparl hereof til next Court and then to plead

- ROBERT DUNLOP & THOMAS DUNLOP, Merchants, Plts. agst
MATTHEW TOOL, Deft.   In Debt

This day came Pt. by GEORGE WYTHE, Gent., his Attorney and Deft. being returned arrested was solemnly called but came not. Therefore on motion of Plt. it is ordered that unless he appears at next Court and answers Plt.'s action, Judgment shall then be entered for the Plts. against him the Deft. and EDWARD SPENCER, Gent., Sherif of this County for the Debt in the Declaration mentioned and costs

- Present. THOMAS CHEW, Gent.

- WILLIAM PICKET, Plt. agst EDWARD WARE, Deft.   In Debt
This day came Plt. by GEORGE WYTHE, Gent., his Attorney and Deft. being re-
turned arrested was solemnly called but came not. Therefore on motion of Plt., it is
ordered that unless he appears at next Court and answers Plt.'s action, Judgment will
be entered for Plt. against him the Deft. and TULLY CHOICE, his Security, for the
Debt in the Declaration mentioned and costs
- RANDAL FUGETT, Plt. agst. JOHN BRAMHAM, Deft. In Case
Continued til next Court
- Ordered that ROBERT SLAUGHTER, HENRY FIELD & PHILIP CLAY-
TON, Gent., or any two of them do examine state and settle the Account of the
Estate of JOHN NEWPORT, deced., in the hands of CHRISTOPHER ZIMMERMAN,
Administrator of the said Estate, and make return thereof to the Court
- WILLIAM RUSSELL, Gent., Plt. agst. CHRISTOPHER ZIMMERMAN,
Admr. &c. of JOHN NEWPORT, deced., Deft. In Case
On motion of Plt. a Commission is awarded him to MORGAN MORGAN,
WILLIAM McMAHAN, LEWIS NEAL & MARCUS CALMES, Gent., or any two or
more of them to examine and take the Deposition of ANDREW CAMPBELL, Gent., a
witness in this Cause de bene esse, Plt. giving Deft. legal notice of the time & place of
executing the same
- ANTHONY STROTHER, Merchant, Plt. agst. CHRISTOPHER ZIMMER-
MAN, Admr. &c. of JOHN NEWPORT, deced.   In Case
This day came the parties by their Attornies and Plt. saith that the Deft. hath and
at the time of exhibiting the Bill aforesaid, had divers goods and chattels which were of
the Testator aforesaid at the time of his death in his hands to be administered whereof he can satisfy Plt. and this he prays may be inquired of by the Country, and Deft.
likewise, Therefore the Trial is referred til next Court
- Present. GOODRICH LIGHTFOOT, Gentleman
- Absent. THOMAS CHEW, Gentleman

p.   Orange County Court 26th of March 1748
107   - ANNE MOOR, PHILIP AYLETT & JAMES POWER, Exrs., &c. of
AUGUSTINE MOOR, deced., Plts. agst. HENRY DOWNS, Deft.   In Debt
This day camd Plts. by GEORGE WYTHE, Gent., their Attorney and Deft. being
arrested was solemnly called but came not. Therefore it is considered by the Court
that Plts. recover against Deft. and EDWARD SPENCER, Gent., Sherif of this County, the Debt in the Declaration mentioned and costs
- RICHARD BRIDGES, Plt. agst THOMAS CHEW, Gent., Deft.   In Debt
This day came the parties by their Attornies and thereupon came also a Jury to

wit,   WILLIAM PANNEL   THOMAS DILLARD   WILLIAM KELLY
        FRANCIS MOOR   GABRIEL JONES   GEORGE DOGGETT
        BRYANT SYSON   JOHN SMITH   WILLIAM BUNTIN
        LAWRENCE STROTHER   ROBERT MASH   &   JOHN CHRISTOPHER
who being elected tried and sworn the truth to speak upon the issue joined, brought in
a Special Verdict in these words, to wit; "We of the Jury do find tht Deft. being Sherif
did by virtue of an Execution take the body of MARGERY PERKINS; We find that
after he had taken the said MARGERY he did let her go at large before the day of
return. We find that he had the said MARGERY before the Court at the time he was
commanded. We find that said MARGERY was in the bounds of the Prison one or two

and twenty days and at the expiration of that time the Gaoler sent word to demand paiment of or security for the Prison Fees which not getting, the Gaoler set her, the said MARGERY, at liberty. We find the Execution and Return hereto annexed. Upon the whole matter, if the Law be for Plt., we find for him the Debt in the Declaration and one penny damage, if not, we find for Deft." And the Cause is continued til next Court for the matters of Law arising thereupon to be argued

   - Present. THOMAS CHEW, Gent.

The Petition of JAMES PENDLETON & PHILIP CLAYTON, Gent., agaisnt WILLIAM KIRTLEY, WILLIAM CLIFT & ROGER ABBET is continued til next Court

   - WILLIAM HUNTER, Gent., Plt. agst GEORGE COOK, Deft. In Debt

This day came Plt. by GEORGE WYTHE, Gent., his Attorney, and Deft. being returned arrested was solemnly called but came not. Therefore on motion of Plt. it is ordered that unless he appears at next Court and answers Plt.'s action, Judgment shall then be entered for Plt. against him the Deft., and ANDREW HARRISON, his Security, and EDWARD SPENCER, Gent., Sherif of this County, for the Debt in the Declaration mentioned and costs

   - ANDREW GAUR, Plt. agst JAMES MAXWELL, Deft. In Chancery

The summons not being served, on motion of Plt. by his Counsel, another summons is awarded him against Deft. returnable here the next Court

   - THOMAS SMITH, Plt, agst AUGUSTINE SMITH, Deft. In Chancery

The Deft. not appearing to answer Plt.'s Bill of Complaint, on motion of Plt. by his Counsel an Attachment is awarded him against the Deft. for his Contempt therein returnable here at next Court

p. <u>Orange County Court 26th March 1748</u>

108 - JOHN MITCHELL, Plt. agst GEORGE DOGGETT, Deft. In Debt

The Deft. not appearing, on motion of Plt. by his Attorney, an Attachment is awarded him against Deft.'s Estate returnable to next Court

   - On Petition of THOMAS FOSTER against GEORGE DOGGETT for two pounds, six shillings and nine pence said to be due by Promisory Note, this day came Plt. by his Attorney and Deft. being served with a copy of the Petition and summoned to appear was solemnly called but came not. Therefore it is considered by the Court that Plt. recover against Deft. the two pounds six shillings and nine pence and his costs by him about his suit in this behalf expended

   - EDWARD SPENCER, Gent.,Plt. agst THOMAS CHEW, Gent., Deft. In Debt

This day came Plt. by GEORGE WYTHE, Gent., his Attorney, and Deft. in his own proper person and Deft. prays and has oyer of the Writing Obligatory in the Declaration mentioned and to imparl thereof til the next Court and then to plead

   - THOMAS FOSTER, Plt. agst WILLIAM NASH, Deft. In Debt

The Deft. not being arrested, on motion of Plt. by his Attorney an Alias Capias is awarded him against the Deft. returnable to next Court

   - ARCHIBALD GORDON & ALEXANDER SCOTT, Plts. agst
JOHN CONNER, Deft. In Debt

The Deft. not being arrested, on motion of Plts. by their Attorney, an Alias Capias is awarded them against the Deft. returnable to next Court

   - The Petition of CHARLES DEWITT against WILLIAM CRAWFORD is dismissed.

- JAMES COLEMAN, TAVERNER BEALE and JOHN WILLIS this day made Report that in obedience to an Order of this Court they have viewed and marked out the most convenient way from the Road in LOUISA County to the Dividing Line of the said Counties to the Main Road in this County near the said WILLIS's Plantation, and it is ordered that the said WILLIS be Overseer of the said Way so laid off and have for his gang to clear the same his own people who are exempted from working on any other Roads

- JOHN DULWOOD & ELIZABETH his Wife, Plts. agst JOHN MORGAN, Deft. In Assault and Battery
   Dismissed being agreed

- Upon Petition of FRANCIS BROWNING against JAMES TURNER, Admr. &c. of JOHN SHELTON, deced., the Deft. not being served with the former Process, on motion of Plt. by his Attorney another summons is awarded him agaisnt the Deft. returnable to next Court

- The Petition of SPENCER BRAMHAM by JOHN BRAMHAM his next Friend, against GEORGE LIVINGSTON & WILLIAM LONG, the Deft., LIVINGSTON, not being served with the former Process on motion of Plt. by his Attorney another summons is awarded him against the Deft. returnable to next Court til which time the Cause is continued against the Deft., LONG,

- Upon Petition of ARCHIBALD GORDON & ALEXANDER SCOTT against JOHN BRAMHAM, this day came Plts. by their Attorney and Deft. confesseth the Plts.'s Petition. Therefore it is considered by the Court that Plts. recover against Deft. four pounds, seventeen shillings and seven pence and their costs by them about their suit in this behalf expended together with a Lawyer's Fee, But this Judgment, the costs excepted, is to be discharged by paiment of two pounds, eight shillings and nine pence half penny with Interest thereon after the rate of five percent per annum to be computed from the first day of November 1746 to the time of paiment and costs

p.   Orange County Court 26th of March 1748
109   - The Petition of JAMES McCULLOCK against ELIE GRIFFIN is dismissed

- FRANCIS BROWN, Plt. against EDWARD SPENCE, Gent., Deft. In Debt
   This day came the parties by their Attornies and Deft. relinquishing his former Plea saith he cannot gainsay Plt.'s action. Therefore it is considered that Plt. recover against Deft. one hundred three pounds current money, the Debt in the Declaration mentioned, and his costs by him about his suit in this behalf expended, and Deft. in mercy, &c., But this Judgment, the costs excepted, is to be discharged by paiment of fifty one pounds, ten shillings together with Interest thereon after the rate of five percent per annum to be computed from the twentieth day of April 1747 to the time of paiment and costs

- EDWARD PRICE, Plt. agst PATRICK LEONARD, Deft.   In Case
   This day came the parties by their Attornies and thereupon came also a Jury to

wit,   JOHN MORGAN   RICHARD SCALES   MICHAEL WHATLEY
        RICHARD VERNON   WILLIAM POUND   JOHN ROBERTS
        WILLIAM HAWKINS   THOMAS FOX   FELIX GILBERT
        THOMAS HUGHES   WILLIAM CHRISTOPHER & RANDAL FUGETT

who being elected tried and sworn the truth to speak upon the issue joined, upon their Oath do say the Deft. is Guilty of the Slander in the Declaration mentioned and they do assess Plt.'s damages by occasion thereof to forty shillings sterling besides his costs; Therefore it is considered by the Court that Plt. recover against Deft. his damages aforesaid in form aforesaid assessed and his costs by him about his suit in this behalf expended, and Deft. in mercy,&c.

    - The Attachment of WILLIAM CROUCHER against JOHN MORGAN is dismissed being agreed by the parties

    - Upon the Presentment of the Grandjury against LAWRENCE BRADLEY, the former Process not being served, another is awarded against him returnable to next Court

    - The several Presentments of the Grandjury against JOHN McCENNY, GEORGE COOK, WILLIAM PANNEL, BENJAMIN HENSLEY, JOHN HENSLEY, WILLIAM POUND and JOHN GILBERT is dismissed

    - Upon Presentment of the Grandjury against CHARLES HOLDSFORD for swearing two Oaths, the said CHARLES being summoned and not appearing to make any excuse for the said offence, it is considered by the Court that he pay to the Churchwardens of Saint Mark's Parish ten shillings for the use of the Poor of the said Parish and that he pay the costs of this Presentment

    - On motion of CHARLES DEWITT, a witness for RICHARD BRIDGES, Plt. against THOMAS CHEW, Gent., Deft., who made Oath that he had attended ten days as an Evidence in that suit, it is ordered that said RICHARD pay him two hundred fifty pounds of tobacco for the same according to Law

    - On motion of JOSEPH DEWITT, a witness for RICHARD BRIDGES, Plt against THOMAS CHEW, Gent., Deft. who made Oath that he had attended eleven days as an Evidence at that suit, it is ordered that said RICHARD pay him two hundred seventy five pounds of tobacco for the same according to Law

    - On motion of ELIZABETH DOWDIE, a witness for RICHARD BRIDGES, Plt. against THOMAS CHEW, Gent., Deft. who made Oath that she had attended eleven days as an Evidence at that suit, it is ordered that said RICHARD pay her two hundred seventy five pounds of tobacco for the same according to Law

    - On motion of MARY BOWMER, a witness for RICHARD BRIDGES, Plt. against THOMAS CHEW, Gent., Deft. who made Oath that she had attended five days as an Evidence at that suit, it is ordered that said RICHARD pay her one hundred twenty five pounds of tobacco for the same according to Law

    - ROBERT SHEDDEN, Plt. agst THOMAS CHEW, Gent., Deft.   In Debt Continued til next Court

    - Absent. WILLIAM RUSSELL, Gent.

p.
110
    Orange County Court 26th of March 1748
    - WILLIAM RUSSELL, Gent., Plt. agst THOMAS WRIGHT, Deft. In Case This day came Plt. by his Attorney and thereupon came also a Jury, to wit

ROBERT MASH	WILLIAM PANNELL	THOMAS DILLARD
WILLIAM KELLY	FRANCIS. MOOR	GABRIEL JONES
GEORGE DOGGETT	BRYANT SYSON	JOHN SMITH
WILLIAM BUNTIN	LAWRENCE STROTHER &	JOHN CHRISTOPHER

who being sworn well & truly to inquire of damages in this suit, upon their Oath do say that Plt. hath sustained damages by occasion of Deft.'s breach of promise in the Declaration mentioned to three pounds, seventeen shillings and eleven pence besides his costs. Therefore it is considered by the Court that Plt. recover against Deft. and

RICHARD WRIGHT, his Security, his damages aforesaid in form aforesaid assessed and his costs by him about his suit in this behalf expended
     - JOHN BEAZLEY, Plt. agst SPENCER BRAMHAM, Deft.
     In Assault and Battery
Continued til next Court at motion and costs of Plt.
     - RICHARD WINSLOW, Gent., Plt. agst WILLIAM RUSSELL, Gent. Deft.
     In Case
Ordered that GEORGE TAYLOR, TAVERNER BEALE and HENRY DOWNS, Gent., or any two of them, do on the Friday next after Easter if fair, if not the next fair day, examine state and settle all matters and Accounts in difference between the parties and make return thereof to the next Court
     - MARGARET GIBSON, Admrx. &c. of JONATHAN GIBSON, deced., Plt.
     agst WILLIAM RUSSELL, Gent., Deft.   In Case
Continued til next Court for Auditors to make their return
     - JOHN SPOTSWOOD, Gent., Plt. agst JOHN CHRISTOPHER, Deft. In Debt
This day came the parties by their Attornies and Deft. relinquishing his former Plea saith that he cannot gainsay Plt.'s action. Therefore it is considered by the Court that Plt. recover against Deft. one thousand pounds of tobacco in one cask, the Debt in the Declaration mentioned, and his costs by him about his suit in this behalf expended, and Deft. in mercy, &c.
       - Present. WILLIAM RUSSELL, Gent.
     - Our Lord the King, agst JOHN GOUGH & ROBERT BICKERS,
     On an Indictment for an Assault and Battery
The Defts. say they are Not Guilty in manner and form as in the Indictment against them is alledged and of this they put themselves upon the Country, and the Attorney for Our Lord the King likewise. Therefore the Trial of the issue is referred til next Court
     - Upon the Indictment of MICHAEL O'NEAL and MARGARET his Wife, the former Process not being served, an Alias venie facias is awarded against them returnable to next Court
     - The Attachment of GEORGE BUCHANAN & COMPANY, against WILLIAM PETTY is continued til next Court
     - On motion of RICHARD REYNOLDS, a witness for JOHN SPOTSWOOD, Gent., Plt. against JOHN CHRISTOPHER, Deft., it is ordered that JOHN SPOTSWOOD pay him seventy five pounds of tobacco for three days attendance at this Court according to Law
     - The Attachment of WILLIAM RUSSELL, Gent. against the Estate of JOSEPH PHILLIPS is continued to be further served

p.   Orange County Court 26th of March 1748
111   - JOHN ASHER having obtained an Attachment against the Estate of
     JOSEPH PHILLIPS who hath privately removed himself out of this County or absconds that Process cannot be served on him for eight hundred pounds of tobacco and cask and twenty five shillings and nine pence, DANIEL CARTER, a Constable in this County, making return that he hath attached four head of cattle and a young Calf, some Corn, a small prcel of household stuff, one Hog, this day came Plt. by his Attorney who made Oath to his Account and Deft. not appearing to replevy the said

effects, therefore it is considered that Plt. recover against Deft. the eight hundred pounds of tobacco and cask and twenty five shillings and nine pence and his costs by him about his suit in this behalf expended, and LAWRENCE STROTHER in whose hands the said Cattle were attached appeared in Court and produced a Bill of Sale for the cattle which being seen by the Court, it is the opinion of the Court that the property of the cattle is vested in the said STROTHER, but it appearing that the eight hundred pounds of tobacco and cask is for Rent due from Deft. to Plt., therefore it is ordered that the Sherif take the effects and make sale of them according to law and of so many of the cattle as with the amount of the other things will be of value sufficient to satisfy the Plt. the eight hundred pounds of tobacco and costs and make return thereof to the next Court

- On motion of JAMES McDANIEL, a witness for JOHN BEAZLEY, Plt. against SPENCER BRAMHAM, Deft., who made Oath that he had attended eight days as a witness in that suit, it is ordered that said JOHN pay him two hundred pounds of tobacco for the same according to Law

- THOMAS CHEW, Gent., in Court acknowledged himself indebted to our Sovereign Lord King George the Second of Great Britain,&c., in fifty pounds to be levied of his goods and chattels lands and tenements to our Lord the King his heirs and successors rendered upon this condition, that if PATRICK RICHEE shall be of good behaviour for a year and a day towards all his Majesty's liege subjects and shall be forth coming in case MICHAEL HANNAGIL shall die within a year and a day of a Wound given him by the said PATRICK from the time the Wound was given for which the said PATRICK stands committed to Gaol of this County, whereupon the said PATRICK is discharged from the custody of the Keeper of the Gaol, and THOMAS CHEW doth undertake to satisfy and pay the fees due for said PATRICK's commitment, confinement and release from the said Gaol

- FIELDING LEWIS, Plt. agst JOHN CHRISTOPHER and THOMAS FOX, Defts.   In Debt
ABRAHAM FIELD, Gent., came into Court and undertook for Defts. that in case they are cast in this suit they shall pay the condemnation of the Court or render their bodies to Prison in discharge thereof or that he will do it for them, and Defts. pray and have leave to imparl thereof til the next Court and then to plead

- On motion of THOMAS WOOTON, a witness for LAWRENCE STROTHER in the suit of JOHN ASHER, Plt. and JOSEPH PHILIPS, Deft., it is ordered that said LAWRENCE pay him twenty five pounds of tobacco for one days attenance at this Court according to Law

- On motion of EDWARD WHITE, a witness for LAWRENCE STROTHER in the suit between JOHN ASHER, Plt. and JOSEPH PHILIPS, Deft., ordered that the said LAWRENCE pay him twenty five pounds of tobacco for one days attendance at this Court according to Law

p.   Orange County Court 26th of March 1748
112   - JAMES BARBOUR, Gent., Plt. agst JOHN SMITH and GEORGE
        ANDERSON, Defts.   On a Scire Facias on a Recognizance of Bail entered
        into the twenty sixth day of September 1746 by which they undertook for
        JOHN SMITH, JUNR. that if he should be cast in an action then depending
        between the Plt. and said JOHN SMITH, JUNR., & TULLY CHOICE, Defts.

he the said SMITH should pay the condemnation of the Court or render his body to Prison in discharge thereof or tht they would do it for him, And JAMES BARBOUR having at a Court held for Orange County the 23d day of July 1747 recovered against the said SMITH & CHOICE, one hundred pounds current mone of Virginia to be discharged by the paiment of twenty five pounds, ten shillings and six pence half penny with Interest on fifty pounds after the rate of five percent per annum from the thirtieth day of June 1744 to the thirtieth day of June 1745, and on forty pounds from thence to the thirtieth day of June 1746 and on thirty pounds from thence to the thirtieth day of June 1747, and on the twenty five pounds, ten shillings and six pence half penny from the time of paiment and costs which amounted to one hundred forty eight pounds of nett tobacco and fifteen shilings or one hundred fifty pounds of tobacco, which JOHN SMITH, JUNR. nor TULLY CHOICE hath paid nor the said Smith rendered himself to Prison in discharge thereof

This day came Plt. by his Attorney and Defendants in their proper person and the Defendants confess the Plaintifs Writ. Therefore on the motion of Plaintif, it is considered by the Court that Judgment be entered for him against the Defendants that he have execution against them according to the form and effect of the recovery aforesaid and for his costs by him in this behalf expended in suing forth and prosecuting this Writ

- Ordered that the Court be adjourned to the fourth Thursday in April next
- The Minutes of these Proceedings were signed
                                              THOS: CHEW

- At a Court held at Orange County Courthouse the Ninth day of May in the twenty first year of the Reign of our Sovereign Lord George the Second of Great Britain, &c., Annoque Domini MDCCXLVIII for the Examination of HUGH GRANT and CATHARINE his Wife, THOMAS LARNEY and BRIDGET LARNEY alias MALEY his Wife who stand committed to the Common Gaol of the said County charged with the felonious stealing and taking away money & goods, the property of GEORGE MOYER
                                  Present
        ROBERT SLAUGHTER   GEORGE TAYLOR
        HENRY FIELD   GOODRICH LIGHTFOOT
                                     PHILIP CLAYTON   Gentlemen

The above named HUGH GRANT and CATHARINE his Wife, and THOMAS LARNEY and BRIDGET LARNEY alias MALEY were led to the Bar and upon examination they severally denied the fact with they stood charged. Whereupon divers witnesses were sworn and examined upon the premises and the Prisoners heard in their own defence. On consideration whereof, and of the circumstances relating to the Crime, it is the opinion of the Court that HUGH GRANT and THOMAS LARNEY and BRIDGET his Wife ought to be tried for the supposed facts at the next Court of Oyer & Terminer to be held at WILLIAMSBURG the second Tuesday in June next and thereupon they are remanded to the Gaol and nothing appearing against the said CATHERINE GRANT she is discharged
BE IT REMEMBERED that EDWARD SPENCER, Gent., GEORGE MOYER

for himself and ANNA BARBARA his Wife, CHRISTOPHER HUTCHINS, WILLIAM HAWKINS and LEWIS TOONE came before the Justices of our Lord the King now here and acknowledged themselves each to owe our Sovereign Lord King George the Second twenty pounds respectively to be levied of their goods and chattels lands & tenements and to our said Lord the King

p.   Orange County Court Called Court 9th of May 1748
113   his heirs and successors rendered upon condition that if they shall personally appear before his Majesty's Justices of Oyer & Terminer in WILLIAMS-BURGH on the second Tuesday in Junr next and shall then and there testify and give evidence against HUGH GRANT, THOMAS LARNEY and BRIDGET LARNEY alias MALEY his Wife, touching the Felony which they stand charged and shall not depart thence without the leave of the last mentioned Justices, then this Recognizance to be void

The Minutes of these Proceedings were signed
ROBT. SLAUGHTER

Memorandum; That at the Courthouse of Orange County on Thursday the twenty sixth day of May in the twenty first year of the Reign of our Sovereign Lord George the Second, King of Great Britain, &c., Annoque Domini 1748, his Majesty's Commission under the Seal of this his Colony and Dominion of Virginia bearing date the fourth day of this Instant directed to

THOMAS CHEW	ROBERT SLAUGHTER	ABRAHAM FIELD
ROBERT GREEN	JAMES BARBOUR	SAMUEL BALL
FRANCIS SLAUGHTER	JAMES POLLARD	ROBERT EASTHAM
ZACHARY TAYLOR	BENJAMIN CAVE	CHARLES CURTIS
WILLIAM RUSSELL	JAMES COLEMAN	GEORGE TAYLOR
RICHARD WINSLOW	HENRY FIELD	RICHARD THOMAS
JOSEPH THOMAS	GOODRICH LIGHTFOOT	PHILIP CLAYTON &
JAMES PENDLETON, Gent.,		

or any four or more of them whereof the said

THOMAS CHEW	ROBERT SLAUGHTER	ABRAHAM FIELD
ROBERT GREEN	JAMES BARBOUR	SAMUEL BALL
FRANCIS SLAUGHTER	JAMES POLLARD	ROBERT EASTHAM
ZACHARY TAYLOR	BENJAMIN CAVE	CHARLES CURTIS
WILLIAM RUSSELL or	JAMES COLEMAN	

should be one to hear and determine all Treasons, Petit Treasons or Misprisions thereof, Felonies, Murders or other offences or crimes whatsoever committed or perpetrated within the County by Letty, a Negro Woman slave belonging to HAN-NAH POTTER, was openly read as was in like manner his Majesty's Dedimus potestatem under the said Seal and of the same date for administering the Oaths &c. to the said Commissioners by virtue of which WILLIAM RUSSELL and GEORGE TAYLOR, Gent., administered the Oaths appointed by Act of Parliament to be taken instead of the Oaths of Allegiance & Supremacy, the Abjuration Oath and the Test unto ROBERT SLAUGHTER, Gent., who subscribed the Test and then WILLIAM RUSSELL and GEORGE TAYLOR, likewise, administered to him the Oath of a Justice of Oyer & Terminer and ROBERT SLAUGHTER thereupon administered the Oaths appointed by Act of Parliament to be taken instead of the Oaths of Allegiance and Supremacy, the Abjuration Oath and Test unto SAMUEL BALL, WILLIAM

RUSSELL, GEORGE TAYLOR & PHILIP CLAYTON, Gent., who also subscribed the Test and then ROBERT SLAUGHTER likewise administered to SAMUEL BALL, WILLIAM RUSSELL, GEORGE TAYLOR & PHILIP CLAYTON the Oath of a Justice of Oyer & Terminer

The Court being thus constituted

ZACHARY LEWIS, Attorney of our Sovereign Lord the King in the Court of the County aforesaid comes here into Court before the said ROBERT SLAUGHTER, SAMUEL BALL, WILLIAM RUSSELL, GEORGE TAYLOR & PHILIP CLAYTON, his Majesty's Justices of Oyer & Terminer for the said County by Special Commission appointed to hear all Treasons, Petit Treasons or Misprisions thereof, murders or other offences or crimes whatsoever commited or perpetrated within the County aforesaid by Letty, a Negro Woman slave belonging to

p.   Orange Court Court Called Court 26th of May 1748
114   HANNAH POTTER, Widow, the 26th day of May in the twenty first year of the Reign of our Sovereign Lord George the Second now King of Great Britain &c., in his proper person and for our said Lord the King gives this Court to understand and be informed that Letty, a Negro Woman slave belonging to HANNAH POTTER of the County of MIDDLESEX, Widow, not having the fear of God before her eyes but led by the instigation of the Devil the first day of August 1746 at the County aforesaid with force and arms of her malice prepensed certain mortal poyson feloniously did mingle with water, bread and meat knowing the poyson aforesaid to be poyson and the same water, bread and meat so mixt corrupt and poysoned then and there feloniously did give to one RICHARD SIMS, which RICHARD SIMS not fearing or distrusting the mixture corruption or poyson aforesaid the same water bead & meat with the poyson aforesaid by the said Letty so poysoned by the procurement and instigation of the said Letty then and there did taste drink eat and swallow down of which said water, bread and meat so with the said poyson as aforesaid mingled poysoned and received the aforesaid RICHARD SIMS did most grieviously languish from the aforesaid first day of August until the fourth day of January in the year aforesaid, said RICHARD SIMS so mortally poysoned with the poyson aforesaid died and the aforesaid Letty the aforesaid RICHARD SIMS falsely and feloniously of her malice aforethough with the poyson aforesaid did kill poyson and murder against the peace of our Lord the now King his crown & dignity, &c., and further the said ZACHARY LEWIS give the said Justices to understand and be informed that the said Letty not having the fear of God before her but led by the instigation of the Devil the last of September 1747 at the County aforesaid with force and arms of her malice forethought certain mortal poyson, feloniously did mingle with cyder, water, bread and meat knowing the poyson aforesaid to be poison the same cyder water bread and meat so mixt corrupt and poysoned then and there feloniously did give to one Simon, a Negro man slave belonging to JOHN GRYMES of MIDDLESEX County, Esqr., which said Simon not fearing or distrusting the mixture corruption or poyson aforesaid the same cyder, water, bread and meat with the poyson aforesaid by the said Letty so poysoned by the Procurement and Instigation of the said Letty then and there did taste drink eat and swallow down of which said cyder water bread and meat so with the poyson aforesaid mingled poysoned and received the aforesaid Simon did most grieviously languish from the aforesaid last day of September until the first day

of April then next following, upon which first day of April in the year aforesaid, the said SIMON so mortally poysoned with the poyson aforesaid, died and the aforesaid Letty the aforesaid Simon falsely and feloniously of her malice forethought with the poyson aforesaid did kill poyson and murder against the peace of our Lord the King his crown and dignity, &c.

Whereupon the said Letty was instantly led to the Bar under the Custody of EDWARD SPENCER, Gent., Sherif of the County aforesaid, (to whose custody before for the Causes aforesaid she was committed and being arraigned of the premises she said she was no wise thereof Guilty and thereof according to the form of the Act of Assembly in cases of this nature made and provided) she did put herself upon the Court upon which divers witnesses were produced, sworn and examined against the said Letty and she heard in her own defence; Whereupon it seems to the Court here that the said Letty is Not Guilty of the murders or any of them as in pleading she hath alledged. Therefore it is considered by the Court that she be thereof discharged and go hence without day

The Minutes of these Proceedings were signed

ROBT. SLAUGHTER

p.   - At a Court held for Orange County on Thursday the twenty sixth day of
115   day of May in the twenty first year of the Reign of our Sovereign Lord
          George the Second by the grace of God, King of Great Britain, &c.
          Annoque Domini MDCCXLVIII Before his Majesty's Justices of the
          Peace for the said County, to wit

ROBERT SLAUGHTER   WILLIAM RUSSELL
SAMUEL BALL   GEORGE TAYLOR
FRANCIS SLAUGHTER   PHILIP CLAYTON &
ROBERT EASTHAM   JAMES PENDLETON,   Gentlemen

- Writings bearing different dates, one the twenty first say of November, the other the tenth day of January last past, the first signed, the other not, said to contain the Last Will and Testament of JOHN FINLESON, Gent., deced., were presented into Court by CATHARINE FINLESON, the Executrix therein named, which being seen, the Court is of opinion that the Writing dated the tenth day of January is the last Will of JOHN FINLESON, And it is ordered that the Sherif make Proclamation and set up Notes according to Law that the Heir at Law may contest the same and that in the mean time the said Will will be lodged with the Clerk in his Office and on the motion of the said Executrix who made Oath according to Law, Certificate is granted her for obtaining a Probat thereof in due form

- Ordered that ROBERT SLAUGHTER, ABRAHAM FIELD, SAMUEL BALL and FRANCIS SLAUGHTER, or any three of them, being first sworn before a Justice in this County do appraise in current money the slaves and personal Estate of JOHN FINLESON, Gent., deced., & return the appraisment to next Court

- An Inventory and Appraisment of the Estate of JOHN LATHAM, deced. returned into Court and ordered to be recorded

- An Indenture of Feoffment between JOHN NOEL of one part and THOMAS KIMBROW of other part was acknowledged by said JOHN and ordered to be recorded

- An Indenture of Feoffment between JOHN NOEL of one part and DAVID

CAVE of the other part was acknowledged by the said JOHN and ordered to be recorded

- An Indenture of Feoffment between DAVID CAVE of one part and THOMAS KIMBROW of other part was acknowledged by said DAVID and ordered to be recorded

JAMES SUGGITT, Foreman	BRYANT THORNHILL	MATTHEW TOOL
JOHN WHARTON	TULLY CHOICE	FRANCIS WILLIAMS
JOHN WILLIS	WILLIAM KELLY	ROBERT TERRIL
WILLIAM CHRISTOPHER	ZACHARY GIBS	THOMAS DILLARD
THOMAS BURK	CHRISTOPHER HOOMES	WILLIAM DUNCAN
JOHN ROBINS &	WILLIAM STROTHER	

were sworn a Grandjury of Inquest for the body of this County and having received their charge, withdrew, and after some short time returning to Court made the following Presentments

"We of the Grand Jury do present SARAH BRIDGES, Wife of RICHARD BRIDGES for a common disturber of the peace;

"We likewise do present ROBERT HUDSON by the Information of JOHN ZIMMERMAN for not keeping the Road in repair from RONE's Quarter to FOX MOUNTAIN,:

And having nothing further to present were discharged

- Indentures of Lease and Release between TIMOTHY HOLDWAY of one part and THOMAS BROWN of other part and a Receipt endorsed on the said Release were acknowledged by the said TIMOTHY and ordered to be recorded, And BRIDGET, Wife of said TIMOTHY, personally appeared in Court and being privately examined as the Law directs, voluntarily relinquished her Right of Dower in the Estate conveyed by the Indentures

- JOHN ASKEW & CHARLES KAVANAUGH are appointed CONSTABLEs the said ASKEW in the room of JOHN CLEVELAND, and the said CHARLES in the room of JOHN RENNOLDS and it is ordered that they be sworn into their said Offices at the next Court

p. 116   Orange County Court 26 May 1748

- Upon Petition of JOHN BRAMHAM, he is allowed to keep ORDINARY at the Courthouse in this County upon his giving security. Whereupon he with ALEXANDER WAUGH, his Security, entered into and acknowledged Bond for his keeping the said Ordinary according to Law, And it is ordered that the Clk. prepare a Licence for him accordingly

- An Indenture of a Marriage Contract between THOMAS WIATT of one part and SUKEY EDMUNDSON, GABRIEL JONES and MARY his Wife, Mother of the said SUKEY was proved as to THOMAS WIATT by the Oath of RICHARD YOUNG, who declared that the other parties were present at the time tht the said WIATT executed the said Indenture but that he can't remember whether they then executed the same

- JOHN FOSTER is by the Court appointed Overseer of the Road in the Room of JOHN FOSTER, JUNR.

- WILLIAM DUNCAN is appointed Overseer of the Road from HILLIN's FORD to SCOTT's ROAD

- Ordered that Process issue against the several persons this day presented by the Grandjury to cause them to come to the next Court to answer the same

- An Indenture of Bargain and Sale between ISAAC NORMAN of one part and JAMES TURNER of other part and the Receipt thereon endorsed were acknowledged by said ISAAC and ordered to be recorded

- An Instrument of Writing between ISAAC NORMAN of one part and FRANCES TURNER of other part and a Receipt thereon endorsed were acknowledged by said ISAAC and ordered to be recorded

- An Indenture of Bargain and Sale between ISAAC NORMAN of one part and JAMES TURNER of other part and a Receipt thereon endorsed were acknowledged by said ISAAC and ordered to be recorded

- JAMES COTTON is by the Court appointed Surveyor of the Road from BLOODWORTH's ROAD and thence by Mr. THOMPSON's upper quarter to THORNTON's MILL; And it is ordered that WILLIAM LOBB, JOHN DILLARD, JAMES DILLARD, PETER COX, COLEMAN BROWN, JOSEPH ABEL, JOHN McKENNY, ROBERT STEWART, LAWRENCE BRADLEY, JOHN HUGHES, ROBERT TREWICK'S male labouring Tithables, Mr. THORNTON's male labouring Tithables where MORDECAI ABRAHAM did live, Mr. THOMPSON's male labouring Tithables at his upper quarter and the male labouring Tithables at the upper Plantation of MARTIN NALL do attend the said COTTON and obey his directions in clearing and keeping the Road in repair

- Upon Complaint of JOHN LATHAM suggesting that PHILIP EDWARDS JONES to whom he was bound by this Court to be instructed in the art & mystery of a Wheelwright and Chair-maker has neglected to instruct him and has misused him. The said JOHN being heard, it is the opinion of the Court that he ought to be removed from the said JONES, Therefore it is ordered that he be bound out to some other good Tradesman

- On motion of ANNE GOUGE, Widow, who made Oath according to Law, Certificate is granted her for obtaining Letters of Administration of the Estate of JOHN GOUGE, deced., on her giving security. Whereupon she with JOHN GOUGE and THOMAS DILLARD, her Securities, entered into and acknowledged Bond for her due and faithful administration of the said Decedent.'s Estate

- Ordered that WILLIAM DUNCAN, FRANCIS BROWNING, FRANCIS STROTHER and JAMES KENNERLEY or any three of them being first sworn before a Justice of this County do appraise in current money the slaves, if any, and personal Estate of JOHN GOUGE, deced., and return the appraisment to the next Court

- Upon motion of WILLIAM DUNCAN & JOHN ROBERTS against SARAH CHAPMAN for whom they became security for her due and faithful administration of her Husband's Estate, suggesting that they are in danger from the same, it is ordered that she give them counter security or render up the Estate to them

p.   Orange County Court 26th of May 1748
117   - JOHN HENDERSON took the Oaths to his Majesty's Person & Government and took the Oath of Abjuration and subscribed the Test and was sworn a CONSTABLE in this County then took the Oath appointed by the Tobacco Law
       - Upon Petition of CHRISTOPHER ZIMMERMAN, JUNR., he is allowed to

keep ORDINARY at his House for one whole year from this time, giving security. Whereupon he with CHRISTOPHER ZIMMERMAN, his Security, entered into and acknowledged Bond for his keeping the Ordinary according to Law; And it is ordered that the Clerk of the Court prepare a Licence for him accordingly

- Indentures of Lease and Release between ROBERT SLAUGHTER, Gent. of one part and THOMAS SLAUGHTER of other part were acknowledged by said ROBERT and ordered to be recorded

- Upon the Attachment brought by RICHARD VERNON against RICHARD McGRAW, LAWRENCE BRADLEY being sworn saith that he hath not any of the Estate of the said McGRAW, therefore he is discharged

- Ordered that THOMAS CHEW, Gent., take the List of Tithables in the upper end of Saint Thomas's Parish where GEORGE TAYLOR, Gent., took them last year

- Ordered that BENJAMIN CAVE, Gent., take the List of Tithables in the lower end of Saint Thomas's Parish where EDWARD SPENCER, Gent., took the same last year

- Ordered that JAMES PENDLETON, Gent., take the List of Tithables in the North Little Fork

- Ordered that PHILIP CLAYTON, Gent., take the List of Tithables in the upper end of the Great Fork

- Ordered that ROBERT SLAUGHTER, Gent., take the List of Tithables in the lower end of the Great Fork

- Ordered that the Surveyors of the Roads in this County continued in their Offices except those this day appointed

- Ordered that the Court be adjourned til tomorrow morning 8 o'clock

- The Minutes of these Proceedings were signed

ROBT. SLAUGHTER

- At a Court continued & held for Orange County on Friday the 27th of May 1748   Present

THOMAS CHEW   WILLIAM RUSSELL
FRANCIS SLAUGHTER   HENRY FIELD   &
BENJAMIN CAVE   GOODRICH LIGHTFOOT, Gentlemen

- Account of the Sale and Administration of the Estate of JOHN NEWPORT, deced., returned into Court by the persons appointed to examine the same and ordered to be recorded

- Upon Petition of GEORGE WELLS, he is allowed to keep ORDINARY at his House in this County for one whole year from this time on his giving security. Whereupon he with TAVERNER BEALE & BRYANT SYSON, his Securities, entered in to acknowledged his Bond for keeping the said Ordinary according to Law, and it is ordered that the Clerk of the Court do prepare a Licence for him accordingly

- Upon Petition of WILLIAM HARVEY, he is exempted from paying County Levy

- ELIZABETH HARDIN, Plt. agst MICHAEL WHATLEY, Deft.   In Debt
This day came the parties by their Attornies and Plt.'s Attorney filed a Bill of Exceptions to the Evidence given at the Trial of the issue joined in this Cause which were signed and sealed by the Justices that were present at the said Trial

- The Information against JOHN WILSON is dismissed
- The Information against JOSEPH CAVE is dismissed

p.   Orange County Court 27th of May 1748
118   - Upon the Indictment against JAMES HEMPHILL for assaulting ROBERT
       YOUNG, ZACHARY LEWIS, Attorney for our Lord the King, produced his
Majesty's Writ of Certiorari directed to the Justices of this Court commanding them
or one of them under their or one of their Seals to send and certify the Record and
Proceedings in this suit with all things touching the same as fully and wholly as the
same is now residing before them to the Honble the Justices of the General Court at
the Courthouse in WILLIAMSBURG on the Sixth day of the next Court which being
seen, it is ordered that the same be sent and certified accordingly
       - WILLIAM KELLY, Plt. agst ROBERT EASTHAM, Gent., Admor, &c. of
       JOHN LATHAM, deced., Deft.   In Case
     This day came the parties by their Attornies and thereupon came also a Jury to
wit,   ISAAC SMITH   JOHN CHRISTOPHER   JOHN FINNEL
       GEORGE HOME   LEWIS TOONE   ROBERT MASH
       LAWRENCE STROTHER   JOHN CARDER   HENRY BOURN
       THOMAS JAMESON   WILLIAM POUND   &   GEORGE COOK
who being elected tried and sworn the truth speak upon the issue joined, (the Plt.
offered to give in Evidence a Note of Hand suggested by him to have been made by
the Testator, LATHAM, in his life time and lodged in Court to maintain his action
aforesaid which was opposed by the Defendant and overruled by the Court as not
legal evidence, it appearing to the Court on the face of the said Note that the same
was Fraudulent or had been altered and clipped by the Plt., although the Plt. by evidence proved that the said Testator about a fortnight before is death had confessed
that he was indebted to the Plt. about five pounds, thirteen shillings and the name
subscribed to the said Note appeared to be the said LATHAM's hand writing) upon
their Oaths do say that the Testator in his life time did not assume upon himself as in
pleading the Deft. hath alledged. Therefore it is considered by the Court that Plt. take
nothing by his Bill but for his false clamour be in mercy, &c., And Deft. go thereof
thence without day and recover against Plt. his costs by him about his defence in this
behalf expended;
     From which Judgment, the Plt. prayed an Appeal to the tenth day of the next
General Court which is granted him. Whereupon he with CHARLES DEWITT and
JAMES GRAVES, his Securities, entered into and acknowledged his Bond for the
prosecution of the Appeal
       - ZACHARY LEWIS, Gent., Attorney for our Lord the King, moved that a
Note which had been offered in Evidence to the Jury in a Trial between WILLIAM
KELLY, Plt. and ROBERT EASTHAM, Admor. &c. of JOHN LATHAM, deced., Deft.
in the possession of GEORGE WYTHE, Gent., Attorney for the said KELLY and had
been handed to the Justices for their Inspection and rejected by the Court might be
lodged with the Clerk in order to file an Information against the said KELLY for a
Fraud supposed to have been committed therein. Whereupon it is ordered that the
Clerk take the said Note into his possession and care
       - On motion of CHARLES DEWITT, a witness for WILLIAM KELLY, Plt.
against ROBERT EASTHAM, Gent., Admr. &c. of JOHN LATHAM, deced., who
made Oath that he had attended five days as an Evidence in that suit, it is ordered

that said WILLIAM pay him one hundred twenty five pounds of tobacco for the said attendance according to Law

   - Upon the Indictment of JOHN GOUGH & ROBERT BICKERS, the said JOHN & ROBERT appeared in Court and confessed the allegations in the Indictment against them to be true. Therefore it is considered by the Court that they make their Fine with our Lord the King by the paiment of five shillings each and that they be taken, &c.

p.   <u>Orange County Court 27th of May 1748</u>
119   - WILLIAM BEVERLEY, Gent., Plt. agst GEORGE HOME, Deft. In Case
   This day came Plt. by his Attorney and Deft. in his proper person and Deft. confesseth the Plt.'s action. Therefore it is considered by the Court that the Plt. recover against Deft. thirty five pounds, three shillings and eleven pence half penny, the Debt in the Declaration mentioned, and his costs by him about his suit in this behalf expended, and Deft. in mercy, &c.

   - The Petition of WILLIAM KELLY against WILLIAM CLARK is dismissed

   - JOHN BRAMHAM, Plt. agst WILLIAM RUSSELL, Gent., Deft.
   In Covenant
This day came the parties by their Attornies, and on the matters of Law arising from the Special Verdict, the Deft. confesseth that the Law is for the Plt. Therefore it is considered by the Court that Plt. recover against Deft. one hundred fifty four pounds current money the damages in the Verdict aforesaid assessed, and his costs by him about his suit in this behalf expended and Deft. in mercy, &c., And Deft. to stay execution on this Judgment filed a Bill of Injunction against the Plt. and EDWARD SPENCER, Gent., and the Plt. is stayed from suing out execution thereupon til the matter is heard in Equity

   - THOMAS CHEW, Gent., Plt. agst JACOB STOVER, HENRY DOWNS & JACOB CASSELL, Defts.   In Chancery
The Defendants having not put in their answer, on motion of Plt., an Attachment is awarded him against them for their Contempt therein returnable to next Court

   - The Attachment of TULLY CHOICE against JOHN MORGAN is continued til the next Court at motion and costs of Plt.

   - DANIEL HART, Plt. agst CHRISTOPHER ZIMMERMAN, Admr., &c. of JOHN NEWPORT, deced., Deft.   In Case
This day came Plt. by GEORGE WYTHE, Gent., his Attorney and Deft. by ZACHARY LEWIS, Gent., his Attorney, and Deft. prays and has leave to imparl hereof til next Court and then to plead

   - WILLIAM HUNTER, Gent., Plt. agst WILLIAM LONG, Deft.,   In Debt
This day came Plt. by ZACHARY LEWIS, Gent., his Attorney and Deft. not being arrested, on motion of Plt. an Alias Capias is awarded him against the Deft. returnable to next Court

   - WILLIAM HENSLEY, quitam &c., Plt. agst JOSEPH PHILIPS, Deft.
   In Debt
This day came Plt. who as well &c., by ZACHARY LEWIS, Gent., his Attorney and Deft. not being arrested, on motion of Plt. an Alias Capias is awarded him against the Deft. returnable to next Court

- WILLIAM HUGHES, Plt. agst JOHN HALEY, Deft.   In Detinue
Dismissed

p.   Orange County Court 27th of May 1748
120   - JAMES DUN, Merchant, Plt. agst JOHN CLAYTON, JUNR., Deft.
       In Case
This day came Plt. by ZACHARY LEWIS, Gent., his Attorney and Deft. not being
arrested, on motion of Plt. an Alias Capias is awarded him against Deft. returnable to
next Court
       - PATRICK LEONARD, Plt. agst WILLIAM POUND, Deft.
       In Assault and Battery
Dismissed, being agreed by the parties
       - ANTHONY STROTHER, Plt. agst THEOPHILUS EDDINS, WILLIAM
       POUND & THOMAS WEATHERBY, Deft.   On a Scire Facias
The Defts., THEOPHILUS & THOMAS, not being warned, on motion of Plt. by his
Attorney, an Alias Scire Facias is awarded him against the Defts. returnable to the
next Court and as to the Deft., POUND, this suit is continued
       - WILLIAM TALIAFERRO, Plt. agst   NICHOLAS PORTER, Deft.   In Case
Dismissed
       - A Writing purporting to be the Last Will and Testament of WILLIAM MOR-
TON, deced., was presented into Court and the Executors therein named not
appearing, ordered that the Sherif summon them to declare whether they will take
upon themselves the burthen of the execution of the same and further that the Sherif
make Proclamation and set up notice according to Law that the Heir at Law contest
the same and that in the mean time the said Will be lodged with the Clk, in his Office
       - EDWARD WHITE quitam, &c., Plt. agst LEWIS DAVIS YANCEY, Deft.
       In Debt
Dismissed being agreed by the parties
       - On motion of JAMES GRAVES, a witness for EDWARD WHITE, who as
well, &c., Plt. against LEWIS DAVIS YANCEY, Deft., it is ordered that said
EDWARD pay im fifty pounds of tobacco for two days attendance at this Court
according to Law
       - On motion of THOMAS DILLARD, a witness for WILLIAM KELLY, Plt.
against ROBERT EASTHAM, Gent., Admr. &c. of JOHN LATHAM, deced., Deft.,
who made Oath that he had attended five days as an Evidence in that suit, it is
ordered that the said WILLIAM pay him one hundred twenty five pounds of tobacco
for his said attendance according to Law
       - The Petition of JAMES DUN against LAWRENCE STROTHER is dismissed
       - The Petition of JAMES DUN against ROBERT SMITH is dismissed
       - The Petition of JAMES DUN against WILLIAM POUND is dismissed
       - GEORGE MOYER, Plt. agst JOHN HANSPARGER, Deft.   In Case
This day came Plt. by his Attorney and Deft. not being arrested, on motion of Plt.
an Alias Capias is awarded him against Deft. returnable to next Court
       - ANN DOGIN, Plt. agst. EDWARD HAMPTON, Deft.   In Case
Dismissed
       - The Petition of JOHN WHARTON against EDWARD WARE is dismissed
       - The Attachment of THOMAS CHAMBERS against JACOB EVERMAN is

dismissed

<u>Orange County Court 27th of May 1748</u>

p.
121   - Upon the Attachment brought by MARGARET RICE, Admrx. &c. of
HENRY RICE, deced., against JOHN SMITH, JUNR., RICHARD WRIGHT,
the Garnishee, being called and not appearing, an Attachment is awarded him against
the said WRIGHT returnable to the next Court
       - The Petition of WILLIAM RUSSELL, Gent. agst ISAAC SMITH is con-
tinued til next Court's Docket
       - The Attachment of ANTHONY STROTHER against JAMES CHISSUM is
continued to be further served
       - Upon the Attachment brought by THOMAS WOOTON against JOHN
WOOTON, BRYANT SYSON being sworn saith he hath not any of the Estate of the
said JOHN therefore he is discharged
       - The Attachment of WILLIAM RUSSELL, Gent., against the Estate of
JOHN SMITH, JUNR. is continued to be further served
           - Present. WILLIAM RUSSELL, Gent.
           - Absent. BENJAMIN CAVE, Gent.
       - The Attachment obtained by WILLIAM HAWKINS against EDWARD
WARE is dismissed
       - ROBERT MARSH having obtained an Attachment against the Estate of
WILLIAM CRIBBEN, who hath privately removed himself out of this County or
absconds that Process cannot be served on him for six hundred pounds of lawful
tobacco fue from said WILLIAM to said ROBERT by Note of Hand. THOMAS
THORNTON and CHARLES LEE being sworn, said THOMAS saith that there are
accounts between him and said CRIBBEN which being seen by the Court, it is the
opinion of the Court that said THORNTON is indebted to said CRIBBEN two hundred ninety eight pounds of tobaccok and the said CHARLES saith that he had a box,
and old Gun barrel, a pair of bullet moulds and a shot bag. This day came Plt. and
Deft. not appearing to replevy the said effects, it is considered by the Court that Plt.
recover against him the six hundred pounds of tobacco and his costs by him about his
suit in this behalf expended, and it is ordered that the said THORNTON pay the Plt.
the two hundred ninety eight pounds of tobacco and that the said LEE deliver the
goods in his hands to the Sherif to be by him sold according to Law and the tobacco
arising from such sale to be paid to the Plt.
       - FIELDING LEWIS, Plt. agst JOHN CHRISTOPHER and
THOMAS FOX, Deft.   In Debt
By Agreement of the parties, it is considered that Plt. recover against Deft. his
costs by him about his suit in this behalf expended except a Lawyer's fee
       - The Attachment of JACOB HOLTSCLAW against ANTHONY LUKE is
continued til next Court
       - Ordered that the Court be adjourned til tomorrow morning 8 o'clock
       - The Minutes of these Proceedings were signed
                                        THOS: CHEW

- At a Court continued and held for Orange County on Saturday the 28th day of May 1748   Present

THOMAS CHEW	WILLIAM RUSSELL
HENRY FIELD	GOODRICH LIGHTFOOT &
PHILIP CLAYTON,	Gentlemen

- An Account of the Administration of the Estate of MARY CURTIS, deced. was returned into Court by MORGAN BRYAN, which being seen and examined by the Court, is ordered to be recorded

- Upon Petition of RICE BOWIN and CATHARINE his Wife against BENJAMIN ROBERTS, it is ordered that the Sherif summon said ROBERTS to appear at next Court to answer the Petition

- The Attachment of ROBERT SEAYRES against WILLIAM JONES is continued til next Court

- The Attachment of THOMAS DILLARD againt GEORGE HOME is discontinued

p. 122   Orange County Court 28th of May 1748

- ROBERT RAE & DANIEL CAMPBELL, Merchants & Partners, Plts. agst GEORGE HOME, Deft.   In Case

By agreement of the parties, this suit is dismissed and it is ordered that Deft. pay unto Plts. their costs by them about their suit in this behalf expended

- JOHN GRYMES & FRANCIS WILLIS, Esqrs., Exrs. &c. of HENRY WILLIS, Gent., deced., Plts. agst GEORGE HOME, Deft. In Case

Continued for Auditors to make their report

- Absent. WILLIAM RUSSELL, Gent.

- BENJAMIN BORDEN, Plt. agst JAMES ARMSTRONG, Deft.   In Debt

Continued til next Court

- JAMES BELL, Plt. agst GEORGE HOME, Deft.   In Case

WILLIAM RUSSELL, Gent., undertakes for Deft. in case he shall be cast in this suit he shall pay the condemnation of the Court or render his body to Prison in discharge thereof, or that he will do it for him; And Deft. prays and has leave to imparl threof til the next Court and then to plead

- HUMPHREY BELL, Plt. agst WILLIAM COX, Deft.   In Debt

The Deft. not being arrested, on motion of Plt. a Plurius Capias is awarded him against the Deft. returnable to the next Court

- JOHN BELFIELD & WILLIAM JORDAN, Gent., Exrs. &c. of THOMAS WRIGHT BELFIELD, Gent., deced., Plts agst WILLIAM MORTON, Deft. In Chancery

Continued til next Court

- DANIEL HORNBY, Gent., Plt. agst WILLIAM MORTON, Deft.   In Debt

Continued til next Court

- JOHN BRAMHAM having obtained an Attachment against the Estate of JOHN SMITH, JUNR. who hath privately removed himself out of the County or so absconded that Process cannot be served on him for thirty pounds due from said SMITH to said BRAMHAM due by Account. BRYANT SISON being sworn saith that he owes said SMITH seven hundred fifty pounds of tobacco. This day came Plt.

who made Oath to his Account, the ballance thereof is seventeen pounds, eleven shillings and ten pence half penny and Deft. not appearing to replevy the said tobacco therefore it is considered that Plt. recover against Deft. the seventeen pounds, eleven shillings and ten pence half penny and his costs by him about his suit in this behalf expended; And it is ordered that said SISON deliver the abovementioned tobacco to the Sherif to be by him sold and the money arising from such sale to be paid to the Plt. in discharge of so much of this Judgment and the costs and Plt. agreeth that Deft. may be at liberty to make out any just discount

    - JOHN BEAZLEY, Plt. agst SPENCER BRAMHAM, Deft.
    In Assault and Battery

This suit is dismissed and it is ordered that Plt. pay unto Deft. his costs by him in his defence in this behalf expended

p.   <u>Orange County Court 28th of May 1748</u>
123   - RICHARD WINSLOW, Gent., Plt. agst ROBERT SEAYRES and
    JOHN SEAYRES, Defts.   In Case

This day came Plt. by his Attorney and Defts. waving their Exceptions, it is considered by the Court that Plt. recover against Defts. and THOMAS CHEW, Gent., late Sherif of Orange County, thirteen pounds, one shilling and ten pence current money, the damages by the Jurors in their Verdict assessed and his costs by him about his suit in this behalf expended, and the Defts. in mercy, &c.

    - JOSEPH MORTON, Gent., Plt. agst WILLIAM RUSSELL, Gent., Deft.
    In Debt

Continued til next Court to be the second Cause on the Docket

    - JARET McCONNICO, who was summoned as an Evidence for JOHN BEAZLEY against JOHN BRAMHAM not appearing, it is ordered that he pay said JOHN three hundred fifty pounds of tobacco unless he shew good cause for his failure at the next Court

    - Absent. THOMAS CHEW, Gent.

    - Present. WILLIAM RUSSELL & GEORGE TAYLOR, Gent.

    - The Information against MICHAEL COOK is continued til next Court

    - JANE WHARTON, Admrx. &c. of THOMAS WHARTON, deced., Plt. agst THOMAS CHEW, Gent., Deft.   In Case

By consent of the parties, it is ordered that ZACHARY LEWIS, Gent., do examine state and settle all matters and accounts in difference between the parties and report thereof to next Court

    - Upon Petition of GEORGE BUCHANAN & WILLIAM HAMILTON, Exrs. &c. of NEIL BUCHANAN, deced. against THOMAS PETTY for a Debt therein said to be due, this day came the parties by their Attornies who being fully heard, it is considered by the Court that the Petition be dismissed and that Deft. recover against Plt. his costs by him about his defence in this behalf expended

    - The Petition of GEORGE BUCHANAN & WILLIAM HAMILTON, Exrs. &c. of NEIL BUCHANAN, deced. against ROBERT KELLY is continued til next Court at costs of Plts.

    - Present THOMAS CHEW, Gent.

    - ROBERT HILL, Plt. agst DANIEL CARTER, Deft. In Assault & Battery

This day came Plt. by ZACHARY LEWIS, Gent., his Attorney and Deft. being returned arrested was solemnly called but came not. Therefore on motion of Plt. it is ordered that unless he appears here at the next Court and answers Plt.'s action, Judgment shall be then entered for Plt. against him, the Deft., and GEORGE DOG-GETT, his Security, for the Debt in the Declaration mentioned and costs

    - JOHN COBURN, Plt. agst WILLIAM LONG, Deft.   In Case

Continued til next Court at motion and costs of Plt.

    - The Petition of RICHARD WINSLOW, Gent., against ISAAC SMITH is continued til next Court

    - ARCHIBALD GORDON & ALEXANDER SCOTT, Plts. agst

    WILLIAM RHODES, Deft.   In Debt

The Deft. not being arrested, on the motion of Pls. by their Attorney, an Alias Capias is awarded them against Deft. returnable to next Court

p.   Orange County Court 28th of May 1748
124   - ARCHIBALD GORDON & ALEXANDER SCOTT, Plts. agst.

    ROBERT ADAMS, Deft. In Debt

The Deft. not being arrested, on motion of Plts. by their Attorney, an Alias Capias is awarded them against Deft. returnable to next Court

    - ARCHIBALD GORDON & ALEXANDER SCOTT, Plts. agst.

    GEORGE DOGGETT, Deft.   In Debt

This day came Plts. by their Attorney and Deft. being returned arrested was solemnly called but came not; Therefore on motion of Plts., it is ordered that unless he appears at next Court and answers Plts.'s action, Judgment sall then be entered for Plts. against him the Deft. and EDWARD SPENCER, Gent., Sherif of Orange County for the Debt in the Declaration mentioned and costs

    - ARCHIBALD GORDON & ALEXANDER SCOTT, Plts. agst

    JOHN SHACKLEFORD, Deft. In Debt

The Deft. not being arrested, on motion of Plts. by their Attorney an Alias Capias is awarded them against the Deft. returnable to the next Court

    - ARCHIBALD GORDON & ALEXANDER SCOTT, Plts. agst

    WILLIAM CHRISTOPHER, Deft.   In Debt

Dismissed being agreed by the parties

    - WILLIAM GAMES, Plt. agst THOMAS FOX, Deft. In Assault & Battery

Dismissed being agreed by the parties

    - WILLIAM GALE of Whitehaven, Merchant, Plt. agst JOHN CARDER, Deft. In Case

JOHN TRIPLET undertakes for Deft that in case he shall be cast in this suit he shall pay the condemnation of the Court or render his body to Prison in discharge thereof or that he will do it for him. and thereupon Deft. prays and has leave to imparl thereof til next Court and then to plead

    - WILLIAM GALE of Whitehaven, Merchat., Plt. agst WILLIAM MORGAN, Deft. In Case

This day came Plt. by his Attorney and Deft. being returned arrested was solemnly called but came not. Therefore on motion of Plt., it is ordered that unless he appears at next Court and answers Plt.'s action, Judgment shall then be entered for Plt. against him the Deft. and EDWARD SPENCER, Gent., Sherif of Orange County, for the Debt in the Declaration mentioned and costs

- GEORGE BUCHANAN & WILLIAM HAMILTON, Exrs. &c. of NEIL
BUCHANAN, deced., Plts agst GEORGE HOME, Deft.   In Case
The Deft. not being arrested, on motion of Plts. by their Attorney and Alias Capias
is awarded them against the Deft. returnable to the next Court
- JOHN LEWIS, Gent., Plt. agst JOSEPH WALSH, Deft.   In Case
The Deft. not appearing, on motion of Plt. by his Attorney, an Attachment is
awarded him against Deft.'s Estate returnable to next Court
- MATTHIAS WILHOIT, Plt. agst WILLIAM SPICER, Deft.
In Assault and Battery
Dismissed

p.   Orange County Court 28th of May 1748
125   - BENJAMIN ROBERTS & WILLIAM PEYTON, Churchwardens of Saint
Mark's Parish, Plts. agst ELEANOR CORNELIUS, Deft.   In Debt
This day came Plts. by their Attorney and Deft. being returned arrested was
solemnly called but came not, therefore on motion of Plts., it is ordered that unless
she appears at next Court and answer Plts.'s action, Judgment that then be entered
for Plts. against her and WILLIAM CRAWFORD, her Security, for the Debt in the
Declaration mentioned and costs
- JOHN PARISH, Plt. agst JOSIAS BAKER, Deft. In Debt
This day came Plt. by ZACHARY LEWIS, Gent., his Attorney and Deft. in custody
of the Sherif and Deft. confesseth Plt.'s action. Therefore it is considered that Plt.
recover against Deft. twenty three pounds, eight shillings and his costs by him about
his suit in this behalf expended, and Deft. in mercy, &c., But this Judgment, the costs
excepted, is to be discharged by paiment of thirteen pounds, four shillings and six
pence with Interest on eleven pounds, fourteen shillings after the rate of five percent
per annum to be computed from the fourth day of September 1746 to time of
paiment and costs
- MATTHIAS WILHOIT, Plt. agst EDWARD STUBBLEFIELD, Deft.
In Assault and Battery
Dismissed
- MATTHIAS WILHOIT, Plt. agst JOHN THOMAS, Deft.
In Assault and Battery
This day came Plt. by ZACHARY LEWIS, Gent., his Attorney, and Deft. being returned arrested was solemnly called but came not. Therefore on motion of Plt. it is
ordered that unless he appears at next Court and answers Plt.'s action, Judgment
shall then be entered for Plt. against him, the Deft., and EDWARD SPENCER, Gent.,
Sherif of Orange County, for the Debt in the Declaration mentioned and costs
- On motion of JOHN TRIPLET, a witness for SPENCER BRAMHAM at the
suit of JOHN BEAZLEY, who made Oath that he had attended five days as a witness
in that suit, it is ordered that said SPENCER pay him one hundred twenty five
pounds of tobacco for his attendance according to Law
- On motion of JOHN CARDER, a witness for SPENCER BRAMHAM at the
suit of JOHN BEAZLEY, who made Oath that he had attended five days as a witness
in that suit, it is ordered that said SPENCER pay him one hundred twenty five
pounds of tobacco for is attendance according to Law

- THOMAS MOOR, Gent. Plt. agst JOHN CLAYTON, JUNR., Deft. In Case
The Deft. not being arrested, on motion of Plt. by his Attorney, an Alias Capias is
awarded him against the Deft. returnable to the next Court
- WILLIAM HUNTER, Gent., Plt. agst FRANCIS WILLIAMS, Deft. In Debt
The Deft. not being arrested, on motion of Plt. by his Attorney, an Alias Capias is
awarded him against the Deft. returnable to next Court
- ARCHIBALD GORDON & ALEXANDER SCOTT, Plts. agst
CHARLES PARKS, Deft.   In Debt
Dismissed

p.   Orange County Court 28th of May 1748
126   - ARCHIBALD GORDON & ALEXANDER SCOTT, Plts. agst
HENRY TILLERY, Deft. In Debt
This day came Plts. by ZACHARY LEWIS, Gent., their Attorney, and Deft. being
returned arrested was solemnly called but came not; Therefore on motion of Plts. it is
ordered that unless he appears at next Court and answers Plts.'s action, Judgment
shall be then entered for Plts. against him the Deft. and WILLIAM CRAWFORD, his
Security, for the Debt in the Declaration mentioned and costs
- ARCHIBALD GORDON & ALEXANDER SCOTT, Plts agst
WILLIAM CRAWFORD, Deft. In Debt
This day came Plts. by ZACHARY LEWIS, Gent., their Attorney, and Deft. being
returned arrested was solemnly called but came not. Therefore on motion of Plts. it is
ordered that unless he appears at next Court and answers Plts.'s action, Judgment
shall be then entered for Plts. against him the Deft., and EDWARD SPENCER,
Gent., Sherif of Orange County, for the Debt in the Declaration mentioned and costs
- ARCHIBALD GORDON & ALEXANDER SCOTT, Plts. agst
WILLIAM WATKINS, Deft.   In Debt
The Deft. not being arrested, on motion of Plts. by their Attorney, an Alias Capias
is awarded them against Deft. returnable to next Court
- ARCHIBALD GORDON & ALEXANDER SCOTT, Plts. agst
WILLIAM WHITMAN, Deft.   In Debt
The Deft. not being arrested, on motion of Plts. by their Attorney, an Alias Capias
is awarded them against Deft. returnable to next Court
- Upon Petiton of JOHN BRAMAHAM, JUNR. against RICHARD JEF-
FERIES for two pounds, ten shillings by Promisory Note, this day came Plt. and Deft.
having been served with a copy of the Petition and summoned to appear was called
but came not. Therefore it is considered by the Court that Plt. recover against Deft.
the two pounds, ten shillings and his costs by him about his suit in this behalf
expended
- Upon Petition of JOHN BRAMHAM against DAVID GRIFFIN for two
pounds, ten shillings by Promisory Note, this day came Plt. and Deft. having been
served with a copy of the Petition and summoned to appear was called but came not.
Therefore it is considered by the Court that Plt. recover against Deft. the two pounds,
ten shillings and his costs by him about his suit in this behalf expended
- The Petition of EDWARD WARE against SAMUEL GREEN is continued til
next Court at motion and costs of Plt.
- WILLIAM HAWKINS, JUNR. who was summoned to appear at this Court

as an Evidence for EDWARD WARE against SAMUEL GREEN, was called but
came not. It is ordered that he pay said EDWARD three hundred fifty pounds of
tobacco for his failure
  - The Petition of EDWARD WARE against RICHARD SCALES is continued
til next Court at motion and costs of Deft.
  - The Petition of EDWARD WARE against LAWRENCE STROTHER is con-
tinued til next Court at motion and costs of Plt.
  - Upon Petition of HENRY HAYNES against JOHN ASKEW, the former
Process not being served, on motion of Plt. another is awarded him against Deft.
returnable to next Court
  - The Attachment of WILLIAM HUNTER, Gent. against THOMAS GIBSON
is dismissed
  - Absent THOMAS CHEW, Gent.
  - THOMAS CHEW, Gent., Plt. agst SUSANNAH RUCKER & PETER
RUCKER, Exrs. &c. of JOHN RUCKER, deced., Defts.   In Case
Continued til next Court at motion and costs of Defts.
  - Present. THOMAS CHEW, Gent.
  - The Attachment of RICHARD VERNON against RICHARD McGRAW is
continued til next Court

p.   Orange County Court 28th of May 1748
127   - ELIZABETH DUFF, Widow, & ROBERT GREEN, Gent., Exrs. &c. of
      WILLIAM DUFF, deced., Plts. against JONAS JENKINS, Deft.   On a Writ
      of Scire Facias on a Judgment obtained the twenty sixth day of May 1744 in
      this County by WILLIAM DUFF against the Deft. for nine hundred ninety nine
      pounds of nett tobacco for Debt and seven shillings and six pence for costs
This day came Plts. by their Attorney and Deft. being returned warned and not
appearing, therefore on motion of Plts. it is ordered that Judgment be entered for Plts.
against Deft., that they have Execution according to the force form and effect of the
recovery aforesaid, and for their costs by them in this behalf for suing forth and
prosecuting this Writ
  - MARGARET RICE, Admrx. &c. of HENRY RICE, deced., Plt. agst
      ELIE GRIFFIN, Deft.   In Case
This day came Plt. by her Attorney and Deft. being returned arrested was solemnly
called but came not. Therefore on motion of Plt., it is ordered that unless he appears
at next Court and answers Plt.'s action, Judgment shall then be entered for Plt.
against him and WILLIAM STROTHER, his Security, for the Debt in the Declaration
mentioned and costs
  - Absent. WILLIAM RUSSELL, Gent.
  - MARGARET GIBSON, Admrx. &c. of JONATHAN GIBSON, Gent., deced.
      Plt. agst WILLIAM RUSSELL, Gent., Deft.   In Case
Continued til next Court for Auditors to make their report
  - WILLIAM RUSSELL, Gent., Plt. agst JANE WHARTON, Admrx. &c. of
      THOMAS WHARTON, deced., Deft.   In Case
Continued til next Court
  - Present. WILLIAM RUSSELL, Gent.
  - The Attachment of JOHN ALLAN against JOHN SMITH, JUNR. is con-

tinued til next Court

    - JAMES HUNTER, Merchant, Plt. agst GEORGE DOGGETT, Deft. In Case
This day came Plt. by his Attorney and Deft. says nothing in bar or preclusion of
Plt.'s action whereby Plt. remains against Deft. altogether undefended. Therefore on
motion of Plt., it is ordered that Judgment be entered for Plt. against Deft. for the
Debt in the Declaration mentioned and costs to be ascertained on Inquiry by a Jury
at next Court

    - RICHARD SHIP, Admr. &c. of THOMAS SHIP, deced., Plt. agst
    GEORGE DOGGETT, Deft.   In Case
The same

    - WILLIAM NASH, Plt. agst JAMES POLLARD, Deft. In Assault & Battery
Continued til next Court

    - CHARLES HARRISON, Plt. agst NICHOLAS JONES, Deft.   In Case
This day came as well Plt. by GEORGE WYTHE, Gent., his Attorney as Deft. by
ZACHARY LEWIS, Gent., his Attorney and Deft. defends the force and injury when,
&c. and prays and has leave to imparl hereof til the next Court and then to plead

p.
128
    Orange County Court 28th of May 1748
    - WILLIAM GALE of Whitehaven, Merchant, Plt. agst
    THOMAS COVINGTON, Deft.   In Case
The Deft. not appearing, on motion of Plt. by his Attorney an Attachment is
awarded him against the Deft.'s Estate returnable to next Court

    - JAMES MADISON, quitam &c., Plt. agst JOSEPH PHILIPS, Deft. In Debt
Continued til next Court

    - EDWARD SPENCER, Gent., Plt. agst THOMAS JONES, Deft.   In Debt
The Deft. not being arrested, on motion of Plt. by his Attorney, a Plurius Capias is
awarded him against Deft. returnable to next Court

    - JOHN BRAMHAM, JUNR by JOHN BRAMHAM his next Friend, Plt. agst
    SAMUEL POUND & THOMAS JAMESON, Defts.   In Chancery
This day came the parties by their Counsel and on motion of Defts. time til next
Court is allowed them to consider Plt.'s Bill and then to plead

    - RICHARD WINSLOW, Gent., Plt. agst. DENNIS BRYNE, EDWARD
    SPENCER & ISAAC SMITH, Defts.   On a Scire Facias
Dismissed, and it is ordered that Plt. pay unto Defts. their costs

    - On motion of MARY ROWLAND, a witness for RICHARD WINSLOW, Gent.
Plt. against DENNIS BRYNE, EDWARD SPENCER & ISAAC SMITH, Defts. who
made Oath that she had attended fifteen days as a witness in that suit, it is ordered
that said RICHARD pay her three hundred seventy five pounds of tobacco for her
said attendance according to Law

    - The Attachment of JAMES HUNTER against VALENTINE BOSTICK is
continued til next Court

    - ISAAC SMITH, Plt. agst FRANCIS WILLIAMS, Deft.   In Chancery
This day came the parties by their Counsel, and on motion of Plt., time til the next
Court is allowed him to consider the Deft.'s Answer and then to reply to it

    - ROBERT SHEDDEN, Merchant, Plt. agst WILLIAM MORGAN, Deft.
    In Debt
This day came the parties by their Attornies and Deft. saith that he hath paid the

Debt in the Declaration mentioned and of this he puts himself upon the Country and Plt. likewise, Therefore the Trial of the issue is referred til next Court

    - ROBERT RAE & DANIEL CAMPBELL, Plts. agst ROBERT FREEMAN, otherwise called ROBERT FREEMAN of Orange County, Deft.   In Debt

This day came Plts. by their Attorney and the Sherif returning that he hath attached one Grubbing Hoe of Deft.'s Estate, and Deft. not appearing to replevy the same, it is considered that Plts recover against Deft. thirty one pounds, two pence current money, the Debt in the Declaration mentioned, and their costs by them about their suit in this behalf expended and Deft. in mercy, &c. And it is ordered that the Sherif make sale of the Grubbing Hoe and pay the money arising from such sale to Plts., But this Judgment, the costs excepted, is to be discharged by paiment of fifteen pounds, ten shillings and one penny with Interest thereon at the rate of five percent per annum to be computed from the twenty eighth day of August 1746 to the time of paiment and costs

    - Absent. THOMAS CHEW, Gent.

p.   Orange County Court 28th of May 1748
129   - RICHARD WINSLOW, Gent., Plt. agst THOMAS CHEW, Gent., Deft.
    In Case

By consent of the parties, it is ordered that JOHN NICHOLAS do examine state and settle all matters in difference between the parties and make return to the next Court

    - WILLIAM PICKET, Plt. agst EDWARD WARE, Deft.   In Debt

This day came Plt. by his Attorney and Deft. being again solemnly called came not. Therefore it is considered that Plt. recover against Deft. and TULLY CHOICE, his Security, eleven pounds current money, the Debt in the Declaration mentioned, and his costs by him about is suit in this behalf expended, and Deft. in mercy, &c.

    - RANDAL FUGET, Plt. agst JOHN BRAMHAM, Deft.   In Case
Constined til next Court

    - ROBERT DUNLOP & THOMAS DUNLOP, Plts. agst
    MATTHEW TOOL, Deft. in Debt

This day came the parties by their Attornies and Deft. saith that Plts. ought not have their action against him because he hath paid the Debt in the Declaration before the exhibiting the Writ aforesaid and thereupon Plts. say that they ought not to be barred from having & maintaining their action against Deft. because they say that Deft. before not at any time since the exhibiting the Writ hath paid the Debt in the Declaration mentioned and this they pray may be inquired of by the Country and Deft. likewise. Therefore the Trial of the issue is referred til next Court

    - ANTHONY STROTHER, Merchant. Plt. agst CHRISTOPHER ZIMMER-MAN, Admr. &c. of JOHN NEWPORT, deced., Deft. In Case
Continued til next Court at motion and costs of Plt.

    - ANN MOORE, Widow, Exrx. & PHILIP AYLETT, and JAMES POWER, Gent., Exrs. &c. of AUGUSTINE MOORE, JUNR., Gent., deced. Plts. against HENRY DOWNS, Deft.   In Debt

This day came Plts. by their Attorney and Deft. being again solemnly called came not. Therefore it is considered that Plts. recover against Deft. and EDWARD SPENCER, Gent., Sherif of Orange County, five pounds, three shillings and two pence

three farthings current money and ninety eight pounds of tobacco and fifteen shillings
or one hundred fifty pounds of tobacco, the Debt in the Declaration mentioned and
their costs by them about their suit in this behalf expended, and Deft. in mercy, &c.
    - RICHARD BRIDGES, Plt. agst THOMAS CHEW, Gent., Deft. In Debt
Continued and to be tried the first day of next Court
    - ANDREW GAUR, Plt. agst JAMES MAXWELL, Deft. In Chancery
The former summons not being served, on motion of Plt. by his Counsel another is
awarded him against the Deft. returnable to the next Court

p.   Orange County Court 28th of May 1748
130   - THOMAS SMITH, Plt. agst AUGUSTINE SMITH, Deft. In Chancery
Continued til next Court
    - JOHN MITCHELL, Merchant, Plt. agst GEORGE DOGGETT, Deft. In Debt
This day came Plt. by his Attorney and Sherif returning that he hath attached one
Grind Stone belonging to Deft. and Deft. not appearing to replevy the same, it is considered by the Court that Plt. recover against Deft. eight pounds, eighteen shillings
current money, the Debt in the Declaration mentioned, and his costs by him about his
suit in this behalf expended, and Deft. in mercy, &c., And it is ordered that the Sherif
make sale of the Grind Stone according to Law and pay the money arising from such
sale to the Plt.
    - WILLIAM HUNTER, Gent., Plt. agst GEORGE COOK, Deft. In Debt
BRYAN SISON & JOHN BRAMHAM came into Court and undertook for Deft.
that in case he shall be cast in this suit he shall pay the condemnation of the Court or
render his body to Prison is discharged thereof, or that they will do it for him; And
Deft. by ZACHARY LEWIS, Gent., his Attorney, comes and defends the force and
injury when,&c., and saith that the Plt. ought not to have and maintain his action
aforesaid against him because he saith that the said GEORGE had before the commencement of the said action paid the Debt in the Declaration mentioned to said
WILLIAM according to the Bill Obligatory therein also mentioned, wherefore he prays
Judgment if said WILLIAM ought to have and maintain his action against him, And
thereupon the Plt. saith that he should not be barred of his action because said
GEORGE had not before the commencement of the action paid the Debt in the Declaration mentioned according to the Bill Obligatory therein also mentioned and this
he prays may be inquired of by the Country, and Deft. likewise. Therefore the Trial of
the issue is referred til the next Court
    - EDWARD SPENCER, Gent., Plt. agst THOMAS CHEW, Gent., Deft.
    In Debt
This day came Plt. by his Attorney and Deft. saith nothing in barr or preclusion of
Plt.'s action whereby Plt. remains against him altogether undefended. Therefore it is
considered that Plt. recover against Deft. nineteen pounds, ten shillings and four
pence current money, the Debt in the Declaration mentioned, and his costs by him
about his suit in this behalf expended and Deft. in mercy, &c., But this Judgment, the
costs excepted, is to be discharged by paiment of nine pounds, fifteen shillings and two
pence with Interest thereon after the rate of five percent per annum to be computed
from the twelfth day of February 1746 to the time of paiment and costs
    - THOMAS FOSTER, Plt. agst WILLIAM NASH, Deft. In
The Deft. not being arrested on motion of Plt. by his Attorney a Plurius Capias is

awarded him returnable to the next Court
- ARCHIBALD GORDON & ALEXANDER SCOTT, Plts. agst
JOHN CONNER, Deft.
The Deft. not being arrested, on motion of Plts. by their Attorney, a Plurius Capias is awarded them against the Deft. returnable to next Court
- The Petition of FRANCIS BROWNING against JAMES TURNER, Admr. &c. of JOHN SHELTON, deced., is continued til next Court

p.   Orange County Court 28th of May 1748
131   - ROBERT SHEDDEN, Plt. agst THOMAS CHEW, Gent., Deft.   In Debt
By agreement of the parties, this suit is dismissed and it is ordered that Deft. pay unto Plt. his costs
- Upon Petition of SPENCER BRAMHAM by JOHN BRAHAM, his next Friend, against GEORGE LIVINGSTON & WILLIAM LONG, the former Process not being served on the Deft. GEORGE, ., on motion of Plt., another is awarded against him returnable to next Court, and as to Deft., LONG, this suit is continued
- RICHARD WINSLOW, Gent., Plt. agst WILLIAM RUSSELL, Gent., Deft.
In Case
Continued til next Court
- Upon the Presentment of the Grandjury against LAWRENCE BRADLEY for swearing two profane Oaths, the Deft. confesseth the same. Therefore it is considered by the Court that said LAWRENCE forfeit and pay to the Churchwardens of Saint Mark's Parish ten shillings for the offence and pay costs
- Upon the Indictment against MICHAEL O'NEAL and MARGARET his Wife an Alias venire facias is awarded against them returnable to next Court
- ARCHIBALD GORDON & ALEXANDER SCOTT having obtained an Attachment against the Estate of WILLIAM PETTY, who hath privately removed himself out of the County or so absconds that Process can't be served on him for twelve pounds, twelve shillings current money due to them from said WILLIAM by Bill. This day came Plts. by their Attorney and Deft. not appearing, it is considered the Plts. recover against Deft. the twelve pounds, twelve shillings and their costs by them about their suit in this behalf expended, But this Judgment, the costs excepted, is to be discharged by paiment of six pounds, six shillings with Interest thereon after the rate of five percent per annum to be computed from the twenty eighth day of October 1746 to the time of paiment and costs, and it is ordered that THOMAS SIMS pay Plt. one pound, four shillings and eight pence which was condemned in his hands as part of the Estate of the Deft.
- Absent. WILLIAM RUSSELL, Gent.
- Present. THOMAS CHEW, Gent.
- WILLIAM RUSSELL, Gent., having obtained an Attachment against the Estate of JOSEPH PHLIPS who hath privately removed himself out of the County or so absconds that Process can't be serve on him for two pounds, fourteen shillings and seven pence half penny current money due to said WILLIAM from said JOSEPH by Account. The Sheriff having returned that he hath attached twenty hogs, this day came Plt. and Deft. not appearing to replevy the Hogs, the Plt. proved his Account to be just by his own Oath. Therefore it is considered that Plt. recover against Deft. two pounds, fourteen shillings and seven pence half penny and his costs by him about his

suit in this behalf expended

    - WILLIAM RUSSELL, Gent., Plt. agst CHRISTOPHER ZIMMERMAN, Admr. &c. of JOHN NEWPORT, deced., Deft.   In Case

Continued til next Court

    - Present. WILLIAM RUSSELL, Gentleman

    - Absent. PHILIP CLAYTON, Gentleman

    - Upon Petition of JAMES PENDLETON & PHILIP CLAYTON, Gent. against WILLIAM KIRTLEY, WILLIAM CLIFT and ROGER ABBETT, this day came Plts. and Defts. having been served with a copy of the Petition and summoned to appear were called but came not. Therefore it is considered by the Court that Plts. recover against Defts. seven hundred pounds of tobacco and their costs by them about their suit in this behalf expended, and Plts. agree that Defts. may hereafter be at liberty to make any just discounts against this Judgment

p.   Orange County Court 28th of May 1748

132   - EDWARD SPENCER, Gent., Sherif of Orange County, excepted against the sufficiency of the Prison

    - Present. PHILIP CLAYTON, Gentleman

    - WILLIAM BEVERLEY, Gent., Plt. agst MATTHEW STANTON, Deft. On a Scire Facias

The Sherif returning that Deft. hath nothing in his Bailiwick whereby he could cause him to know nor is he found within the same, therefore on motion of Plt. by his Attorney, an Alias Scire Facias is awarded him against him returnble to next Court

    - JAMES McCRACKEN, Plt. agst JOHN TRADAN & RICHARD WINSLOW Gent., late Sherif of Orange County, Defts.   On a Scire Facias

The Sherif returning that Defts. hath nothing in his Bailiwick whereby he could cause them to know nor are they found within the same, Therefore on motion of Plt. by his Attorney, an Alias Scire Facias is awarded him against Defts. returnable to next Court

    - The Petition of JOHN KING against JOHN BRAMHAM is dismissed

    - The Petition of JOHN KING against THOMAS FOX is dismissed

    - EDWARD WHITE, Plt. agst EDWARD STUBBLEFIELD, Deft. In Assault and Battery

This day came as well Plt. by ZACHARY LEWIS, Gent., his Attorney as Deft. by GEORGE WYTHE, Gent., his Attorney and Deft. prays and has leave to imparl hereof til next Court and then to plead

    - EDWARD WHITE, Plt. agst WILLIAM SPICER, Deft. In Assault & Battery

The Deft. not being arrested, on motion of Plt. by his Attorney, an Alias Capias is awarded him against Deft. returnable to next Court

    - Upon Petition of FIELDING LEWIS against THOMAS FOX for four pounds, ten shillings and a penny half penny said to be due by Promisory Note, this day came Plt. by his Attorney and Deft. having been served with a copy of the Petition and summoned to appear was called but came not. Therefore it is considered that Plt. recover against Deft. the four pounds, ten shillngs and a penny half penny and his costs by him about his suit in this behalf expended, together with a Lawyer's fee

    - The Petition of WILLIAM PICKET against JOHN CAVE is continued til next Court

- JOHN MITCHELL, Plt. agst THOMAS WOOTON, Deft.   In Case
Dismissed
- GEORGE MOYER, Plt. agst JOHN HANSBARGER, Deft.   In Case
The Deft. not being arrested, on motion of Plt. by his Attorney an Alias Capias is
awarded him against the Deft. returnable to the next Court
- ANDREW BARCLAY, Plt. agst TULLY CHOICE, Deft. In Case
ISAAC SMITH undertakes for Deft. that in case he shall be cast in this suit he
shall pay the condemnation of the Court or render his body to Prison is discharge
thereof or that he will do it for him; and Deft. prays and has leave to imparl hereof til
next Court and then to plead
- BENJAMIN SMITH, Plt. agst WILLIAM McDONAUGH, Deft.   In Debt
Dismissed

p.   Orange County Court 28th of May 1748
133   - ANTHONY STROTHER, Merchant, Plt. agst WILLIAM BECKHAM,
         Deft.   In Case
Continued til next Court
- HEZEKIAH RHODES, Plts. agst JOHN GOUGH, Deft.
In Assault and Battery
This day came Plt. by ZACHARY LEWIS, Gent., his Attorney and Deft. being re-
turned arrested was solemnly called but came not. Therefore on motion of Plt., it is
ordered that unless he appears at next Court and answers Plt.'s action, Judgment shll
then be entered for Plt. against him, the Deft., and TIMOTHY CROSTHWAIT, his
Secrity, for the Debt in the Declaration mentioned and costs
- JOHN ROBERTS, Plt. agst JOHN INNIS, Deft.   In Debt
Dismissed by agreement of the parties and it is ordered that Deft. pay Plt. his costs
- SOLOMON RYAN, Plt. agst JOSEPH EDDINGS, Deft.   In Case
Dismissed
- ROBERT HARRIS, Survivor, of LOUISA County, Plt. agst
JOHN BRAMHAM & HENRYPENDLETON, Defts.   On a Scire Facias
on a Recognizance entered into the 26th day of June 1747 in this Court by the
Defts. whereby they undertook for JOSEPH WALSH that in case he should be
cast in a certain action upon the Case brought by Plt. against said JOSEPH
and then depending in said Court, he should pay the condemnation of the Court
or render his body to Prison in discharge thereof or they would do it for him. And
said ROBERT afterwards at a Court held for said County having recovered
against said JOSEPH two thousand one hundred pounds of tobacco for
damages in the said suit and one hundred eighty nine pounds of nett tobacco &
fifteen shillings or one hundred fifty pounds of tobacco for costs, which said
JOSEPH hath not paid nor rendered himself to Prison in discharge thereof, nor
the Deft. for him
This day came Plt. by his Attorney and Defts. being returned warned and not appearing, it is considered that Plt. recover against Deftsl the two thousand two hundred
eighty nine pounds of tobacco and fifteen shillings or one hundred fifty pounds of
tobacco and his costs by him about his suit in this behalf expended, and Defts. in
mercy &c.
- The Attachment of MATTHEW TOOL against WILLIAM MILLER is

dismissed being agreed by the parties

    - The Attachment of JOHN TAYLOE, Gent., against WILLIAM MILLER is dismissed, being agreed by the parties

    - Upon the Attachment of ANTHONY STROTHER against ELLIS MARCUS the Garnishees not appearing, a summons is awarded against them returnable to next Court

    - The Attachment of ANTHONY STROTHER against JOHN GARHART is dismissed

    - The Attachment of PETER HITT against JACOB MILLER is dismissed

    - Upon Attachment of TULLY CHOICE against WILLIAM EDDINS, WILLIAM GIVENS the Garnishee not appearing, on motion of Plt. an Attachment is awarded him against him returnable to next Court

    - NINIAN BOOG, Plt. agst. WILLIM BELL, Deft.   In Debt
The Deft. not being arrested, on motion of Plt. by his Attorney an Alias Capias is awarded him against Deft. returnable to next Court

p.   <u>Orange County Court 28th of May 1748</u>
134   - GEORGE BUCHANAN & WILLIAM HAMILTON, Exrs. &c. of NEIL
       BUCHANAN, deced., Plts. agst JOHN ROBINS, Deft.   In Debt
This day came Plt. by ZACHARY LEWIS, Gent., their Attorney and Deft. being returned arrested was solemnly called but came not. Therefore on motion of Plts. it is ordered that unless he appears at next Court and answers Plts.'s action, Judgment shall then be entered for Plts. against him, the Deft. and JOHN WILLIS, his Security, for the Debt in the Declaration mentioned and costs

    - The Attachment of WILLIAM POUND against BENJAMIN TWENTYMAN is continued til next Court

    - Ordered that the Court be adjourned to the fourth Thursday in next month

    - The Minutes of these Proceedings were signed
W. RUSSELL

(Orange County Order Book, 1747-1754 will be continued in another book beginning on page 134 with the Court held the 23d day of June 1748.)

ABBETT / ABBIT.
  James 1,
  Roger 38, 50, 83, 109,
ABELL.
  Joseph 40, 93,
ABRAHAM.
  Mordecai 93,
ADAMS.
  Robert 53, 79, 101,
  Susannah 71,
ALLAN.
  John 39, 50, 77, 104,
  John, Mercht. 11, 26,
ALLEN.
  Thomas 60,
ANDERSON.
  George 60, 87,
  George deced. 13,
  George Junr. 56,
  Susannah Admrx. of George, deced. 13,
  William 47, 74,
APPLEBY.
  Robert 19,
ARMSTRONG.
  James 9, 24, 42, 66, 99,
ASHER.
  Charles 68,
  John 17, 31, 45, 86, 87,
ASKEW.
  John 59, (apptd. Constable -92), 104,
AYLER.
  Henry 73,
AYLETT.
  Philip an Exr. of Augustine Moor deced. 82,
      106,

BALL,
  Samuel Gent. (Justice -1), (Justice of Oyer &
      Terminer -89, 90), 91,
BARBOUR.
  James Gent. 5, 16, 87, 88,
BARCLAY.
  Andrew 110,
BARDINE.
  Richard 69,
BARNETT.
  John 23,
BATTAILE.
  Lawrence 64,
BEALE.
  Taverner 54, 60, 84, 86, 94,
BEARBACK.
  Mary 58,
BEAZLEY.
  James 56,
  John 14, 44, 69, 86, 87, 100, 102,

BECKHAM.
  William 110,
BELFIELD.
  John an Exr. of Thomas Wright Belfield, deced.
      10, 25, 38, 42, 66, 76, 99,
  Thomas Wright, deced. 10, 25, 38, 42, 50, 66,
      76, 99,
BELL.
  Elizabeth 56,
  Humphrey 8, 10, 12, 13, 24, 29, 42, 46, 66,
      68, 99,
  Humphrey of London, Mercht. 9, 11, 13, 26,
      29, 68, 69,
  James 9, 24, 42, 99,
  William 29, 32, 35, 48, 56, 76, 111.
BELL ISLAND FORD
  75,
BEVERLEY.
  Harry 56,
  John 30,
  William Gent. 4, 9, 23, 24, 41, 63, 96, 109,
BICKERS.
  Robert (Indicted -55), 86, 96,
BIRD.
  Samuel 71,
BLACKEY.
  John 56,
BLANKENBECKLER
  Zacharias 6, 59,
  Zachary (apptd. Constable -2),
BLANTON.
  John 14, 30, 44,
BLEDSOE
  John 58,
  William Junr. 41,
BOBO.
  Spencer 27-29, 74, 75,
BOHANNON.
  Elliott 75,
  Robert 9, 24, 46, 61,
BOOG.
  Ninian 111.
BOOTEN.
  John 61,
BORDEN.
  Benjamin 9, 24, 42, 66, 99,
BOSTICK.
  Vallentine 4, 23, 41, 79, 105,
BOTTS.
  John deced. (Inv. retd.-2),
BOURN(E)
  Andrew 17, 31, 48,
  Henry 27-29, 60, 67, 69, 70, 95,
  John 8, 9, 31, (G.J.-55), 63,
  Robert 17, 19,

BOWEN.
  Catharine Wife of Rice 99,
  Christopher 41,
  John 44,
  Rice 99,
BOWMAN.
  Mary (an infirm witness -47),
BOWMER.
  Mary 85,
BRADFORD.
  Rachel Wife of Richard 21,
  Richard 21,
BRADLEY.
  Lawrence 39, 50, (prstd -55), 77, 85, 93, 94,
    108,
  Patrick 40,
BRAMHAM.
  John 4, 14, 17, 19, 28, 38, 43, 44, 47, 50,
    (Goaler -58), 59, 60, 63, 66, 70, 73, 76,
    80, 82, 84, (Ord. Lic. -92), 96, 99, 100,
    103, 105-110,
  John Junr. (apptd. Under Sheriff-40), 62, 80,
    103, 105,
  Spencer 14, 30, 44, 69, 84, 86, 87, 100, 102,
    108,
  Spencer Thadeus 28,
BRANCHES.
  Cattail 6,
BREEDINCROSS
  Richard 10,
BRIDGES.
  Anne 15, 31, 37, 45,
  Richard 14, 34, 47, 67, 82, 85, 92, 107,
  Sarah 46,
  Sarah Wife of Richard (prstd.-92),
  William deced. 3, 11, 25,
BROWN.
  Coleman 93,
  Daniel 47, 69, 70, 74, 75, 80,
  Francis 36, 49, 84, 93,
  Thomas 75, 92,
BROWNING.
  Francis 84, 108,
BRUCE.
  Elizabeth 1,
BRYAN.
  Morgan 99,
BUCKHAM.
  Elizabeth Admrx. of Simon, deced. 19, 20,
  Simon deced. 19, 20,
  Stephen 20,
BUCKHANNON./ BUCHANAN
  George 30, 62,
  George an Exr. of Neil, deced. 15, 100, 102,
    111.
  George & Co. 2, 7, 23, 30, 41, 45, 86,

BUCKHANNON / BUCHANAN (contd.)
  Neil deced. 15, 18, 69, 100, 102, 111.
BUFORD.
  John 73,
BULLARD.
  Ambrose 59,
BUNTIN(E).
  William 11, 25, 82, 85,
BURDYNE.
  Richard 2,
BURK.
  Thomas 4, 23, 31, 44, 46,(G.J.-92),
BYRNE.
  Dennis 9, 24, 27, 45, 46, 80, 81, 105,

CALMES.
  Marcus 82,
CAMPBELL.
  Daniel Mercht. 2, 7, 14, 24, 30, 41, 45, 54, 66,
    75, 80, 81, 99, 106,
  Dougald 4,
CARDER.
  John 52, 74, 75, 79, 95, 101, 102,
CARPENTER.
  William deced. (Inv. retd. -21),
CARROL.
  William 6,
CARTER.
  Daniel (apptd. Constable -1), 18, 33, 45, 62,
    69, 86, 100,
  William 64,
CASSELL.
  Jacob 3, 61, 96,
CATLETT.
  William 38,
CAVANAUGH.
  Anne Wife of Charles 57,
  Charles 53, 57,
CAVE.
  59,
  Benjamin 1, 58,
  Benjamin Gent. (Ord. Lic.-2), (Justice -61), 62,
    73, 94,
  David 92,
  John 109,
  Joseph 3, 23, 41, 63, 95,
  Robert 73,
CHAMBERS.
  Thomas 97,
CHAMPE.
  John Gent. 4,
CHANDLER.
  Timothy 57,
CHAPMAN.
  Sarah 93,

CHEEK.
John 7,
Judith Wife of John 7,
CHEW.
Thomas 14,
Thomas Gent. 3, 10, 15, 16, 23, 29, 31, 34,
42, 45, 49, 51, 61, 67, 70, 76, 81-83,
85, 87, 94, 96, 100, 104, 106-108,
Thomas Gent., Sheriff 3, 10, 12, 13, 16-18,
20, 26, 35-37, 47, 48, 50, 51, 78, 100,
CHISSUM
James 41, 97,
William 41,
CHOICE.
Tully 5, 7, 22, 52, 53, 59, 62. 82, 87, 88,
(G.J.-92), 96, 106, 110. 111.
CHRISTOPHER.
Anne Wife of John 40,
John 8, 9, 13, 17, 19, 24, 29, 33, 40, 44, 45,
62, 67, 69, 71, 74, 80, 82, 85-87, 95,
98,
Nicholas 6, 15,
William 2, 5, 84, (G.J.-92), 101,
CLARK.
William 22, 23, 41, 63, 96,
CLAYTON.
John Junr. 22, 32, 33, 43, 49, 53, 97, 103,
Philip 28,
Philip Gent. (Justice -7), 9, 10, 14, 24, 38, 39,
50, 54, 79, 82, 83, (Justice of Oyer &
Terminer 89, 90, 94, 109,
CLEVELAND.
Alexander (exempt from Levy -41),
John 60, 92,
CLIFT.
William 39, 40, 50, 83, 109,
COBURN.
John 12, 26, 46, 70, 101,
COFER.
Thomas 56,
COFEY.
William Junr. 3,
COLEMAN.
James 84,
Robert 40,
Sarah Wife of Robert 40,
Thomas 17, 31, 46, 70, 71,
CONNER.
James 53, (G.J.-55),
John 83, 108,
CONWAY.
Francis Son & Heir of Francis, deced. 40,
Francis deced. 40,
COOK.
Daniel 21,
George (prstd-55), 62, 83, 85, 95, 107,

COOK (contd.)
James (make Oath for 50 acres of land a head
right -21),
Michael 6, 7, 24, 45, 69, 100,
Shem 37, 49,
COOPER.
Abraham 2,
John 3,
CORNELIUS
Eleanor 102,
COTTON.
James 93,
COUNTIES:
Augusta 34,
Essex 60,
Gloucester 14,
King George 9, 41,
King & Queen 60,
King William 68,
Louisa 84, 110,
Middlesex 90,
Spotsylvania 36, 44, 60, 68,
COUNTY LEVY
58-60,
COVINGTON.
Thomas 4, 24, 52, 79, 105,
COWNE.
William Gent. 8,
COX.
Peter 93,
William 10, 24, 42, 66, 99,
CRAWFORD.
William 12, 26, 32, 83, 102, 103,
CRIBBEN.
William 98,
CROSS.
Richard Breedin 10,
CROSTHWAIT.
Timonty 15, 50, (Ord. Lic.-64), 110,
Timothy Admr. of William, deced. 29, 37, 54,
William deced. 29, 38, 54,
CROUCHER
63,
William 85,
CUDDEN.
William 13,
CURTIS.
Mary deced. 99,

DAVIS.
Joseph 56,
Mathew 56,
Thomas 27-29,
DEAR.
Jeremiah 43,

DEATHERAGE.
  Anna Wife of William 74,
  William 22, 74,
DEWITT.
  Charles 4, 23, 38, 44, 75, 83, 85, 95,
  Charles Junr. 22, (apptd. Under Sherif -74),
  Joseph 85,
  Martin 11, 67,
DICK.
  Charles 12,
  Charles Mercht. 9,
DILLARD.
  James 93,
  John 23, 93,
  Thomas 44, 60, 65, 74, 81, 82, 85, (G.J.-92),
      93, 97, 99,
DOGAN.
  Ann 97,
  John 53,
DOGGETT.
  George 5, 11, 12, 14, 18, 25, 30, 51, 77, 78,
      81-83, 85, 101, 105, 107,
  George of Spotsylvania Co. 44,
  Richard 11, 25,
DOUGLASS.
  George 59,
DOWDE / DOWDIE
  Elizabeth (an infirm witness -47), 85,
  Thomas 22, 44, 67, 68,
DOWNS / DOWNES.
  Henry 3, 37, 38, 50, 53, 59, 61, 62, 73, 77,
      82, 86, 96, 106,
  Henry Gent. 1, 73,
  Richard 73,
DUETT.
  Martin 25, 42, 46, 60,
DUFF.
  Elizabeth Widow & an Exr. of William deced.
      104,
  William deced. 104,
DULWOOD.
  Elizabeth Wife of John 84,
  John 84,
DUN.
  James 17, 18, 31, 45, 97,
  James Mercht. 97,
DUNCAN.
  William 58, (G.J.-92), 92, 93,
DUNLOP.
  Robert 51, 78, 81, 106,
  Thomas 51, 78, 81, 106,
DURRETT.
  Richard 56,

EARLY.
  James 18, 31,
  John 36, 49, 70,
EASTHAM.
  George 77,
  Robert 22,
  Robert Gent. (Justice -1), 47, 57, 58, 81,
  Robert Admr. of John Latham, deced. 35, 54,
      95, 97,
EASTHAM's FORD
  75,
EDDINS / EDDINGS
  Joseph 110,
  Theophilus 40, 97,
  William 111.
EDMONDS.
  Joseph 72,
EDMONDSON.
  Sukey (Marriage Agreement with Thomas
      Wiatt -92),
  Thomas 14,
ERWIN.
  Edward 4,
EUBANK.
  John 72,
EVE.
  Joseph 31,
EVERMAN.
  Jacob 97,

FALMOUTH
  Town of 41,
FARGUSON.
  Samuel 15, (G.J.-55), 58, 64, 75,
FARRELL.
  Sylvester 41,
FIELD.
  Abraham Gent. (Justice -1), 2, 87, 91,
  Henry Gent. (Justice -1), 2, 41, 82,
  Henry Gent. Gdn. of Wm. Stanton, Infant,
      Orphan of Tho: Stanton, deced. 21,
  John 48, 80,
  Keene / Cain / Kane 11, 25, 28, 44, 46, 68,
FINLESON
  Catharine Exrx. of John deced. 91,
  John Gent (Justice -1),
  John Gent, deced. (Will prstd to Court -91),
FINNEL.
  John 8, 10, 53, 56, 57, 95,
FINX.
  Mark 57,
FISHBACK.
  Frederick 43,
FLESHMAN.
  Peter 6,

FLINCH.
  Anthony 35, 48,
FLINCHBACK.
  Anthony 76,
FORRESTER.
  John 4, 71,
FOSTER.
  Anne Wife of Thomas 40,
  George 80,
  John 92,
  John Junr. 92,
  Thomas 21, 40, 83, 107,
FOX.
  Thomas 8, 17, 19, 27, 44, 59, 60, 71, 84, 87,
        98, 101, 109,
FRANKLYN.
  Edward 50, 72, 77,
FRAZIER.
  William 30,
FREDERICKSBURG
  Town of 7, 73,
FREEMAN.
  Robert 14, 22, 30, 38, 81, 106,
FROGG.
  John 4,
FUGETT
  Randal 47, 48, 81, 82, 84, 106,

GAHAGAN.
  Thomas (G.J.-54), 59, (imported from Ireland,
        Oath for head right -74),
GAINES.
  James 43, 57, 58,
  MaryWife of James 57,
GALE
  William 79,
  William of Whitehaven, Mercht. 52, 101, 105,
GAMES.
  William 101,
GARDINER.
  Francis 57,
GARHART.
  John 36, 37, 111.
GARNETT.
  Anthony 21,
  James 40,
GARR
  Lawrence 22,
GARTH's FORD
  73,
GAUR.
  Andrew 23, 83, 107,
GERMANNA.
  Ferry at 59,

GHOLSTON.
  Anthony 22, 33, 43,
  William 53,
GIBBS.
  Zachariah 2, 5, 27-29, 32, 34, (G.J.-92),
GIBSON.
  Margaret 19, 34, 47, (Widow -75),
  Margaret Admrx. of Jonathan, deced. 37, 49,
        51, 59, 76, 86, 104,
  Jonathan deced. 37, 49, 51, 59, 76, 86, 104,
  Jonathan Gent. 40,
  Thomas 2, 5, 104,
GILBERT.
  Felix 84,
  John (prstd.-55), 85,
GIVENS.
  William 111.
GLASPY.
  Andrew 3,
GODFREY.
  Thomas 41,
  Thomas Servant to Wm. Kelly 73,
GORDON.
  Archibald 20, 33, 83, 84, 101, 108,
  John 52, 78,
GOUGE.
  Anne Widow, Admrx. of John deced. 93,
  John deced. 93,
GOUGH.
  John (Indicted -55), 67, 70, 86, 96, 110,
GRANT.
  Catharine (Trial of 20, 21),
  Catherine Wife of Hugh, (Trial of 88, 89)
  Hugh (Trial of 88, 89),
GRAVES.
  James 95, 97,
  Thomas 17, 31, 48,
GREEN.
  Eleanor Wife of Robert, Gent. 57,
  Robert Gen. Churchwarden of St. Mark's
        Parish 6,
  Robert Gent. (Justice -1), 10, 15, 31, 34, 41,
        47, 57, 58, 70,
  Robert an Exr. of Wm. Duff, deced. 104,
  Samuel 103, 104,
GRIFFIN,
  David 2, 5, 8-10, 37, 49, 103,
  Eli(e) 17, 27-29, 32, 35, 36, 48, 52, 76, 84,
        104,
GRYMES.
  John Esqr. an Exr. of Henry Willis, Gent.,
        deced. 7, 9, 24, 66, 99,
  John Esqr. of Middlesex Co. 90,

HACKLEY.
  John 75,

HALEY.
  Edward 57,
  John 97,
HAMILTON.
  William an Exr. of Neil Buckhannon, deced. 15,
        100, 102, 111.
HAMPTON.
  Edward 97,
HANNAGIL.
  Michael 87,
HANNAN.
  Thomas 10, 24, 28,
HANSPARGER.
  John 97, 110,
HARDIN.
  Elizabeth 19, 34, 47, 80, 94,
HARDING.
  57,
HARRIS.
  Elizabeth Wife of Robert 21,
  Robert 15, 21, 28,
  Robert of Louisa Co. 110,
HARRISON.
  Andrew 16, 26, 43, 44, (G.J.-55), 59, 60, 83,
  Battail 14,
  Charles 52, 79, 105,
HARVIE.
  Francis 59,
HARVEY.
  William (exempt fr Levy -94),
HAWKINS.
  Benjamin (G.J.-55),
  Joseph 43, 58,
  Philemon 32,
  William 84, 89, 98,
  William Junr. 103,
HAYNES.
  Henry 104,
HEAD.
  Anthony 6,
HEDGMAN.
  Nathaniel 14, 30, 45,
HEMPHILL.
  James 4, 41, 63, 95,
HENDERSON.
  John (apptd. Constable -93),
  William 59, 60, 64, 65, 70,
HENSLEY.
  Benjamin (prstd -55), 85,
  John (prstd -55), 85,
  William 96,
HERNDON.
  James 21, 23, 74, 80,
HIATT.
  John 64,

HILDRUP.
  Samuel of Fredericksburg 7,
HILL.
  Robert 10, 12, 15, 18, 29, 30, 32, 37, 45, 69,
        100,
  Russell 16, 17, 22, 39, (apptd. Constable -80),
HILLIN's FORD
  92,
HILLING.
  Keziah Wife of Nathaniel 22,
  Nathaniel 22,
HITT.
  Peter 111.
HOBSON.
  John 11,
  John deced. 25, 42,
HOGG.
  Eleanor Wife of John, Admrx. of John Savage
        5,
  John 5,
HOLCOM.
  John 22,
HOLDWAY.
  Timothy 92,
HOLSFORD.
  Charles (prstd-55), 85,
HOLTSCLAW
  Jacob 98,
HOME(S) / HOOMES
  Christopher 14, 16, 24, 28, 32, 39, 75, (G.J.
        -92),
  George 4, 7, 9, 16, 23, 24, 39, 41, 42, 50, 60,
        65, 66, 74, 75, 95, 96, 99, 102,
HORD.
  Thomas 41,
HORNBY.
  Daniel 38, 39, 42, 50,
  Daniel Gent. 10, 16, 25, 67, 76, 99,
HOUISON.
  Thomas 10, 13,
HOWELL.
  Samuel 68,
HUBBARD / HUBARD
  Jane 5,
  Mathew 48, 53,
HUDSON.
  Robert 92,
  Rush 60, 62,
HUFFMAN.
  Henry 74,
HUGHES.
  John 39, 93,
  Thomas 17, 19, 84,
  William 8, 16, 31, 45, 97,

HUNTER.
  James 4, 23, 41, 79, 105,
  James Mercht. 51, 77, 105,.
  William an Exr. of John Taliaferro, deced. 40,
  William 64, 96,
  William Gent. 51, 77, 83, 103, 104, 107,
HUNTON.
  James Mercht. 14,
HUTCHINS.
  Christopher 89,

INGRAM.
  John 8, 27, 44, (G.J.-55), 71,
INNIS.
  John 110,

JACKSON.
  Elizabeth Wife of William 35, 50,
  Robert Gent. 25, 35, 48, 76,
  William 35, 50, 67, 71,
JAMESON.
  Thomas 62, 67, 80, 95, 105,
JARMAN.
  Thomas 64,
JEFFERIES.
  Richard 103,
JENKINS.
  Jonas 51, 54, 75, 78, 80, 104,
JOHNSTON.
  Elizabeth Wife of William 55,
  Peter 66,
  William 25, 55, 63,
JONES.
  Edward 65,
  Gabriel 82, 85, 92,
  John 58, 62,
  Mary Wife of Gabriel, Mother of Sukey
      Edmundson -92),
  Nicholas 3, 17, 48, 52, 79, 105,
  Philip Edwards 93,
  Thomas 53, 79, 105,
  Thomas Gent. 21,
  William 2, 4, 5, 23, 41, 74, 75, 99,
JORDAN.
  William an Exr. of Thomas Wright Belfield,
      deced. 10, 24, 38, 42, 66, 76, 99,
JUSTICES
  BALL, Samuel 1,
  CAVE, Benjamin 61,
  CLAYTON, Philip 7,
  EASTHAM, Robert 7,
  FIELD, Abraham 1,
  FIELD, Henry 1,
  FINLESON, John 1,
  GREEN, Robert 1,
  LIGHTFOOT, Goodrich 9,

JUSTICES (contd.)
  PENDLETON, James 2,
  RUSSELL, William 7,
  SLAUGHTER, Francis 1,
  SLAUGHTER, Robert 1,
  SPENCER, Edward 13,
  TAYLOR, George 1,

KAVANAUGH.
  Charles 52, 78, (apptd. Constable -92),
KELLY.
  Robert 100,
  William 13, 17, 23, 35, 40, 41, 54, 63, 73, 74,
      82, 85, (G.J.-92), 95-97,
KENNERLEY.
  James 93,
KIMBROW.
  Bradley 55,
  Thomas 91, 92,
KING.
  John 109,
  Joseph 6,
  Robert 6,
KINKEAD.
  David 4, 11,
  David Admr. of John Hobson, deced. 25, 42,
KIRK.
  Joseph 2, 8,
KIRTLEY.
  Francis 18, 31, 45, 69, 75,
  Francis Junr. 18, 31,
  William 12, 39, 50, 83, 109,

LACY.
  John 64,
LAMB.
  Richard 62,
LAND.
  William 59,
LARNEY.
  Bridget alias Maley, Wife of Thomas (Trial of
      -88, 89),
  Thomas (Trial of -88, 89),
LATHAM.
  John 13, 65, 93,
  John deced. 35, 54, (Inv. retd. -91), 95, 97,
LATON.
  John 22,
LAWLER.
  Michael 22,
LEE.
  Charles 98,
  Hancock Gent. 4, 22, 66,
  Mary Wife of Hancock, Gent. -4), 22,

LEONARD.
  Patrick 35, 49, 52, 84, 97,
  Walter 23,
LEVILL.
  Robert 21,
LEWIS.
  Fielding 75, 87, 98, 109,
  John 75, 102,
  John an Exr. of John Washington, deced. 14,
      29,
  Zachary, Attorney 11-14, 16-19, 22, 25, 27,
      29, 30, 33-37, 49-51, 53, 54, 62, 67,
      77-79, 96, 97, 100, 102, 103, 105, 107,
      109-111.
  Zachary King's Attorney 59, 90, 95,
LIGHTFOOT.
  Goodrich Gent. (Justice -9), 59,
  William 16, 31, 45, 69,
LINCH.
  John 38,
LINES.
  Robert 68,
LIVINGSTON,
  George 12, 22, 26, 84, 108,
LOBB.
  William 93,
LOCKER.
  Thomas 52,
LOCKHART
  Samuel of Augusta Co. 30,
LONG.
  William 12, 26, 46, 52, 70, 84, 96, 101, 108,
LOVELL.
  Ann, Single Woman 6,
  Gabriel 6,
LOVING.
  Gabriel 15, 31,
LUCAS
  William Junr. 64,
  William Senr. 64,
LUDWELL.
  Philip Esqr. 3,
LUKE.
  Anthony 98,
LYNCH.
  John 12, 51, 81,
LYNN.
  William 18,
LYNES
  Robert 17, 31, 45,

McCENNY.
  John (prstd -55), 85,
McCOLLESTER,
  Findley 38, 65,

McCONNICO.
  Jaret 100,
McCRACKEN.
  James 109,
McCULLOCK
  Anne 52,
  James 84,
McDANIEL.
  James 14, 18, 77, 87,
McDONAUGH.
  William 1, 2, 11, 23, 26, 37, 49, 110,
McGEE.
  Thomas 57,
McGRAW / McGRAUGH
  Richard 38, 39, 50, 77, 94, 104,
McKAY
  a Merchant 63,
McKENNY.
  John 93,
McMAHAN
  William 82,

MADISON.
  James 53, 79, 105,
MALLORY.
  John 43, (G.J.-55),
MARCUS.
  Ellis 18, 34, 46, 56, 74, 111.
MARKS.
  John 81,
MARSH.
  John 19,
  Robert 74, 75, 98,
MARTIN.
  Hugh 8,
MASH.
  Robert 81, 82, 85, 95,
MAULDIN.
  Richard 51, 73, 75,
MAXWELL.
  James 22, 83, 107,
MAYFIELD.
  Abraham Junr. 56,
MEDLEY.
  Isaac 22,
MICHAEL.
  Francis (G.J.-55),
  John 24,
MILLER.
  Jacob 18, 111.
  William 12, 110, 111.
MINOR.
  William 4, 75,
MICAL.
  John 9,

MITCHEL
 James 21,
 John 83, 107,
MOOR
 Anne an Exr. of Augustine, deced. 82, 106,
 Augustine deced, 82, 106,
 Evin 75,
 Francis 19, 23, 31, 59, 67, 75, 82, 85,
 Harbin 8-10, 19, 67,
 Thomas Gent. 103,
MORGAN.
 Charles 1, (G.J.-55),
 John 16, 31, 45, (Indicted -55), 62, 69, 74, 75,
  84, 85,
 Mary Wife of John 16, 31, 45, (Indicted -55),
  69,
 Morgan 82,
 Peter 67,
 Valentine 53,
 William 52, 67, 68, 74, 75, 79-81, 101, 105,
MORPHIS.
 John 8-10,
MORRIS.
 William (imported from Great Britain, Oath
  for head rights -80),
MORTON.
 Elijah (apptd. Constable -61),
 Jeremiah 32, 58, 59, 69, 70, 75,
 John 27, 28, (apptd. Constable -29), 42,
 Joseph Gent. 100,
 Joseph Gent. (of King George Co. -9),
 William 10, 25, 66, 67, 99,
 William deced. (Will prstd -97),
MOUNTAINS:
 Fox 92,
 Mount Poney 62,
 Southwest 59, 73,
MOYER.
 Anna Barbara Wife of George 89,
 George 88, 97, 110,
MULLIN.
 Richard 6,

NALL.
 Martin 93,
NASH.
 William 5, 11, 18, 26, 28, 32, 45, 46, 51, 69,
  78, 83, 105, 107,
NEAL.
 Lewis 82,
NEALAND.
 John 4,
NEGROES.
 In suit 54,
 Trial & Punishment for Hog Stealing 73,

NEGROES (contd.)
 Trial of Letty for poisoning Richard Sims and
  a Negro man, Simon, she found not
  guilty -89, 90.
 Whipped for Felony 64,
NEWMAN.
 Thomas 27, 28,
NEWPORT.
 John 8, 16,
 John deced. 1, (Inv. retd. -21), 35, 47, 56, 82,
  (Acct. of Sales retd.-94), 96, 106, 109,
NICHOLAS.
 John 37, 54, 56, 70, 106,
NIX
 John 59,
NIXON.
 Henry 61,
NOEL.
 John 56, 91,
NORMAN.
 Isaac 93,

O'NEAL.
 Margaret Wife of Michael (Indicted -55), 86,
  108,
 Michael (Indicted -55), 86, 108,
ORDINARIES.
 John Bramham at the Courthouse 92,
 Benjamin Cave, Gent. 2,
 Timothy Crosthwait 64,
 Joseph Reynolds 74,
 George Wells 94,
 Christopher Zimmerman, Junr. 93, 94,

PANNILL / PANEL(L)
 William 5, 67, 81, 82, 85,
PARK.(S)
 Charles 103,
 Thomas 17, 45,
PARSONS
 George 44,
PEARSON.
 Michael 73,
PENDERGRASS.
 John 7,
PENDLETON.
 Elizabeth Wife of James 64,
 Henry 2, 110,
 James 22, 24, 28, 64,
 James Gent. (Justice -2), 9, 10, 14, 39, 47, 50,
  54, 58, 59, 79, 83, 94, 109,
PERKINS.
 Margery 82, 83,
PETTY.
 Thomas 15, 45, 69, 100,
 Thomas Junr. (exempt from Levies -2), 22,

PETTY (contd.)
  William 2, 7, 18, 20, 23, 33, 41, 62, 86, 108,
PEYTON.
  William 40,
  William Churchwarden of St. Mark's Par. 102,
PHILLIPS.
  Jemima Wife of Leonard 56,
  Joseph 17, 31, 38, 43, 45, 48, 53, 79, 86, 87,
        96, 105, 108,
  Leonard 56,
PICKET(T)
  Henry 17, 31, 46, 56, 70, 71,
  James 4,
  Micajah 2, 11, 25, 35, 37, 42, 50, 67,
  William 77, 82, 106, 109,
PINNION.
  Richard 74, 75,
  William 17,
POLLARD.
  Elizabeth 22, 33, 43,
  James 14, 26, 51, 69, 78, 105,
PORTER.
  Benjamin 24, 40,
  Nicholas 97,
PORTEUS.
  James 36, 37,
POTTER.
  Hannah Widow of Middlesex Co. 89, 90,
POUND.
  John 48, 69, 70,
  Samuel 12, 17, 20, 36, 44, 62, 69, 70, 80,
        105,
  William 17, 28, (prstd -55), 60, 67, 84, 85,
        95, 97, 111.
POWELL.
  Ambrose 8-10, 22, 23, 26-29, 32, 74, 75,
  Honorias 34, 38, 50, 76,
POWER.
  James an Exr. of Augustine Moor, deced 82,
        106,
PRATT.
  Jonathan 21, 74, 75,
PRICE.
  Arjalon 17, 19,
  Edward 19, 35, 49, 81, 84,
  Mungo 3,
PRYER.
  Richard 75,

QUIN(N).
  Darby 1,
  Richard 1,

RAE.
  Robert, Mercht. 2, 7, 14, 24, 30, 41, 45, 54,
        66, 75, 80, 81, 99, 106,

RAINS.
  John 8,
RATES for Liquors, Lodging, Diet, &c.
  72.
RAWSON.
  William 22,
RAY.
  Andrew 12,
  John 9, 24, 54, 79,
RENNOLDS.
  John 92,
REYNOLDS.
  Cornelius 68,
  John 2, 5, 59,
  Joseph 8-10, 12, 67, 69, 70, (Ord. Lic.-74),
  Richard 86,
RHODES.
  Hezekiah 110,
  William 101,
RICE.
  Amon Bohannon 65,
  Fisher 65,
  Henry deced. 17, 36, 48, 74, 76, 98, 104,
  Margaret Admrx. of Henry, deced. 17, 36, 48,
        76, 98, 104,
  Michael 65,
  Samuel 27-29, 32, 65,
  William (apptd. Constable -60), 65, 73,
RICHEE.
  Patrick 65, 87,
RIVERS:
  Rappahannock 27, 28,
ROADS.
  Bloodworth's 6, 93,
  Fredericksburg 59,
  Old Germanna 22,
  Scott's 92,
  Southwest Mounain 57,
  Tombstone to the Trapp 62,
ROANE.
  William Gent. 57,
ROBERTS.
  Benjamin 40, 75, 99,
  Benjamin Churchwarden of St. Mark's Par:
        102,
  George 44, 60,
  John 84, 93, 110,
ROBINS.
  John (G.J.-92), 111.
RONE's QUARTER
  92,
ROSS.
  Andrew 14, 15, 30, 45,
  David (Headright claim -61),

ROSSE.
  Alexander (imported from Great Britain, Oath
          for head right -74),
ROSSON.
  Jeremiah 16, 39,
ROWLAND.
  Edward (imported from Great Britain, Oath
          for head right -74),
  Mary 81, 105,
RUCKER.
  James 60, 71, 81,
  John deced. 15, 31, 45, 76, 104,
  Peter (G.J.-55), 60,
  Peter deced, who was Exr. of John, deced. 15,
          31, 45. 76, 104,
  Peter deced. 15, 31,
  Reuben 51,
  Susannah Exrx. of Peter, deced 15. 31, 44, 76,
          104,
  Thomas 34, 47, 51, 56, 74, 75,
  William 56,
RUMSEY.
  William 4,
RUNS
  Battle Spring 2,
  Elk 73,
  Muddy 62,
  Wilderness 40, 60,
RUSH.
  Margaret 64, 74,
  William 9,
RUSSELL.
  William 4,
  William Gent. 4, (Justice -7), 11, 13, 22, 23,
          25, 28, 30, 35, 37, 38, 42-44, 46, 47,
          49, 50, 58, 60, 62, 63, 66-68, 70, 76,
          82, 85, 86, (Justice of Oyer & Terminer
          -89, 90), 96, 98-100, 104, 108, 109,
  William Gent. Churchwarden of St. Mark's
          Parish 6,
RYAN.
  Solomon 110.

SAMPSON.
  John 6, 65,
SANDERS.
  John Winell 63,
  Thomas 16, 31, 45,
SAVAGE.
  John deced. 5,
SCALES.
  Richard 84, 104,
SCOTT.
  Alexander 20, 33, 50, 61, 83, 84, 101,103,
          108,
  Anthony 75,

SCOTT (contd.)
  Samuel 2,
  Thomas 51, 75,
SCRATCHWELL.
  Samuel 81,
SEAYRES.
  John 16, 43, 53, 67, 79, 100,
  Robert 4, 16, 23, 41, 43, 53, 67, 99, 100,
SELSER.
  Matthias of Augusta Co. 34,
SHACKLEFORD.
  John 101,
SHEDDEN.
  Robert 35, 49, 80, 85, 105,
SHELTON.
  John deced. 84, 108,
SHEPPARD.
  John 6,
SHERMAN.
  Lucy 1,
  Robert 1,
SHIP.
  Richard 17,
  Richard Admr. of Thomas deced. 3, 23, 51, 78,
          105,
  Thomas deced. 3, 23, 51, 78, 105,
SHORT.
  Samuel 5, 17-19,
SIMS.
  Joanna Admrx. of Richard, deced. 1, 37, 49,
  Richard deced. 1, 37, 49, 89, 90,
  Robert Junr. 2,
  Thomas 5, 7-10, (G.J.-55), 62,
SINGLETON.
  Daniel (G.J.-55), 58,
SKILLION.
  William deced. (Inv. retd. -24),
SLAUGHTER,
  Francis Gent. (Justice -1), 91,
  George 72,
  Robert Gent. (Justice -1), 25, 59, 60, 80, 82,
          Justice of Oyer & Terminer 89-91), 91,
          94,
  Thomas 2, 5, 94,
SLEET.
  John 20,
SMALL.
  Oliver 3,
SMITH.
  Anne Servant to John Lacy -64,
  Augustine 83, 107,
  Benjamin 110,
  George Junr. 15,
  George Senr. 5,

SMITH (contd.)
  Isaac 9, 10, 15, 22, 24, 27, 29, 30, 32, 36,
      44-46, 54, 61, 62, 65, 67, 69, 70, 80, 81,
      95, 98, 101, 105, 110,
  John 17, 19, 34, 35, 38, 45, 47, 50, 60, 67,
      69, 70, 75, 77, 82, 85, 87,
  John Junr. 5, 7, 12, 13, 17, 19, 24, 29, 31, 38,
      39, 41, 45, 50, 68, 77, 87, 88, 98, 99,
      104,
  Robert 97,
  Thomas 56, 57, 83, 107,
SOUTHALL.
  Edward deced. 24,
SPARKS.
  Henry 22,
SPENCER.
  Edward 9, 24, 27, 40, 45, 46, 50, 60, 64, 80,
      81, 105,
  Edward Gent. 3, (Justice -13), 20, 36-38, 49,
      53, 58, 59, 62, 70, 79, 88, 94, 96, 105,
      107,
  Edward Gent. apptd. Sheriff -40, 74, 81-84,
      91, 101, 103, 106, 109,
SPICER.
  William 102,
SPOTSWOOD.
  Alexander Esqr., deced. 61,
  John Gent. 17, 18, 31, 33, 36, 45, 49-51, 59,
      69, 70, 78, 86,
STANTON.
  Matthew 109,
  Thomas 59,
  Thomas deced. 21,
  William Orphan of Thomas 21,
STEPHENS.
  William 26, 31,
STEVENS.
  Mumford 44, 52, 57, 58, 61, 73,
  William 16, 48, 60, 64,
STEWART.
  Joseph 10,
  Robert 93,
STOVER.
  Jacob 96,
  Jacob deced. 3, 23, 61,
  Jacob Admr. of Jacob deced. 3, 23, 61,
STROTHER.
  Anthony 4, 5, 18, 97, 98, 111.
  Anthony Gent. 34, 46, 47, 56, 66, 74,
  Anthony Mercht. 6, 15, 35, 82, 106, 110.
  Christopher 3, 23,
  Francis 3, 53, 93,
  Lawrence 81, 82, 85, 87, 95, 97, 104,
  William 17-19, 37, 53, (G.J.-92), 104,
STUART.
  Anne, Single Woman 8,

STUBBLEFIELD
  Edward 74, 77, 102, 109,
  George 50,
  Thomas 75,
SUGGITT.
  Elizabeth Dau. of James 26,
  James 2, 8-10, 12, 23, 26, 32, 40, 44, 52,
      (G.J. foreman -55, 92),
SUTTON.
  Christopher 48,
SYSON / SISON
  63,
  Bryan(t) 8-10, 19, 20, 23, 31, 44, (G.J.-55),
      59, 67, 69, 70, 73, 81, 82, 85, 94, 98,
      99, 107,

TALIAFERRO
  Francis 56, 57,
  John deced. 40,
  Lawrence an Exr. of John deced. 40,
  Mary an Exr. of John, deced. 40,
  William 57, 97,
TAPP.
  William 46, 48, 60, 65.
TAYLOE.
  John Gent. 111.
TAYLOR,
  Erasmus 26, 29, 32, 56,
  George Gent. (Justice -1), 22, 54, 58-60, 67,
      86, (Justice of Oyer & Terminer 89, 90),
      94,
  Zachary 54, (Old Ordinary -59),
TEAL.
  Edward 9, 24,
TENNANT
  22,
TERRENCE.
  Leonard 2, 5,
TERRILL
  Robert 21, (G.J.-92),
THOMAS.
  John 6, 73, 102,
  Joseph 37, 54,
  Joseph Gent. 36, 48,
  Mary Wife of John 73,
THOMPSON.
  John, Revd. 57,
  Mr. 93,
THORNHILL.
  Bryant 1, (G.J.-55, 92),
THORNTON.
  Frances Wife of Francis, Gent. 4, 22,
  Francis Gent. 4, 20, 22, 36, 48, 66,
  Francis Gent. of Spotsylvania Co. 36,
  John 22,
  Luke 19,

THORNTON (contd.)
  Mary 8, 24, 41,
  Mr. 93,
  Thomas 8-10, 13, 29, 39, 44, 48, 50, (G.J.
        -55), 67, 69-71, 74, 75, 78, 98,
TILLERY.
  Henry 103,
TOOL(E)
  Mathew 15, 17, 23, 27-29, 32, 34, (G.J.-55),
        64, 74, 81, (G.J.-92), 106, 110,
TOONE.
  Lewis 74, 75, 89, 95,
TOWLES.
  Stockley 5, 22, 23, 67,
TRADAN.
  John 109,
TREWICK.
  Margery 78,
  Robert 54, (G.J.-55), 67, 75, 78, 93,
TRIPLETT.
  John 44, 101, 102,
TURNER.
  Frances 93,
  James 93,
  James Admr. of John Shelton, deced. 84, 108,
  Nathan 48, 52,
TUTT.
  James 65,
  Richard Gent. 57,
  William 65,
TWENTYMAN.
  Benjamin 111.
TYLER.
  Francis 20, 26,

UNDERWOOD.
  Daniel 1,
  John (G.J.-55),

VERNON.
  Richard 14, 32, 34, 38, 39, 50, 60, 69, 70, 76,
        77, 81, 84, 94, 104,

WALKER
  Charles 65,
WALLACE.
  Michael Gent. 4, 22,
WALLIS.
  Humphrey of Spotsylvania Co. 68,
WALLOCK.
  Martin 15, 32, 34,
WALSH.
  Joseph 15, 28, 102,

WARE.
  Edward 13, 16, 26, 31, 48, 51, (G.J.-55), 57,
        58, 60, 81, 82, 97, 98, 103, 104, 106,
  Henry 58,
  Lucy Wife of Edward 57, 58,
WAREHOUSES:
  Royston's 10,
WASHBOURN.
  John 58,
WASHINGTON.
  John, late Sheriff of Gloucester Co., deced. 14,
        29,
  Warner Gent. an Exr. of John of Gloucester Co.
        deced. 14, 29,
WATKINS.
  Solomon 74,
  William 56, 103,
WATTS.
  Easther Wife of Thomas 1,
  Edward 23, 52, 61, 62,
  Joell 23,
  Thomas 1,
WAUGH.
  Alexander 10, 12, 21, 27-29, 32, 37, 40, 56,
        57, 67, 92,
WEATHERBY.
  Thomas 20, 57, 97,
WELLS,
  George 59, 67, (Ord. Lic. -94),
WHARTON.
  Jane Widow & Admrx. of Thomas deced. 10,
        11, 13, 25, 29, 30, 42, 46, 59, 67, 70,
        100, 104,
  John 2, 11, 13, 25, 46. 63, (G.J.-92), 97,
  John an infirm witness 43,
  Thomas 15, 31,
  Thomas deced. 10, 11, 25, 29, 30, 42, 46, 59,
        67, 70, 100, 104,
WHATLEY.
  Michael 8-10, 17-20, 34, 47, 56, 74, 80, 84,
        94,
WHEELER.
  Diana Exrx. of John, deced. 11, 25, 42,
  John deced. 11, 25, 42,
WHITE.
  Edward 14, 87, 97, 109,
  James Taylor 50, 61,
  William (apptd. Constable -2), 11, 25, 59, 75,
WHITING.
  Beverley an Exr. of John Washington, deced.
        14, 29,
WHITMAN.
  William 103,
WIATT.
  Thomas (Marriage -92),

WILHITE.
  John 22,
  Tobias 22,
WILHOIT.
  Matthias 102,
WILLIAMS.
  Francis 4, 36, 54, 60, 62, 65, 80, (G.J.-92),
        103, 105,
  Jemima Single Woman 6,
  James 3, 6,
  John 38,
  Katherine Wife of Thomas 64,
  Joseph 46,
  Thomas 64,
WILLIAMSBURG
  88, 89, 95,
WILLIS.
  Francis an Exr. of Henry, Gent., deced. 7, 9,
        24, 66, 99,
  Henry Gent., deced. 7, 9, 24, 41, 66, 99,
  John 8, 18, 27, 33, 40, 44, 49, 71, 84, (G.J.
        -92), 111.
  John Gent. 37,
  Mildred deced. 53,
WILSON.
  John 3, 23, 41, 63, 73, 95,
WINSLOW.
  Richard 9, 13, 15, 16, 64, 74,
  Richard Gent. 4, 23, 24, 27, 29-31, 42, 43,
        45, 46, 51, 59, 60, 66-68, 70, 80, 81, 86,
        100, 101, 105, 106, 108, 109,
WISDOM.
  Ann Wife of John 56,
  John 56,
WOOTON.
  John 98,
  Thomas 67, 69, 70, 87, 98,
WRIGHT.
  Richard 1, 86, 98,
  Thomas 4, 38, 50, 85,
WROE.
  William Exr. of Wm. Bridges, deced. 3, 11, 25,
WYLIE.
  Allan an Infant (Apprentice -43),
WYTHE.
  George, Attorney 11-14, 16, 17, 19, 22, 25,
        27, 29, 31, 33-37, 51, 52, 54, 62, 79,
        80-83, 95, 96, 105, 109,

YANCEY.
  John 2, 74,
  Lewis Davis 58, 65, 97,
YARBROUGH.
  Richard 14, 16, 17, 26, 27, 39,
YATES.
  Thomas 7, 24, 41,
YEARLY.
  Jeremiah 73,
YOUNG.
  Richard 92,
  Robert 95,
YOUNGER.,
  Joseph deced. 4,
  Mary Exrx. of Joseph deced. 4,
YOWELL.
  Christopher 6,
  Davis 6,
  James 6,

ZACHARY.
  David 56,
ZIGLER.
  Leonard 44,
ZIMMERMAN.
  Christopher 7, 8, 19, 37, 94,
  Christopher Admr. of John Newport, deced. 1,
        35, 47, 56, 82, 96, 106, 109,
  Christopher Junr. 2, (Ord. Lic. -93),
  Christopher Junr. Under Sheriff -52, 53,
  John 6,